Cursor AI for Web Design

First Edition

The Complete Beginner's Guide to Building Websites with AI, No Coding Required

Chris Barin

<packt>

Cursor AI for Web Design

First Edition

Portfolio Director: Ashwin Nair
Relationship Lead: Sneha Shinde
Content Engineer: Kinnari Chohan
Project Manager: Ruvika Rao
Technical Editor: Arjun Varma
Indexer: Tejal Soni
Proofreader: Kinnari Chohan
Production Designer: Aparna Bhagat
Growth Lead: Priyadarshini Sharma

First published: August 2026

Production reference: 1060826

Published by Packt Publishing Ltd.
Grosvenor House
11 St Paul's Square
Birmingham
B3 1RB, UK.

ISBN 978-1-80808-491-1
www.packtpub.com

To everyone with a dream, keep rocking!

– Chris Barin

Contributors

About the authors

Chris Barin is a professional web and app designer, an Adobe Certified Instructor, and a Certified Photoshop Expert with nearly 10 years of experience. Self-taught, he has earned the trust of over 300,000 students worldwide with a hands-on, no-nonsense approach focused on getting maximum results with minimal effort. He started out as a freelance web designer and today runs a 20-strong Android design studio whose apps have surpassed 100 million downloads. In this book, he brings that same practical, beginner-friendly style to vibe coding, showing how anyone can build and launch real websites with Cursor and AI, without writing code.

Table of Contents

Preface

Not long ago, building a website or an app meant one of two things: spending months or years learning to code, or spending thousands of dollars hiring a team to build it for you. Either way the barrier was high, the timeline was long, and most people with a good idea never made it past the idea stage.

That has changed. Today you can describe what you want in plain English, and artificial intelligence writes the code for you. This is called *vibe coding*: you imagine something, you describe it in simple terms, and the AI builds it. You don't need to know Python, JavaScript, or any other programming language. You bring the idea and the judgment; the AI does the heavy lifting.

This book is built around Cursor, one of the best vibe coding platforms available today. Working in Cursor is like having a team of senior developers at your fingertips, available 24/7, infinitely patient, ready to build whatever you describe, all for the price of a single monthly subscription. You write a prompt, the AI takes over, you review the result and give feedback, and it improves on the spot.

What can you actually build this way? Websites, portfolios, and landing pages; software-as-a-service (SaaS) products with a real frontend, backend, and database; mobile apps; and tools such as browser extensions, bots, and plugins. If it runs in a browser or lives online, there is a good chance you can build it with Cursor.

I want to be honest with you from the start: this is early technology, and being early comes at a price. Things change fast, new features ship almost every week, and at some point you *will* get stuck. You'll hit confusing errors, follow instructions that don't match what's on your screen, and run into problems that are specific to your own computer. That is not a failure of this book, nor of yours; it is simply the cost of being early.

And being early is exactly where your advantage lies. It's like investing in a company before everyone else has heard of it: there is uncertainty, but the head start is enormous. The people who learn this now, while it's still uncomfortable, will be far ahead of the crowd that waits until it becomes easy and everyone else piles in.

I'm a designer, not a developer, and I consider that an advantage for teaching you. I won't fill your head with jargon, theory, or computer-science concepts you don't need. Instead, I focus on getting real results fast, through practical examples and hands-on exercises. Throughout the book, I'll keep things simple; sometimes I'll deliberately oversimplify because the goal is for a complete beginner to follow along and actually build something.

By the end of the book, you will have done exactly that. We start from a single prompt and an empty folder and build a portfolio page. We compare the leading AI models, Claude, Gemini, and GPT, so you learn to pick the right one for the job. We set up the tools and accounts that make Cursor far more capable. And then we build a complete vet-clinic website from scratch: making its contact form send real emails, publishing it to the internet through GitHub and Vercel, connecting it to a custom domain, and debugging the inevitable real-world problems along the way. We'll also cover the things most tutorials skip, how credits and costs really work, the security risks of handing too much control to AI, and why AI gets you 80 to 90 percent of the way quickly while the final polish takes patience.

You won't write code. You won't even need to read it. What you will develop is the ability to think clearly, describe what you want, and guide these tools to a finished, working product, and that is a skill that will serve you whether you want a better job, freelance income, or a business of your own. This is your head start. Let's get to work.

Who this book is for

This book is for complete beginners. You do not need any programming experience, and you do not need to know how to code; that is the entire point of vibe coding.

It's written for anyone who wants to build websites, apps, and digital products without spending years learning to program: aspiring freelancers and entrepreneurs, designers and other creatives, small-business owners, side-hustlers, and curious makers who have an idea and want to bring it to life. If you've ever wanted to launch a portfolio, a landing page for a local business, a simple SaaS tool, or a plugin, and perhaps turn that into a job, freelance work, or a business, this book is for you.

What you do need is a willingness to think logically, to describe clearly what you have in mind, and , above all, to stay patient when things don't work on the first try. Those are the real skills of vibe coding, and you'll build them as you work through the book.

What this book covers

Chapter 1, Welcome to Vibe Coding with Cursor, explains what vibe coding means, why Cursor matters, what beginners can build, and the mindset needed to succeed without learning traditional programming first.

Chapter 2, Your First Website in Cursor, walks through creating a simple portfolio landing page from a prompt, working in Agent mode, accepting changes, previewing the result, changing the color scheme, adding a map, and understanding the first AI-assisted workflow.

Chapter 3, Choosing What to Build, explores small, useful software ideas, niche tools, landing pages for local businesses, simple SaaS concepts, plugins, and the importance of execution over originality.

Chapter 4, Setting Up Your Vibe Coding Toolkit, covers installing and understanding the practical role of Python, Node.js, PowerShell, Git, GitHub, Docker, Vercel, Resend, and Supabase without overwhelming the reader with unnecessary theory.

Chapter 5, Rules, MCPs, and Giving Cursor Better Instructions, covers setting up Cursor rules, understanding user rules versus project rules, configuring MCPs, adding keys safely, and using tools such as GitHub, filesystem, memory, and sequential thinking.

Chapter 6, Getting Around Cursor Like a Beginner-Friendly Builder, explains Cursor's interface, project folders, the chat panel, terminal, Agent mode, file references, model selection, and the workflow for starting and switching projects, including debugging.

Chapter 7, Choosing the Right AI Model for the Job, compares Claude, Gemini, and GPT models, examining their personalities, strengths, weaknesses, costs, common mistakes, and why testing the same prompt across models is essential.

Chapter 8, Costs, Credits, and Working Without Range Anxiety, explains Cursor credits, requests, free trials, paid plans, model cost differences, when extra credits make sense, and why credits should be treated as an investment in learning and output.

Chapter 9, Ensuring Your Projects Are Secure, addresses security risks, API keys, giving AI too much control, why full access can be dangerous, how to protect sensitive information, and how to stay cautious while still moving fast.

Chapter 10, The 80/20 Reality of AI-Built Websites, examines why AI can get you 80 to 90 percent of the way quickly, why the final details can be frustrating, how to avoid perfectionism, how to guide design polish, and why Figma-to-Cursor workflows still need caution.

Chapter 11, From Local Project to Live Website, takes you through building a full vet clinic website, using a better prompt and PRD, making the contact form work with Resend, fixing images, uploading to GitHub, deploying with Vercel, connecting a domain, translating and updating the site, and debugging production issues.

To get the most out of this book

This book assumes no prior programming knowledge. If you can use a computer, browse the web, and describe what you want in plain language, you have everything you need to begin.

A few things will make your experience smoother:

- **Patience and a hands-on mindset.** This is early-stage technology. You will hit errors that are specific to your own machine, and learning to work through them calmly is part of the skill. Work along at your own pace, pause often, and don't expect everything to go perfectly the first time.
- **A Cursor account.** You can start on the free trial; for the best experience and access to the strongest models, such as Claude 4 , the Pro plan (around $20 per month at the time of writing) is recommended.
- **A few free accounts.** Over the course of the book, you'll create free accounts with GitHub, Vercel, Resend, and Supabase. Each takes only a minute, and we set them up together.

The examples in this book are demonstrated on a Windows PC, but Cursor and the supporting tools we use are all cross-platform, so you can follow along just as well on macOS or Linux; only small details, such as a few installation steps and commands, will differ. In *Chapter 4*, we install and set up everything Cursor needs to do its best work: Cursor itself, Python, Node.js, PowerShell, Git, and Docker, so don't skip it, because having these in place from the start saves you from error after error later on.

We also configure Cursor itself, setting up *rules* (so the AI follows your preferences on every project) and *MCPs* (which let the AI do more on its own, such as creating a GitHub repository and uploading your project automatically). All the prompts, rules, and configuration files used in the book are provided so you can follow along exactly.

If you are using the digital version of this book, we advise you to download the companion files for this book and paste the prompts and configuration from there rather than retyping them. When you copy a key or a command, paste it precisely; a single extra space in an API key can cause problems that are hard to spot, and you often won't get an error message telling you why.

Finally, a word of realism: this field changes constantly, and some details, model names, prices, button labels, menu positions, will look different by the time you read this. That's expected. This book teaches you principles and a way of working, not just a fixed sequence of clicks, so that you can adapt as the tools keep evolving.

Conventions used

There are a number of text conventions used throughout this book.

`CodeInText`: Indicates code words in text, database table names, folder names, filenames, file extensions, pathnames, dummy URLs, user input, and Twitter handles. For example: "To confirm the installation worked, open Command Prompt and type `py.`:"

A block of code is set as follows. This is the `.env.local` file that stores the keys your contact form needs in order to send emails through Resend:

```
RESEND_API_KEY=your_actual_key_here
FROM_EMAIL=delivered@resend.dev
TO_EMAIL=your_resend_registered_email@example.com
```

When we wish to draw your attention to a particular part of a code block, the relevant lines or items are set in bold:

```
{
  "mcpServers": {
    "github": {
      "command": "npx",
      "args": ["-y", "@modelcontextprotocol/server-github"],
      "env": {
        "GITHUB_PERSONAL_ACCESS_TOKEN": "---add your own key----"
      }
    }
  }
}
```

Any command-line input or output is written as follows:

```
node --version
```

Bold: Indicates a new term, an important word, or words that you see on the screen. For instance, words in menus or dialog boxes appear in the text like this. For example: "In the chat panel, set the mode to **Agent**, and once the model has finished, click **Accept All** to save your progress."

> **Note**
>
> Warnings or important notes appear like this.

> **Tip**
>
> Tips and tricks appear like this.

Get in touch

Feedback from our readers is always welcome.

General feedback: If you have questions about any aspect of this book or have any general feedback, please email us at `customercare@packt.com` and mention the book's title in the subject of your message.

Errata: Although we have taken every care to ensure the accuracy of our content, mistakes do happen. If you have found a mistake in this book, we would be grateful if you reported this to us. Please visit `http://www.packt.com/submit-errata`, click **Submit Errata**, and fill in the form.

Piracy: If you come across any illegal copies of our works in any form on the internet, we would be grateful if you would provide us with the location address or website name. Please contact us at `copyright@packt.com` with a link to the material.

If you are interested in becoming an author: If there is a topic that you have expertise in and you are interested in either writing or contributing to a book, please visit `http://authors.packt.com/`.

Reviews

Please leave a review. Once you have read and used this book, why not leave a review on the site that you purchased it from? Potential readers can then see and use your unbiased opinion to make purchase decisions, we at Packt can understand what you think about our products, and our authors can see your feedback on their book. Thank you!

For more information about Packt, please visit `packt.com`.

Free benefits with your book

This book comes with free benefits to support your learning. Activate them now for instant access (see the *How to Unlock* section for instructions).

Here's a quick overview of what you can instantly unlock with your purchase:

How to Unlock

Scan the QR code (or go to `packtpub.com/unlock`). Search for this book by name, confirm the edition, and then follow the steps on the page.

UNLOCK NOW

Note: Have your invoice handy. Purchases made directly from the Packt website don't require an invoice.

Share your thoughts

Once you've read *Cursor AI for Web Design*, we'd love to hear your thoughts! Scan the QR code below to go straight to the Amazon review page for this book and share your feedback.

https://packt.link/r/1808084918

Your review is important to us and the tech community and will help us make sure we're delivering excellent quality content.

1

Welcome to Vibe Coding with Cursor

Building websites and apps used to require years of coding experience, a team of developers, or a serious budget. Vibe coding changes that starting point. Instead of writing every line of code manually, we describe what we want in plain English and use AI to generate, improve, and launch the project.

In this book, we will use Cursor to do exactly that. Cursor gives us a practical way to build websites and apps with AI, even without traditional programming knowledge. The process is not always smooth, and it will require patience, but it opens the door to building real projects much faster than before.

By the end of this chapter, you will understand what vibe coding is, why Cursor has become one of the most exciting tools for beginners, and how this book will help you move from idea to working website without needing to become a traditional programmer first.

You will also learn something just as important: vibe coding is not magic. It can feel magical when it works, but it still requires patience, clear thinking, and a willingness to troubleshoot problems. That mindset will matter throughout the book.

In this chapter, we will cover:

- What does vibe coding mean?
- What Cursor does
- What kinds of projects can you build?
- Why do beginners now have a serious advantage
- Why patience matters more than technical knowledge at the start
- How to think about this book and the projects ahead

Note

Download the PDF version of this book

Your purchase includes a DRM-free PDF copy of this book, the code bundle, and a range of exclusive benefits. To unlock everything, follow the *Free benefits with your book* section in the *Preface*.

The big idea behind vibe coding

For a long time, building a website or an app meant you needed one of two things: serious coding skills or enough money to hire people who had those skills.

A simple website could take days or weeks. A more advanced app could take months. You needed designers, developers, hosting, databases, emails, deployment workflows, and a long list of technical decisions that were difficult to understand as a beginner.

Vibe coding changes that.

Vibe coding means creating websites, apps, tools, and software by describing what you want in plain language and letting AI produce most of the code for you. You imagine the result, explain it clearly, and work with the AI until the project becomes real.

That does not mean you sit back and do nothing. It means your role changes.

Instead of writing every line of code yourself, you become the person who guides the project. You describe the goal. You review the result. You give feedback. You test what the AI built. You ask it to fix problems. You keep refining until the project works.

In traditional coding, the beginner's biggest obstacle is syntax. You need to know the correct words, symbols, file structure, commands, and programming concepts before you can make useful things. In vibe coding, your first skill is communication. You need to explain what you want clearly enough that the AI can build it.

That is why this book is not about memorizing programming languages. It is about learning how to think, prompt, review, debug, and launch.

Why Cursor feels like a team of developers

Cursor is an AI-powered code editor. That sounds technical, so let's simplify it.

Think of Cursor as the workspace where your project lives. It lets you open a folder, describe what you want, and ask AI models to create or modify the files inside that folder. Those files become your website, app, or tool.

The important part is that Cursor not only chats with you. It can also work directly inside your project. It can create files, edit code, run commands, explain issues, and suggest fixes.

That is what makes it different from simply asking a chatbot to "write me a website." A chatbot can give you code, but you still have to know where to put it, how to run it, how to fix it, and how to connect everything. Cursor brings the AI into the same space as the project itself.

In this book, we will use Cursor as the main tool for building. The workshop script describes Cursor as a platform that helps you build software with AI without needing to know how to code, and that is the core learning promise we will preserve throughout the book.

When Cursor works well, it can feel like you have a team of developers sitting beside you.

You can ask it to create a portfolio page. It can write the HTML, CSS, and JavaScript. You can ask it to change the color scheme. It can update the styling. You can ask it to add a map. It can embed one. You can ask it to make the site work on mobile. It can adjust the layout.

Later in the book, you will go further. You will create a more complete website, connect a form to email, upload the project to GitHub, deploy it with Vercel, and connect a domain.

That does not mean Cursor is perfect. It will make mistakes. It may misunderstand your instructions. It may create something that looks good but does not actually work. It may say a task is complete when it is only partly complete. It may ask you to do something manually. It may get stuck. It may need several attempts.

This is why the right mindset matters. Cursor gives you speed, but you still need judgment. It gives you code, but you still need to test the result. It gives you a shortcut, but not a guarantee.

What can you build with vibe coding?

The exciting answer is: a lot.

Cursor can help you create websites, landing pages, portfolios, simple web apps, internal tools, SaaS prototypes, plugins, dashboards, and browser-based tools. The script gives examples such as mobile apps, portfolio websites, landing pages, SaaS products, Chrome extensions, Discord bots, internal tools, and WordPress plugins.

As a beginner, though, the best starting point is not a massive app.

The best starting point is a small, focused project. It can be any of the following or beyond:

- A one-page portfolio
- A landing page for a local business
- A simple image tool
- A form that sends emails

- A booking page
- A small calculator
- A niche utility for a group of people with a specific problem

The reason is simple: small projects teach you the full workflow without burying you in complexity.

A small website still teaches you how to prompt. It still teaches you how to organize files. It still teaches you how to preview the result. It still teaches you how to fix bugs. It still teaches you how to deploy. It still teaches you what to do when the AI gets confused.

Once you can do that with a small project, you can build confidence. Then you can increase the difficulty.

Why this matters for beginners

The old path into building software was intimidating. You had to pick a language. Then a framework. Then a code editor. Then a package manager. Then a deployment platform. Then a database. Then authentication. Then APIs. Each step had its own errors, tutorials, outdated screenshots, version differences, and confusing terminology.

Many people quit before building anything useful.

Vibe coding gives beginners a new entry point. You can begin with the outcome rather than the syntax. You can say:

```
Create a modern landing page for a vet clinic with a services section,
testimonials, a contact form, and a map. In the main menu, show a register button.
Use whatever tech stack you think is best.
```

That is a normal sentence. Cursor can turn that sentence into a starting point.

The starting point may not be perfect, but it gives you something to react to. That is powerful because it is much easier to improve something visible than to stare at a blank screen.

This book will keep that practical approach. You will not start with theory. You will start by building.

You are not trying to become a traditional developer overnight

One of the most important ideas in this book is this: you do not need to understand everything at once.

You will see files with names such as index.html, package.json, .env.local, and README.md. You will see terms such as React, Next.js, Tailwind, Node.js, GitHub, Vercel, Resend, Supabase, APIs, and MCPs.

Some of these will sound strange at first.

That is okay.

You are not expected to master all of them immediately. At the beginning, you only need a practical understanding of what each thing does.

For example:

- Cursor is where you build
- GitHub is where you store and version your project
- Vercel is where you publish it
- Resend helps your forms send emails
- Supabase can help with databases and user accounts
- Node.js helps modern web projects run
- Python and Git can help tools work correctly behind the scenes

You will learn these ideas through use, not through abstract lectures.

Clear thinking, patience, and execution

Since AI writes the code, it is tempting to think the human role becomes less important. Actually, the opposite is true. Your thinking becomes more important.

AI needs direction. It needs constraints. It needs examples. It needs feedback. It needs to know what matters and what does not. It needs you to notice when something looks wrong, when something does not work, or when it has quietly skipped part of the task.

A vague prompt can still produce something, but it may not produce what you imagined.

For example, this prompt is weak:

"Make me a website."

This prompt is better:

"Create a one-page portfolio website for a freelance web designer. Use a clean blue and white color scheme, a hero section with a call-to-action button, a portfolio section with six projects, a testimonials section, a contact form, and a footer with social links. Make it responsive for mobile."

The second prompt gives Cursor a direction. It describes the type of site, the audience, the layout, the style, and the expected sections.

The more clearly you think, the better the AI can help. I also feel like this needs to be said early: **you will get stuck.**

Not because you are doing something wrong. Not because you are not technical enough. Not because the tool is useless.

You will get stuck because this field is moving quickly. Interfaces change. Buttons move. Models behave differently from one week to the next. A tutorial might say "click Save," but your screen might not show a Save button. A tool might work perfectly on one computer and fail on another. A model might build a website in three minutes one day and struggle with a basic task the next.

That is part of working early with fast-changing tools.

The space is changing rapidly, so the course may become outdated in places, and the real goal is to teach principles rather than only button-by-button instructions. Patience is essential because learners will face issues specific to their computer, operating system, tools, or setup.

That message is important enough to repeat:

Your success will not come from avoiding every error. It will come from learning how to investigate, adapt, and keep moving when errors happen.

When something goes wrong, beginners often assume they are stuck forever. In vibe coding, being stuck is usually temporary. The process is simple:

1. Read the error or observe the problem.
2. Copy the exact message where possible.
3. Paste it into Cursor or another AI assistant.
4. Explain what you were trying to do.
5. Ask for a step-by-step fix.
6. Try the suggested fix.
7. Test again.
8. Repeat until it works.

You do not need to pretend you understand everything. You can say:

```
I am using Cursor. I tried to run this project, but I got this error: {paste the
error here}. Explain what it means in simple terms and give me the safest fix step
by step.
```

That kind of prompt is often enough to move forward.

There is a reason vibe coding feels both exciting and frustrating: it is still early.

The tools are powerful, but not always polished. AI models can produce impressive work, but they can also hallucinate. They may claim something is done when it is not. They may create fake-looking features. They may build a form that says "message sent" even though no email is actually being sent. They may create layouts that look good on desktop but break on mobile.

This is uncomfortable, but it is also where the opportunity is.

When a tool is mature, clear, stable, and easy for everyone, competition increases. When a tool is powerful but still messy, the advantage goes to people who are willing to learn it early, tolerate the frustration, and build practical experience. That is the tradeoff.

You need to remember you are not learning vibe coding because it is perfectly smooth. You are learning it because it gives you leverage. Many beginners get stuck trying to find the perfect idea. That is usually the wrong place to start.

Most profitable tools are not brilliant, once-in-a-generation ideas. Many are simple solutions to specific problems. Compressing images. Renaming files. Scheduling social posts. Creating a small plugin. Building a better landing page for a local business. Making a form easier to use. Helping a niche audience do one annoying task faster.

I will strongly emphasize that execution matters more than the idea itself. It gives examples of small, niche tools and local business websites as realistic opportunities, and it encourages learners to solve specific problems rather than chase the next huge startup idea.

This is an important business lesson. A simple idea, well executed, can beat a brilliant idea that never launches.

For this book, that means we will focus on shipping—not endlessly planning, not endlessly polishing, not waiting for the perfect concept.

We will build, test, fix, and publish.

What this book will help you build

The book will move in stages.

First, you will build a simple portfolio landing page. This will help you understand the basic Cursor workflow: create a folder, open it in Cursor, write a prompt, let the AI generate files, accept changes, preview the website, and request improvements.

Next, you will set up the tools that make Cursor more useful. This includes Python, Node.js, PowerShell, Git, GitHub, Docker, Vercel, Resend, and Supabase. You will not become an expert in each tool, but you will understand why they are part of the workflow.

Then, you will configure Cursor itself with rules and MCPs. This helps the AI behave more consistently and gives it more ability to work with your files and services.

After that, you will compare models. This matters because Claude, Gemini, and GPT-style models can behave differently. Some are more autonomous. Some ask more questions. Some are better at design. Some are better at debugging. Some are faster. Some are cheaper. The best way to understand them is to test the same prompt and compare the results.

Then, you will learn about costs, security, and realistic expectations. These chapters matter because beginners often worry too much about credits and too little about sensitive keys. We will correct both of those habits.

Finally, you will build a more complete website and publish it. This is where the workflow becomes real: local project, working form, GitHub, Vercel, domain, production fixes, and updates.

The core workflow

The workflow you will learn can be summarized like this:

1. Start with a clear project idea
2. Create a clean folder for the project
3. Open that folder in Cursor
4. Write a detailed but natural prompt
5. Let Cursor generate the first version
6. Accept and review the changes
7. Preview the website locally
8. Test the design and functionality
9. Ask Cursor to fix or improve specific things
10. Upload the project to GitHub
11. Deploy it with Vercel
12. Connect a domain
13. Keep improving the live project

That is the path from idea to launched website.

The details can get messy, but the flow itself is simple.

Cursor is where you build. GitHub is where you store. Vercel is where you publish. Resend helps emails work. Supabase comes in when projects need databases or accounts. The script uses that same high-level chain when explaining how a project moves from Cursor to GitHub to Vercel and eventually to a live website with a domain.

What you should not expect

This book will not turn you into a senior developer.

It will not teach every programming concept. It will not explain every line of generated code. It will not cover every possible error. It will not guarantee that your screen always matches the screenshots or that every model behaves the same way. That is not the goal. The goal is to make you capable of building and launching practical projects with AI assistance.

That means you will learn just enough technical knowledge to guide the AI, understand the workflow, protect yourself from common mistakes, and ship useful work.

You will still need patience. You will still need to test everything. You will still need to ask good questions. You will still need to be skeptical when the AI says something is done.

But you will not be starting from zero anymore.

What you should expect

You should expect to build real things.

They may not be perfect at first. They may not look exactly like the design in your head. They may need several rounds of fixes. The final 10 or 20 percent may take longer than expected. The important thing is that you will have something working. Something you can improve. Something you can show. Something you can publish. Something you can potentially sell, use in a portfolio, or turn into a larger project.

A working project teaches more than a perfect plan.

> Note
>
> **A note on perfectionism**
>
> Vibe coding can make you impatient.
>
> When the first version appears in minutes, you may expect every refinement to be just as fast. Sometimes it is. Often, it is not.
>
> Changing a color may be easy. Fixing a spacing issue across desktop and mobile may take multiple attempts. Making a form truly work may require an API key, environment variables, deployment settings, and careful testing. Making images load correctly may require debugging paths, optimization, or hosting behavior.
>
> Do not let that discourage you. The early version gives you momentum. The later refinements teach you judgment.
>
> The script repeatedly warns that the last 10 to 20 percent can be the hardest part and that perfectionism can slow you down. The better habit is to launch, gather feedback,

> and polish based on real needs rather than obsessing over every detail before anyone sees the project. That is how we will approach the book projects.

Your role as the builder

Throughout this book, think of yourself as the builder, not merely the "user." A user clicks buttons and waits.

A builder decides what matters. You will decide what the project should do. You will decide whether the design is good enough. You will decide whether the form actually works. You will decide whether an AI-generated answer makes sense. You will decide when to start a new chat, when to continue, when to switch models, and when to stop polishing.

Cursor is powerful, but it does not replace your judgment. That is good news. It means you remain in control.

Summary

Vibe coding lets you build software by describing what you want in plain language and using AI to generate and modify the code. Cursor is the workspace that makes this practical because it combines a code editor, project files, AI chat, Agent mode, and model access in one place.

This book will teach you how to use Cursor as a beginner, create your first website, set up the tools that make projects work, compare AI models, manage costs, protect sensitive information, debug problems, and publish a real website with GitHub, Vercel, Resend, and a domain.

The most important lesson in this chapter is not technical. It is mental: you need patience, clear communication, and a willingness to test everything.

You do not need to know how to code before starting.

You do need to think clearly, describe what you want, review what the AI creates, and keep going when something breaks.

That is the real foundation of vibe coding.

Practice exercise

Before moving on, write down three project ideas you could build with Cursor. Keep them small. For example:

- A portfolio website for a photographer
- A landing page for a local dentist
- A tool that resizes or renames images
- A simple booking page for a service business
- A one-page site for a restaurant, lawyer, vet, or repair shop

Choose one idea that feels useful but not overwhelming. In the next chapter, we will use that kind of thinking to build a first website in Cursor.

2

Building Your First Website in Cursor

In this chapter, we will create our first website in Cursor.

This first project is not meant to be perfect, advanced, or production-ready. It is meant to show the basic workflow of vibe coding in a practical way. We will start with an empty folder, open that folder in Cursor, give the AI a prompt, let it generate the files, accept the changes, and then preview the website in a browser. After that, we will make a few simple changes to the result so we can understand how the AI-assisted workflow actually feels.

This is the first time we're moving from an idea to something visible on the screen. Vibe coding is not just about writing a prompt and hoping for the best. It is about giving the AI a clear task, watching what it does, accepting or refining the result, and then continuing from there. The website we create here will be simple, but the workflow is the foundation for everything that follows.

We will cover the following main topics in this chapter:

- Creating the project folder
- Opening the prompt in Cursor
- Starting the generation
- Previewing the first website
- Checking the mobile version
- Making the first change
- Adding a map to the website
- Creating a personal version

Before starting, this chapter should be approached in two passes. The first pass is for watching and understanding the flow. The second pass is for working along slowly. Cursor can move quickly, and trying to follow every action the first time around can become frustrating.

Creating the project folder

Every new project in Cursor starts with a folder.

This is an important habit to build from the beginning. All projects should be organized into their own folders, because Cursor will create and edit files inside the folder that is currently open. Keeping each project in a separate folder helps avoid confusion later, especially when there are several websites, apps, or experiments on the same computer.

For this project, we will create a new empty folder on the computer. The folder can be named anything. In this example, the folder is called **portfolio**, but the name does not matter. The important part is that it starts empty.

On Windows, it is better to avoid creating the project folder inside the main partition where Windows is installed, because that can sometimes create issues. A separate location is usually safer and cleaner.

Once the folder is created, Cursor can be opened and maximized so it takes up the full screen. Then we open the newly created folder inside Cursor. At this stage, nothing has been generated yet. We have simply prepared the space where the project will live.

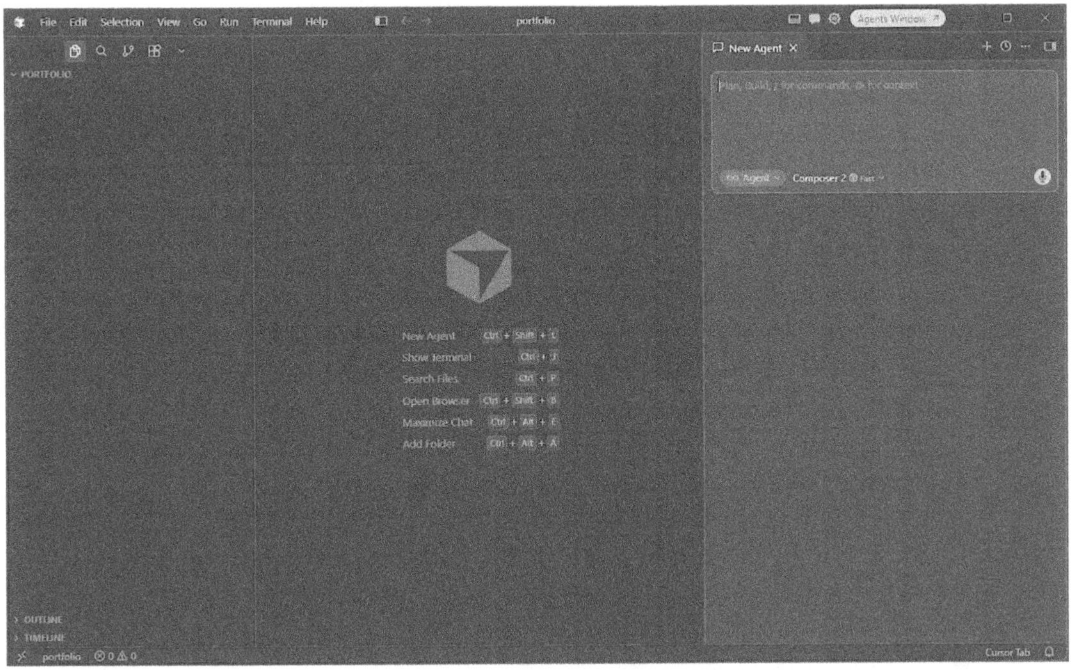

Figure 2.1: The Empty Portfolio folder

The empty folder matters because it gives the AI a clean starting point. There are no existing files to confuse the project structure, no old assets, and no previous code. Cursor is working inside one defined project space.

Opening the prompt in Cursor

Attached to the course is a text file containing the task for this first website. This task is the prompt. It describes what we want the AI to build.

The prompt is pasted into the chat area on the right side of Cursor. This right-side panel is where we communicate with the AI. It is the main place where the vibe coding workflow happens.

After pasting the prompt, we *do not* immediately press Enter. First, two settings need to be checked.

- The first setting is the mode. We are using **Agent mode**. This is important because Agent mode means the AI will create the code for us. For this course, that is the mode we will use. The other modes are not the focus here, because the goal is not to manually improve code as a developer. The goal is to tell Cursor what we want and let the AI do most of the work.
- The second setting is the model. Do not use **Auto** mode. Disable that setting to get access to the most used models that are available in Cursor. In this example, the selected model is **Gemini 2.5 Pro/Composer 2**. The same model should be used if it is available. If it is not available, one of the other options shown in Cursor can be used. The models will be explained in more detail later, so for now, the important part is to continue with the flow and see how the process works.

The prompt for this first project is:

```
Create a modern portfolio landing page for me, Chris Barin, 36, from Bucharest,
Romania. I have 14 years of experience in design, I'm an Adobe Certified
Instructor, and I specialize in web and app design. I prefer a red and black color
scheme, nice animations, and a portfolio section with 5 categories. Use
placeholder images for now. It will be one single page with a main menu at the top
that takes you down to that particular section. My office address is: Soseaua
Giurgiului 230, sector 4, Bucuresti. Add dummy reviews.
Add a contact form for people to message me and show my phone number: 0720.123.123
as well as all my social media profiles. Use best practices to build the landing
page.
```

The prompt is written in plain language. It describes the person, the location, the experience, the color scheme, the page structure, the portfolio section, the contact form, the phone number, social media profiles, dummy reviews, and the office address.

This is enough for Cursor to begin. The prompt is not written like technical documentation. It is not full of programming terms. That is intentional. We are describing the desired outcome in natural language and letting Cursor translate that into code.

It is also important to understand that the generated design may look different each time. Even with the same prompt and the same model, AI-generated results can vary. That is normal. The goal is not to reproduce the exact same design pixel by pixel. The goal is to understand the workflow.

If the project does not work at all, that is also not a reason to panic. Some systems may need additional setup first. In that case, this exercise can be revisited after the setup section later in the course.

Starting the generation

Once the prompt is submitted, Cursor begins generating the website.

The right-side panel shows that it is working. This generating state tells us the AI is processing the task and creating the project files. There is a stop button in case we want to interrupt it, but for this exercise, there is usually no reason to stop the generation.

Inside the panel, the model may show different kinds of text. Some models explain a lot. They may show what they are thinking through, what they plan to do, and how they are approaching the task. In the interface, some of this text may appear in a lighter, washed-out gray. After a while, clearer text appears. The washed-out text represents the model's thought process or planning, while the clearer text is the actual response.

It can feel like watching the AI think through the task. That is one of the fascinating parts of this workflow. We are not only getting a final file; we can also observe the model's approach as it decides what to create.

The AI says it will start with an index file. That is a useful first signal because the index file is typically the main file for a simple website. At this point, we can already see that the model has understood the task well enough to start building the structure of the page.

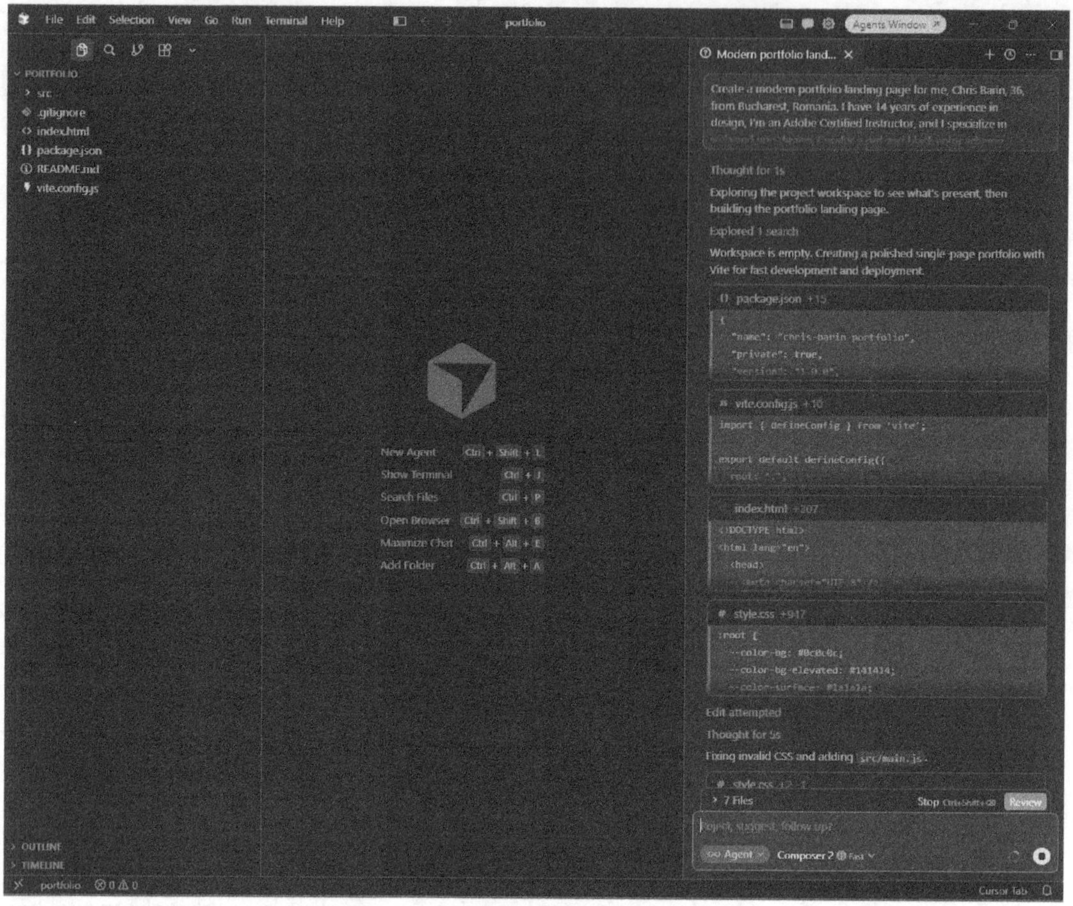

Figure 2.2: Model generating the first index file

After a few seconds, the index file appears in the project.

It appears in two places. On the left side of Cursor, it appears in the file explorer, inside the folder we created earlier. The folder was empty before. Now it contains a generated file. In the middle of the screen, the contents of that file are visible.

This is the first visible sign that Cursor has moved from prompt to code.

Most of the time, though, the focus will remain on the right-side panel. The file explorer and code editor are useful, but for vibe coding, the chat panel is where the main interaction happens.

After creating the index file, Cursor moves on to the CSS. The CSS controls the styling of the website. It determines how the page looks: colors, spacing, layout, visual presentation, and related styling. This part may take a few seconds. In a video, this may be sped up because generation can take a while.

Next, Cursor creates a JavaScript file. We do not need to understand every line of code. We do not need to read the code as developers. But it is useful to observe what the AI is doing. Watching the sequence helps us understand how Cursor approaches a project: first, the main page structure, then the styling, then the behavior.

At this stage, the AI is doing the heavy lifting. We gave it the task, and now it is creating the foundation of the website.

Depending on the selected model and your prompt, you may see a message that you have to approve. Cursor is asking you for permission to install a tool and use it. In most situations, you should allow it.

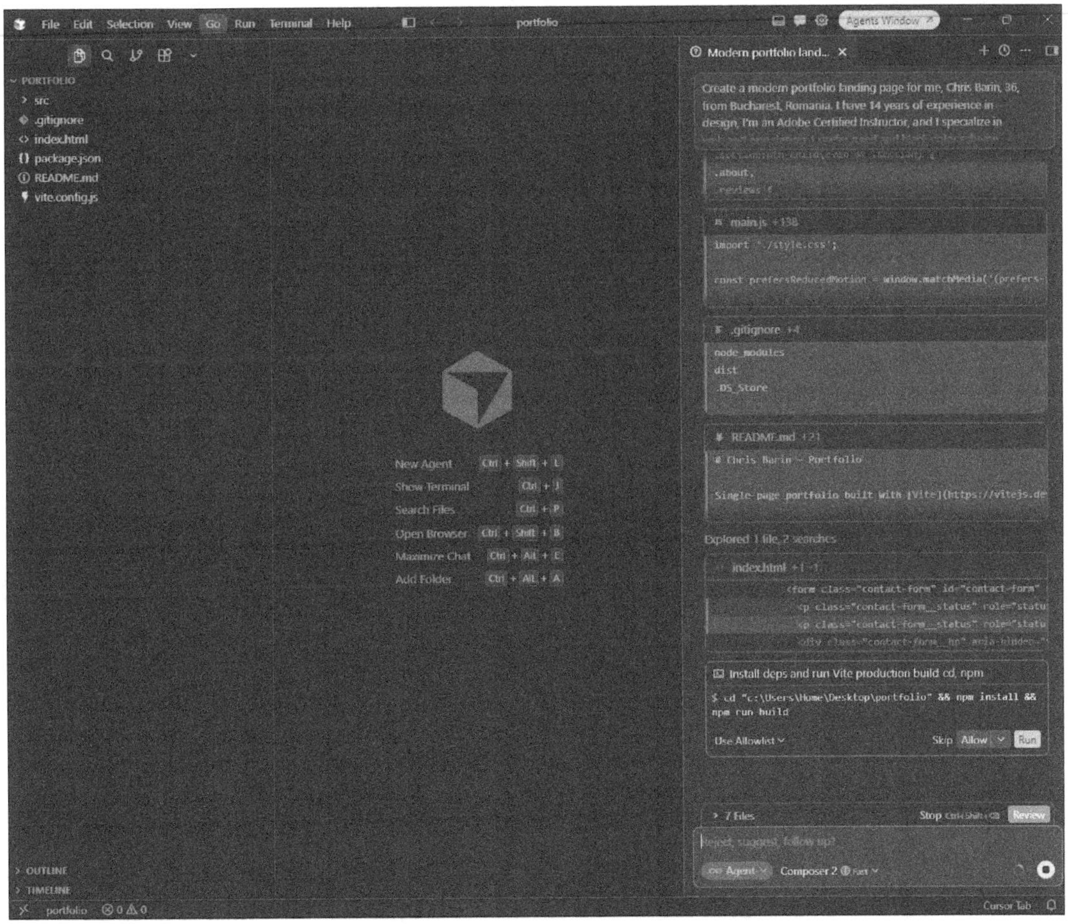

Figure 2.3: Approve permission to install a tool

The model decides what tools it needs, so don't worry if you see a lot of similar messages or none at all.

Reading the AI's summary

When Cursor finishes, it usually provides a summary or a set of instructions.

These instructions are for us. They explain what has been created and what may still need attention. In this first project, Cursor may mention that images need to be added, because we did not provide any actual image files. It may also explain that the contact form will not really work yet because it is not connected to anything. That is fine for now.

The first goal is to create a working visual version of the website. A fully working contact form will come later in the course. For now, it is enough to understand that the AI can build the structure and appearance of a simple landing page, but some features need additional setup.

When the generation is finished, the interface no longer says that the AI is generating. A button appears that says **Keep all**. This button is important. Cursor has created or modified files, but those changes still need to be accepted. Clicking **Keep all** commits the generated changes and saves the progress.

> **Note**
>
> This is a pattern we will use constantly. Cursor proposes changes, and we accept them when we want to keep them. Accepting changes is part of the workflow.

Here's what you'll see on your screen:

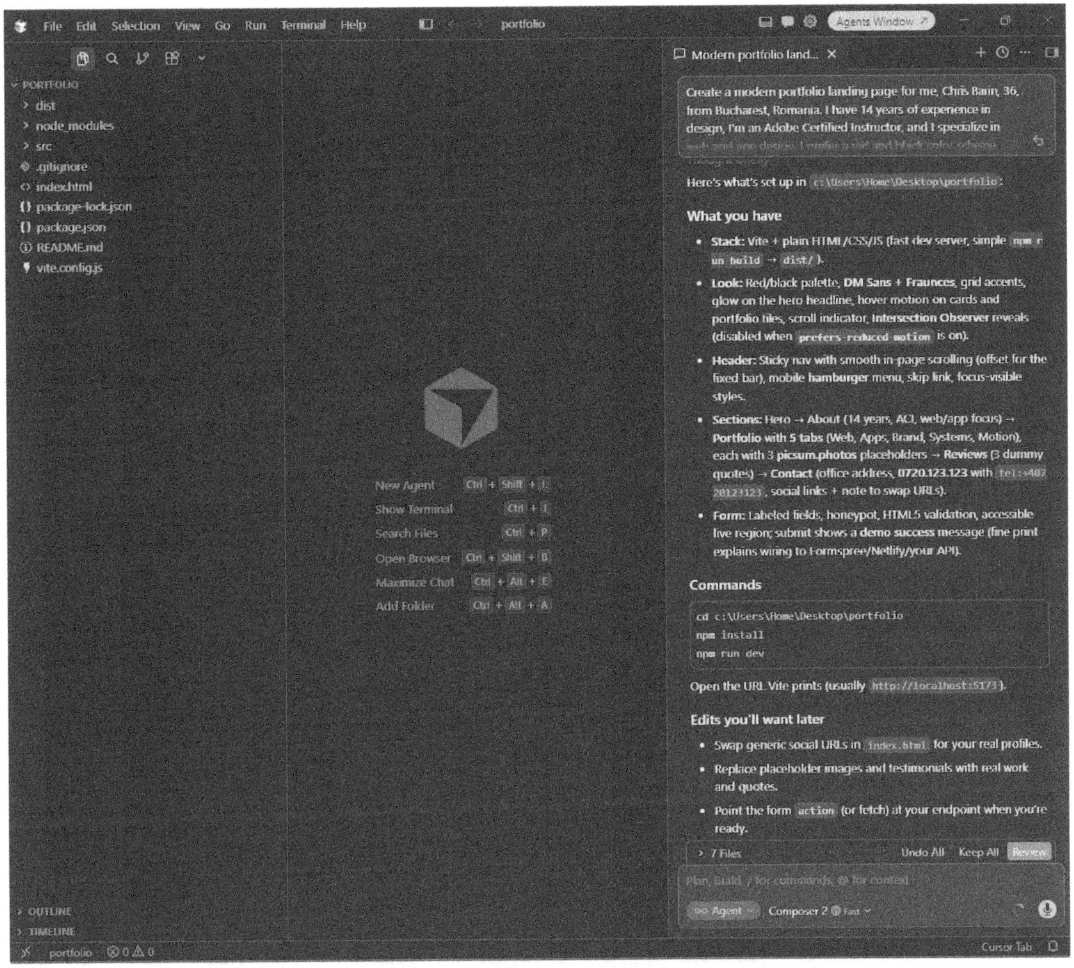

Figure 2.4: Accept all button after Cursor finishes generating the website

The summary may say that a basic version of the website is done and that it can be launched by opening the index.html file. This gives us the next step: previewing the website in the browser.

Previewing the first website

To preview the website, we go back to the project folder and open the index.html file.

In this example, Firefox is used, but any browser can be used. Opening index.html displays the generated website.

This is the first real result of the workflow. A few minutes earlier, we had an empty folder and a prompt. Now we have a website that can be opened in a browser.

The result is not expected to be beautiful or final. It probably will not look like a polished professional website yet. But that is not the point. The important thing is that there is now something visible and usable. We have a starting point.

Because we did not provide images, the AI does not download any images on its own. The website may therefore look empty in places where images were expected. That is normal. The prompt asked for placeholder images, and the AI handled the layout with that limitation.

Even with those limitations, the AI followed the instructions from the text file. It created a portfolio landing page, included the requested sections, and produced something that can be opened in a browser.

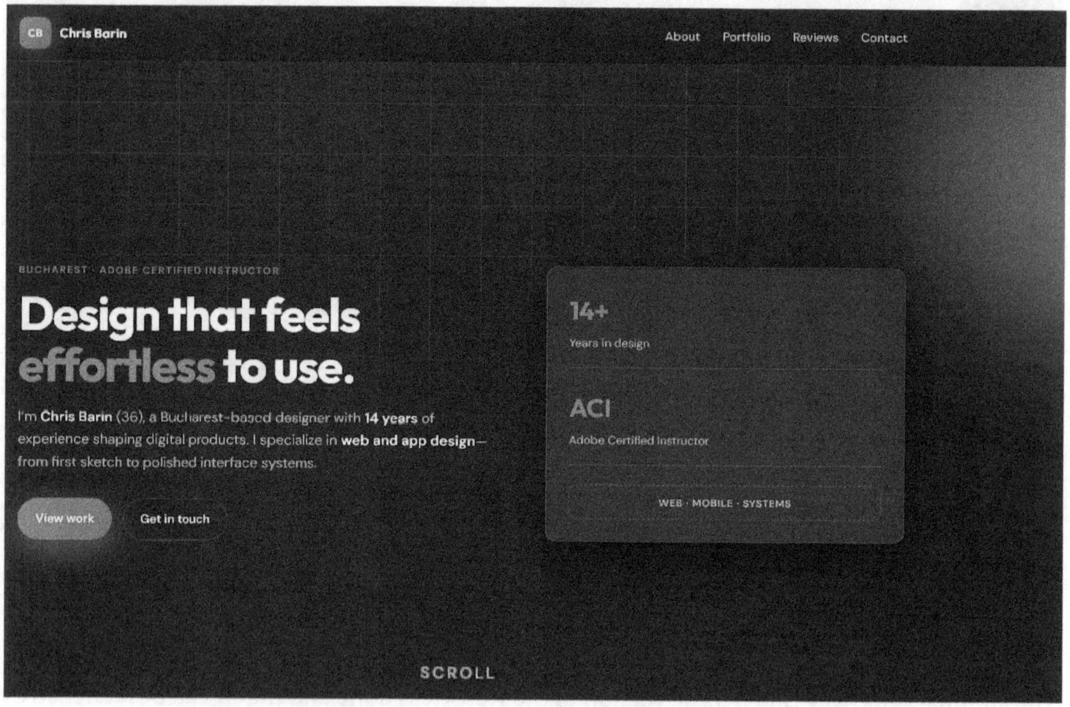

Figure 2.5: The first generated portfolio landing page opened in a browser

This is the core of vibe coding. We think about what we want, describe it in plain language, submit the prompt, and get a working starting point. The first version is rarely perfect, but we can build on it.

Checking the mobile version

The AI may also say that the website is optimized for mobile use. We should check that.

In Firefox, we can right-click the page and choose Inspect. The inspection tools include a mobile preview option. This allows the website to be viewed as if it were on a phone. If that button is difficult to find, the browser window can simply be resized to a narrow width that resembles a phone screen.

The goal is to see whether the layout still works on a small screen.

In this example, the website also looks good on mobile. That is not surprising, because the AI was asked to use best practices and said it optimized the page for mobile use.

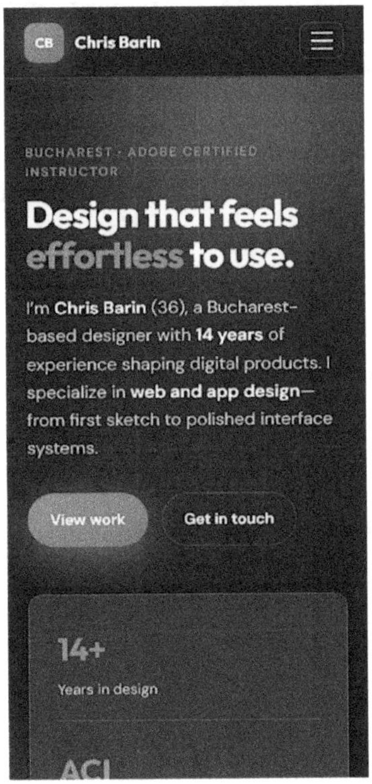

Figure 2.6: The generated website in mobile preview mode

This is a simple but important check. A website should not only look acceptable on a desktop screen. It should also respond properly to smaller screens. Cursor can handle a lot of that automatically, especially when the prompt asks for best practices, but the result should still be checked.

Making the first change

Now that the first version is working, we can ask Cursor to change something.

The original prompt asked for a red and black color scheme. In this example, the result feels too dark. So we ask the AI to change the color scheme to blue and white.

```
Change the color scheme from red and black to blue and white. The current design
feels too dark, so make it brighter, cleaner, and more balanced while keeping the
overall layout and content the same.
```

The instruction can be written naturally. We do not need to use technical terms or explain exactly which CSS properties should change. The request can simply say that the color scheme should be changed to blue and white.

Cursor understands the request and starts editing the CSS file.

As it edits, the interface shows red and greenish lines. The red lines represent code that will be removed. In this case, those are the old color values. The greenish lines represent the new code that will be added. In this case, those are the new colors.

This makes the change visible even without reading the code deeply. The old color scheme is being removed, and the new color scheme is being inserted.

When the change is complete, we need to accept the edits again. This is the same pattern as before: Cursor proposes the change, and we accept it.

After accepting the change, we return to the browser and refresh the page.

The website now uses a white and blue color scheme.

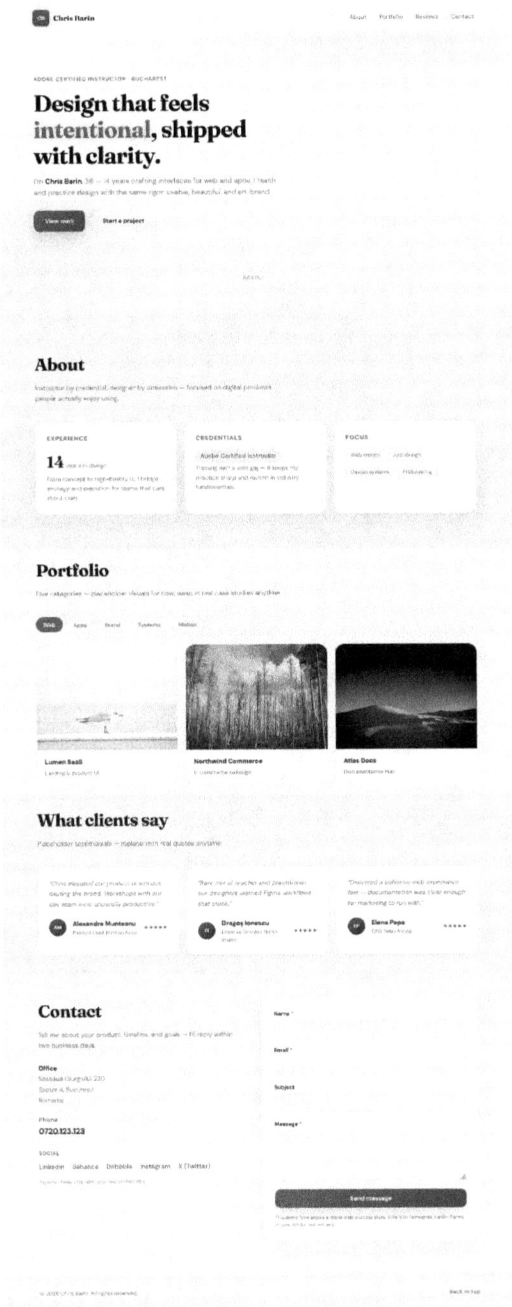

Figure 2.7: The portfolio website after the color scheme has changed to blue and white

Depending on the model and prompt, your website may not be visible by opening the index.html file. Instead, you may see Cursor guide you to open a link that looks like this: `http://localhost:5173/`

This is normal. If you're ever confused about how to preview your website, simply ask Cursor for help.

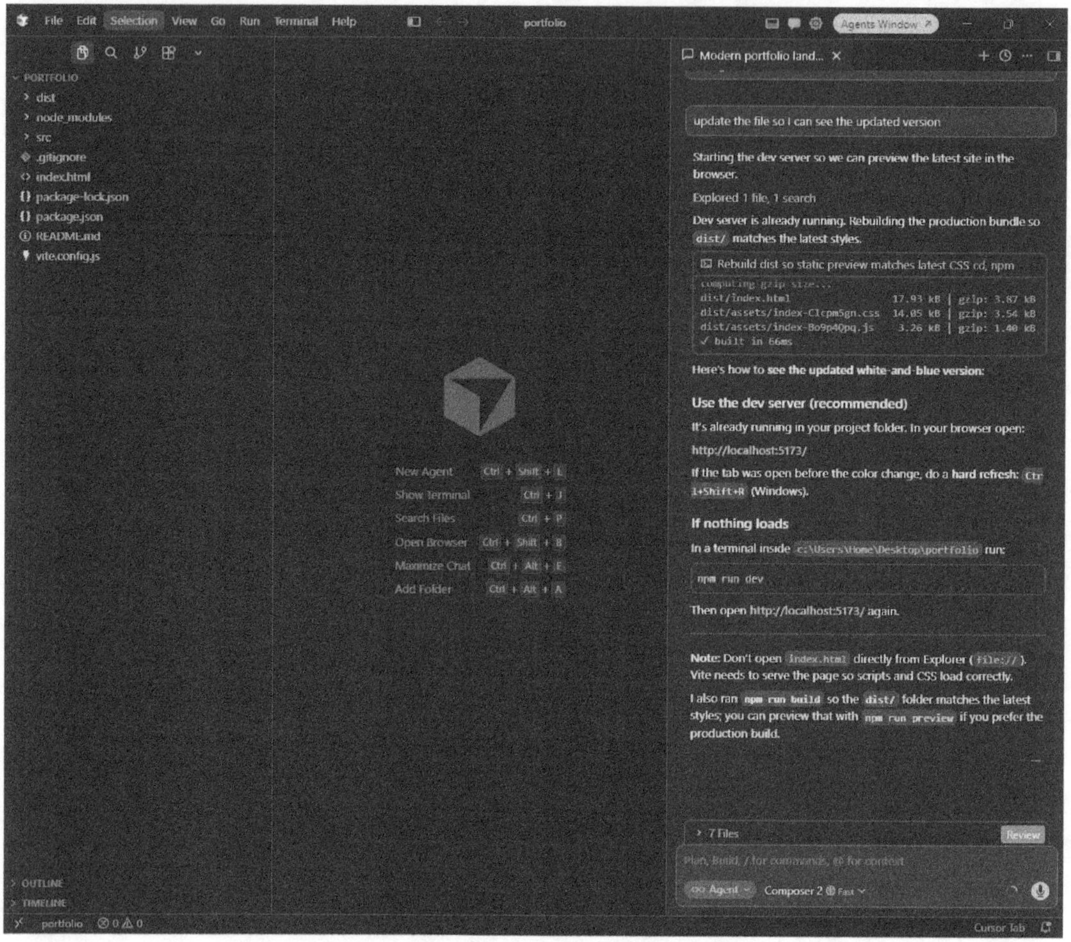

Figure 2.8: Asking Cursor how to preview the website

If the browser is still in mobile preview mode, that is not a problem. We can right-click and inspect again, turn off the mobile preview, close the inspection tools, or reopen the page. The point is simply to confirm that the new color scheme has been applied.

This is a small change, but it shows a key part of the workflow. We are not rebuilding the website manually. We are giving Cursor a design instruction in plain language and letting it update the project.

Note

Understanding how Cursor shows changes

The red and green lines are worth noting.

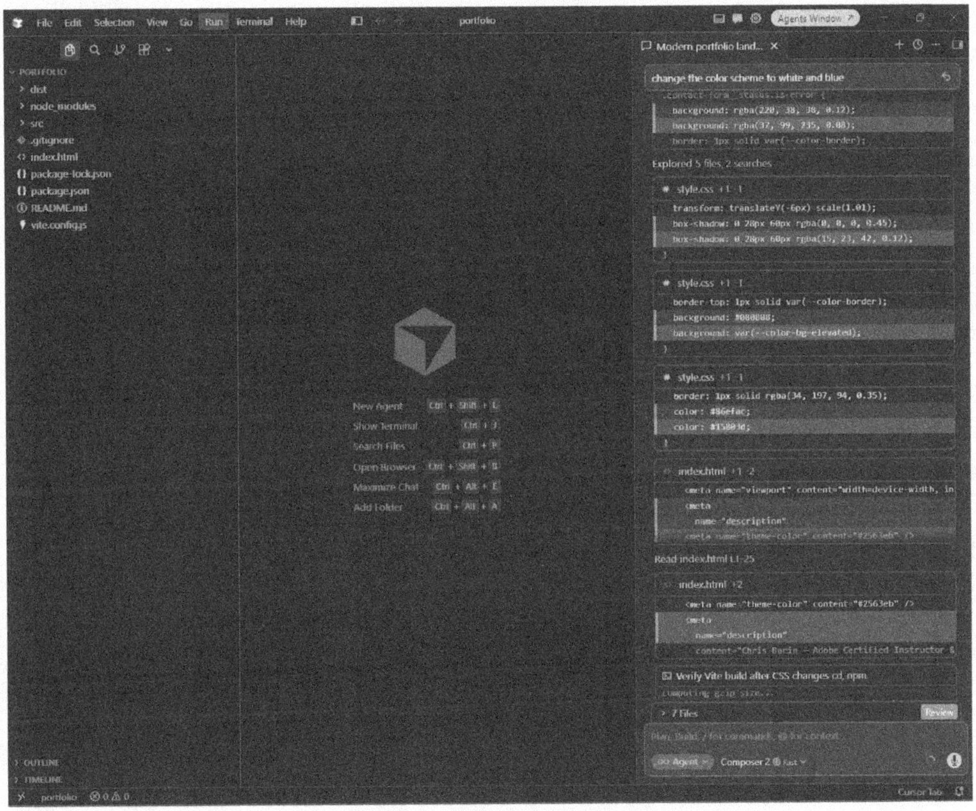

Figure 2.9: The red and green lines

When Cursor edits a file, it does not simply hide the work from us. It shows what is changing. Red means something is being removed. Green means something is being added.

> This gives us a rough sense of what the AI is doing, even if we are not reading the code line by line. When we ask for a color change and see old color values removed and new ones added, the change makes sense.
>
> We do not need to understand every technical detail, but we should get used to watching the pattern. The AI receives an instruction, edits the relevant files, shows the proposed changes, and waits for us to accept them.
>
> This is how the project evolves.

Adding a map to the website

The final change in this first workflow is to add a map instead of showing only the address.

The original prompt included the office address:

```
Soseaua Giurgiului 230, sector 4, Bucuresti
```

At first, the website may show the address as plain text. Now we ask Cursor to add a map instead.

This is a useful test because it moves beyond simple colors. We are asking Cursor to add a more functional element to the page.

There are limitations. AI cannot implement absolutely everything we can imagine, and later projects may involve features that require setup, accounts, keys, or additional services. But a map is a reasonable request for this first project. Results will vary depending on the model you've initially selected. Some may ask for permission to run various scripts or use certain tools, while others may fail altogether, and other models will work flawlessly.

```
Show the updated website with a map added to the page. Use a clean blue-and-white
color scheme. Show the browser refreshed after Cursor accepts the changes.
```

Cursor updates the website. Again, we accept the changes. Then we refresh the browser using the refresh icon, *F5*, or *Ctrl+R*.

The website now includes a functional map that can be zoomed in and out.

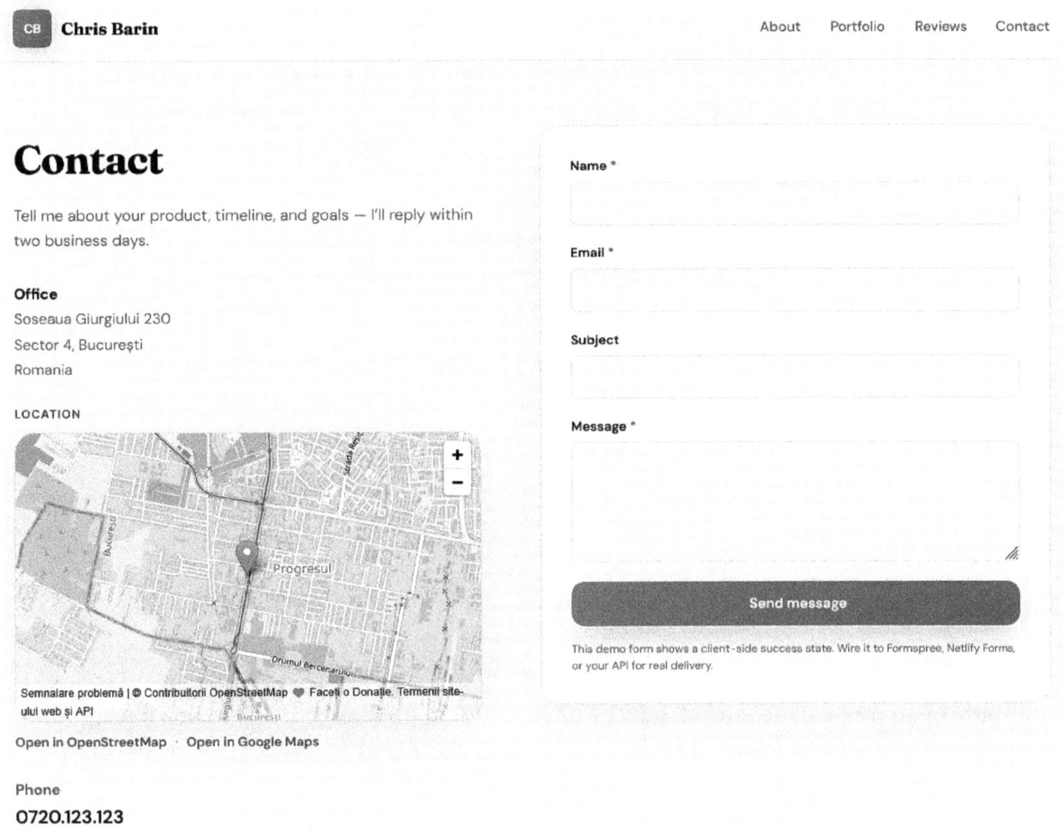

Figure 2.10: The contact section showing the embedded map

This is a strong example of the vibe coding loop. We created a first version, noticed something that could be better, described the change, accepted the update, and checked the result in the browser.

We imagined it, described it, and got it. Then the work became refinement.

> **Note**
>
> This first project introduces the basic Cursor workflow.
>
> We start with a folder. We open that folder in Cursor. We paste a prompt into Agent mode. We choose a model. We let the AI generate the files. We accept the changes. We open the result in the browser. We inspect the result, then continue improving it with natural language instructions.
>
> The important point is not that the website is perfect. It is not. The design may be basic. The images may be missing. The contact form may not actually work yet. But the workflow is real.
>
> We now have a website that exists as files on the computer and can be opened in a browser. We have also changed its color scheme and added a map without manually writing the code ourselves.
>
> That is the foundation of vibe coding.

Creating a personal version

After completing the first version, the next step is to create a personal version.

The starting prompt can be reused, but the details should be changed. The name, background, location, contact information, preferred colors, and other personal details can be adjusted.

The workflow is the same:

1. Create a new folder on the computer
2. Open that folder in Cursor using Open Folder
3. Paste the adjusted prompt
4. Make sure Agent mode is selected
5. Choose the model – don't leave it set to **Auto**
6. Run the prompt
7. Accept the generated files
8. Open the result in the browser or as instructed by Cursor

Once the website is generated, a screenshot of the full design can be captured.

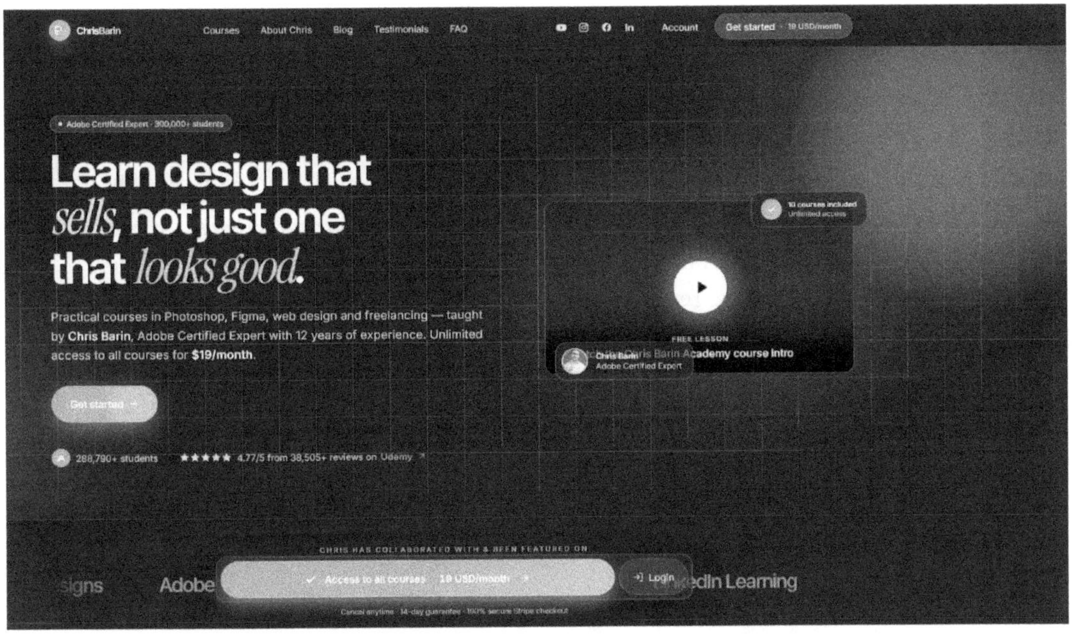

Figure 2.11: An example final personalized portfolio website created from the adapted prompt

Some people may run into errors. Cursor may stop working, ask for additional tools, or show messages that are difficult to understand. That is normal at this stage. This book will soon go through the setup needed to reduce those issues.

For now, the important thing is to understand the flow and try the first project. Even if something breaks, that becomes part of the learning process.

Summary

In this chapter, we created the first website in Cursor from a simple prompt.

We started with an empty folder, opened it in Cursor, used Agent mode, selected a model, and gave the AI a portfolio landing page prompt. Cursor generated the website files, including the main page, styling, and behavior. We accepted the generated changes, opened the website through index.html, checked the desktop and mobile versions, changed the color scheme, and added a functional map.

The result was not perfect, and it was not meant to be. The real lesson is the workflow. Vibe coding is an iterative process: describe what should be built, review what the AI creates, accept the changes, preview the result, and keep refining.

This first website gives us something real to build on.

Practice exercise

In this exercise, you'll create a simple personal portfolio website using Cursor. This does not need to be a professional designer portfolio, and you do not need to sell services or have client work to show. The goal is to practice turning an idea into a working website with AI assistance.

Your portfolio can be about you as a developer, learner, student, writer, creator, or professional. It can include projects you have already built, things you are currently learning, or even placeholder projects you plan to replace later.

Ask Cursor to help you create a portfolio website with the following sections:

- A homepage introduction
- An About section
- A Projects section
- A Skills or Tools section
- A Contact section

3

Choosing What to Build

Before diving into how Cursor works, there's a question worth addressing first: what should *you* build?

Not everyone who comes to vibe coding has a product idea ready to go. Most people aren't entrepreneurs with a startup vision sitting in their back pocket. That's completely fine; it's exactly why this chapter exists.

But one principle needs to land before anything else, because without it, the examples that follow are easy to misread: **Ideas are worthless. Execution is everything.**

This isn't meant to be provocative. It's just how successful small software products actually get built and why the ones that fail usually do. The quality of an idea, on its own, determines almost nothing. What matters is whether you build something, get it in front of people, and keep improving it after that first version ships. Keep that in mind as you read through everything that follows.

We will cover the following main topics in this chapter:

- The Threshold for a Viable Idea Is Lower Than Expected
- Niche Revenue: The PDF to Excel Converter
- Execution Beats Originality: The Case of Pallyy
- Single Features, Real Products
- Niche Over Scale
- Local Businesses as a Market
- Building in Public

Note

Download the PDF version of this book

Your purchase includes a DRM-free PDF copy of this book, the code bundle, and a range of exclusive benefits. To unlock everything, follow the *Free benefits with your book* section in the *Preface*.

The threshold for a viable idea is lower than expected

The instinct when thinking about what to build is to aim for something original. Something that has not been done before, or that solves a problem in a genuinely novel way. That instinct, while understandable, is not particularly useful at the start. The most instructive examples of small software businesses that actually work tend to be the ones that look almost embarrassingly simple in concept.

Consider `iLoveIMG.com`. This website does one primary thing: it shrinks images. If there has been any time spent working in Photoshop or any similar design application, the problem is familiar. Exporting a finished graphic or photograph often produces file sizes in the range of two, three, or five megabytes. Those sizes are too large for web use, too slow to load, and wasteful of storage.

iLoveIMG addresses that directly: drag the file in, drop it, and the output is roughly 80% smaller with no meaningful loss in visible quality. The platform also handles quick image resizing, and there are a few additional features beyond those two. The price is between four and seven dollars per month. It is not a complex tool. It is not a unique idea. Image compression has been a solved technical problem for decades. And yet the platform has a large paying user base, and it is good enough that even seasoned designers, people who know perfectly well how to compress images manually, sign up for it because the convenience is worth the cost.

`[IMAGE PLACEHOLDER: Screenshot of iLoveIMG.com showing the drag-and-drop image compression interface and feature list]`

The lesson from iLoveIMG is not about image compression specifically. It is about the relationship between simplicity, convenience, and willingness to pay. People pay for tools that save them time, reduce friction, and sit exactly where they need them. The underlying technology does not have to be impressive. The product just has to work, and it has to be easy to use.

Niche revenue: the PDF-to-Excel converter

Along similar lines, there is a platform that converts PDF files into Excel spreadsheets. The target audience is extremely specific: accountants, bookkeepers, finance teams, and anyone who regularly receives financial data locked inside a PDF and needs to work with it in a spreadsheet. That is a narrow slice of users. It is not a tool that most people will ever need. And yet, by focusing on that narrow slice and solving the problem well, the platform generates approximately $38,000 per month.

That number is worth sitting with for a moment. Thirty-eight thousand dollars per month from a tool that converts one file format into another, aimed at a category of users that most software products ignore entirely. The narrowness of the focus is not a weakness. It is exactly why the product works. The people who need it really need it, they are willing to pay for it, and there are enough of them to sustain a serious business.

There is another tool that renames phone photos automatically. Most smartphones name photos sequentially: IMG_0001, IMG_0002, IMG_0003. This tool replaces those meaningless filenames with something descriptive and human-readable, which is particularly useful for anyone sitting on thousands of vacation photos that currently carry no useful information in their names. Again: super specific service, narrow audience, real problem, real revenue.

Execution beats originality: the case of pally

Pallyy.com is an instructive case study in what execution over originality actually looks like in practice. The platform helps users schedule and publish content across multiple social media channels from a single dashboard. It is not a new idea. Social media scheduling tools have existed for years. There are probably fifty other platforms that do something meaningfully similar to Pallyy. Some charge more, some charge less, some have more features, some have fewer.

Figure 3.1: Screenshot of the Pallyy.com homepage showing the scheduling and publishing dashboard

The founder of Pallyy built and ran the entire platform alone, without a team, for years. He documented the journey publicly as he went. At the time of writing, the platform generates over one million Australian dollars per year. He is now in the process of considering selling it.

This is what the execution argument looks like when it plays out over time. The idea was not special. The competitive landscape was crowded. None of that prevented the platform from reaching that level of revenue, because the person behind it focused on building something that worked, kept improving it, grew an audience, and stayed consistent over a long period. The fifty other platforms doing similar things are not a reason why Pallyy could not succeed. They are proof that the market exists and that people are willing to pay.

The practical advice that follows from this: focus on the design side. Take something that has already been done a hundred times, add a genuinely well-considered design and a cleaner user experience, and there is a business in that. Promotion and audience-building are separate disciplines, but the starting point is the quality of what gets built and how it feels to use it, not whether the idea has been done before.

Single features, real products

Some of the most successful small software products are built around a single feature, expanded over time once the core proves itself. Basecamp is a useful example here because it looks like a complex project management platform from the outside, but it is fundamentally organized around one thing: messages. At its core, it functions as a structured way to keep communication and to-do lists organized, not unlike Notion in some respects. The additional layers of functionality were added incrementally, after the original value was established.

Figure 3.2: Screenshot of Basecamp interface showing the message board and task structure

That model of starting with one concrete feature and expanding from there is widely applicable. An app that reminds someone to stand up from their desk once an hour is a real product. It sounds trivial. It probably takes a weekend to build. But there is a specific group of people who want exactly that, who have tried to remember to do it on their own and failed, and who would pay a small amount per month for a reliable reminder system. How to monetize it, how to build an audience around it, how to promote it: those are separate questions. The starting point is recognizing that products built around a single specific behavior, done well, can generate income.

WordPress plugins are a clear illustration of this pattern. There is a plugin that does nothing more than pull social media posts into a WordPress website and display them inline. That is its entire function. It generates significant passive income for its creator. There is another plugin that adds a customizable announcement bar to the top or bottom of a site, a simple strip of text with a background color and a close button. There is one that simplifies the installation of Google Analytics or Facebook Ads tracking code for site owners who do not want to touch their theme files. Each of these does one small thing. Each of them earns money because that one thing is useful enough to a specific enough group of people that they will pay rather than figure it out themselves.

The WordPress ecosystem is a good place to notice this pattern because the plugin marketplace makes the commercial outcomes visible. But the same logic applies to browser extensions, standalone web tools, email automation utilities, and any other category where a small, focused tool can slip into someone's existing workflow without requiring them to change everything around it.

Niche over scale

There is a temptation, especially when first thinking about building a product, to try to build for everyone. A general-purpose tool, a broad platform, something that could theoretically be useful to a large number of people. That temptation is worth resisting, at least in the beginning, because serving everyone well is difficult and the path to the first paying customers is much longer.

A horoscope platform was vibe-coded live on TikTok. The creator streamed the process of building it, the audience watched, and the platform did well. A wallpaper app was built for fans of a specific subgenre of anime, not anime broadly, but a particular style within it. Neither of these products was trying to compete with Uber or DoorDash, or any other company operating at a massive scale. They did not need to. Getting to one thousand, five thousand, or ten thousand dollars per month does not require building for the entire market. It requires solving a problem for a small, specific group of people who care about that problem deeply enough to pay for a solution.

The narrower the niche, the more clearly the product can speak to the people who need it. The messaging is simpler, the value proposition is more obvious, and the path to finding the first users is more direct. A tool for a specific type of anime fan does not need to convince everyone it is worth using. It needs to convince a subset of a passionate community that it solves something they have been dealing with. That is a much more achievable goal than building for the general public and hoping enough people notice.

Local businesses as a market

Not every application of vibe coding leads to a software product. There is another path that is often overlooked, particularly by people who are not natural entrepreneurs: building websites for local businesses.

The portfolio website built in *Chapter 2* took a matter of minutes from prompt to result. That same capability can be turned into a service business. The exercise is straightforward: find a hundred local businesses in any city or town. Dentists, restaurants, lawyers, auto repair shops, veterinary clinics, service businesses of all kinds. Look at their websites, if they have them at all. A significant proportion will have websites that are outdated, slow, visually poor, or not functional on mobile. These businesses are doing real volume and generating real revenue. They are simply not technical, and they have not prioritized their web presence because building a website historically required hiring someone with specialized skills.

The outreach model is flexible. Platforms exist that list every dentist or every accountant in a given city or region. The list is not hard to find. What matters more than the list is the approach: email outreach, phone calls, showing up in person, finding the decision-maker, and making the offer clearly. The pricing structure is equally flexible. Charging a flat fee of around a thousand dollars for a finished site is one option. Charging a recurring monthly fee in the range of eighty dollars for ongoing maintenance and updates is another. Both models can work. The right choice depends on the specific business, the relationship, and the local market.

In many parts of the world, restaurants, law firms, service shops, and veterinary clinics represent businesses that earn well but whose digital presence does not reflect that. Their customers find them through word of mouth or outdated directory listings. A well-built, fast, mobile-optimized website with a clear contact form and accurate information is genuinely valuable to them, and many of them know it. They just have not had an affordable, reliable path to getting one.

A web design service built on vibe coding can differentiate in ways that traditional agencies cannot easily match. Specialization is one approach: pick an industry that is personally familiar, learn its language, and its customers' expectations, and build a portfolio within that vertical. A specialist who has built twenty websites for veterinary clinics knows exactly what that client needs, can deliver faster, and can speak credibly to the outcome. That is a meaningful advantage over a generalist agency quoting the same project.

The competitive window for this type of work is real but not unlimited. More people are learning to vibe code, and as the tools become more accessible, the market for this kind of service will attract more competition. Prices will compress over time. Someone who is building and delivering these sites now, accumulating experience, and client references, will be in a substantially stronger position than someone who waits until the process becomes easy for everyone. That lead is worth acting on, but it does not require panicking. The market is large enough that there is more than enough work to go around for the foreseeable future. Starting with a few smaller, lower-stakes projects before taking on paid client work is the right approach: get comfortable with the delivery workflow, understand where the friction points are, and then bring that experience to client engagements.

Building in public

There is a practice that has developed into a recognizable movement in the independent software world: building in public. The concept is simple. Founders post about what they are building openly on social media, in real time, as the project develops. What went wrong this week, what got fixed, what the revenue looks like at each milestone, what decisions were made, and why. It is simultaneously a marketing strategy, a form of accountability, and a source of community feedback.

Social media is full of people doing exactly this with small tools, niche products, and local service businesses. Looking at their profiles reveals that these are ordinary people, not technical prodigies or business school graduates. They had an idea, they shipped something, and they kept going. What makes their public documentation useful is not the eventual outcome; it is the granular, unfiltered detail of the process: the weeks where nothing worked, the first paying customer, the decision to raise prices, the features that users did not care about at all. That kind of documentation is far more instructive than a retrospective success story.

The building in public dynamics also creates a direct line between the work and the audience. People who follow along with the journey become potential customers. They feel invested in the outcome. They are more likely to sign up when the product launches and to refer others who might benefit from it. It is a form of pre-marketing that costs nothing beyond the time spent writing and posting consistently.

Even a tool as apparently trivial as converting square image corners into rounded ones can generate a hundred dollars per month in passive revenue. That sounds almost too small to bother with. But a hundred dollars per month from one tool, built once, running without ongoing effort, is a meaningful starting point. It is proof that the workflow produces income. It is experience with the process of shipping, promoting, and maintaining a product. And it is the kind of result that, posted publicly as part of a building-in-public journey, attracts attention and builds credibility for whatever comes next.

The founder of Pallyy documented every step of building that platform over several years. He was the only developer, managing every aspect of the product alone, for the entire time. That story is instructive not just as motivation but as a benchmark for what a solo builder can accomplish over time. The difference now is significant: with Cursor and the models it connects to, the same kind of solo-founder path does not require years of accumulated coding skill. The knowledge of a thousand senior developers is accessible for somewhere between fifteen and fifty dollars a month. The time required to get from idea to first working version is dramatically compressed compared to what the founder faced when he started.

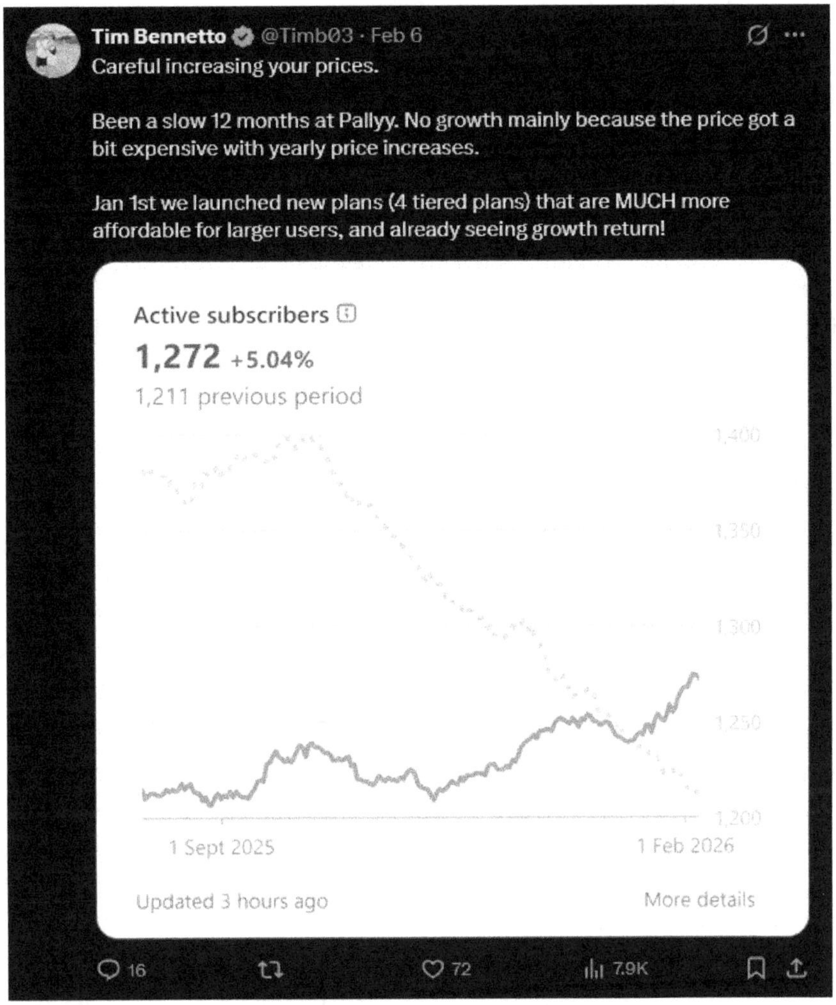

Figure 3.3: A year-long lesson in pricing

Note

Starting Somewhere

The question of what to build does not need to be resolved before getting started. In fact, waiting for the perfect idea before touching the tools is one of the most reliable ways to never ship anything. What this chapter is meant to establish is that the bar for a viable idea is much lower than most people assume, and that the factor that determines whether a product earns money is not whether the concept is original or impressive.

> The tools built by solo founders generating real revenue are not remarkable in their conception: a PDF converter, an image compressor, a scheduling dashboard. These are unremarkable ideas executed with consistent attention to quality and user experience. A well-designed, well-functioning solution to a specific problem is worth more than a brilliant concept that never becomes a working product.
>
> The practical path forward is to start small. Build something that solves a problem that is personally familiar. Post the process publicly if that is comfortable. Accept that the first version will be imperfect and that the process of refining it is where the real learning happens. The project that feels too simple to be worth building might turn out to be exactly the right place to begin.

Summary

This chapter covered the question of what to build when there is no obvious starting point, and established the core principle that underpins the rest of the course: execution matters more than the quality of any idea. The examples explored here, from image compression tools to social media schedulers to WordPress plugins, share a common characteristic. None of them required an original concept. All of them required someone to build the thing, ship it, and keep improving it.

Small, focused tools that solve a specific problem for a defined audience can generate meaningful revenue without requiring large teams, large budgets, or large ambitions. iLoveIMG shrinks images. A PDF-to-Excel converter serves accountants. Pallyy schedules social media posts, and fifty competitors doing the same thing did not prevent it from reaching seven figures in annual revenue. The pattern is consistent across every example: specificity and execution win over novelty.

For those without a product idea, building websites for local businesses is a direct and accessible path. The capability demonstrated in *Chapter 2* with the portfolio site is the same capability that can be turned into a paid service for restaurants, law firms, clinics, and any other business category where the web presence lags behind the actual quality of the operation.

The building-in-public movement offers both a marketing strategy and a source of ongoing inspiration. Following founders who document their process publicly provides a realistic view of what the journey looks like, including the setbacks, and a reminder that the people generating income from these tools are not exceptional. They are consistent.

The final point to carry forward is that the threshold for starting is lower than it appears. A project that earns a hundred dollars per month from a tool that rounds image corners is not a sign of low confidence or a lack of ambition. It is proof that the process works, experience that compounds, and a foundation to build on.

Chapter 4 moves from ideas to infrastructure. Before Cursor can operate at full capability, a set of supporting tools needs to be installed and configured: Python, Node.js, PowerShell, Git, GitHub, Docker, Vercel, Resend, and Supabase. None of them require deep technical understanding to set up, and having them in place before starting a real project avoids the compounding frustration of hitting missing-dependency errors mid-build.

Practice exercise

Before moving on, take twenty minutes to do the following. Open a browser and search for three local businesses in your area that operate in any of the categories mentioned in this chapter: restaurants, law firms, dental practices, veterinary clinics, auto repair shops, or any other service business that is likely to have an outdated or poorly maintained website.

For each business, visit their website, and note down three things. First, the business type, and what they do. Second, the specific problems visible on their site: slow loading, no mobile optimization, outdated design, missing contact information, broken pages, or no website at all. Third, what a replacement or improved site would need to include, and what a reasonable price for that work might look like, whether a flat fee or a monthly arrangement.

The goal of this exercise is not to build anything or contact anyone. It is to practice the habit of looking at the world around and identifying where the gap between a business's actual quality and its digital presence is large enough to represent a real opportunity. That gap is the business. Getting comfortable spotting it is the first step toward acting on it.

Keep the notes somewhere accessible. The businesses identified here may become the first outreach targets once the delivery workflow covered in later chapters is solid enough to take on paid work confidently.

4

Setting up Your Vibe Coding Toolkit

Before we continue building in Cursor, we need to set up a few tools on the computer. These tools help Cursor do a better job, especially when the goal is to do the least amount of manual work possible.

This does not mean giving complete control to AI. Instead, we are going to install well-known software that gives Cursor a stronger foundation. When Cursor needs to create, run, test, or publish a project, these tools reduce the chances of it getting stuck.

The goal is not to become technical right now. The goal is practical: create websites as fast as possible, with fewer errors, fewer wasted credits, and less lost momentum.

There is a temptation to skip setup and go straight into building. That is understandable because installing tools is not the exciting part. But if Cursor keeps running into missing software, broken commands, or unavailable accounts, every small issue becomes a distraction. The work slows down, the credits get used up, and the frustration builds.

It is much better to prepare the computer now.

We will cover the following main topics in this chapter:

- Installing Python
- Installing Node.js
- Installing PowerShell 7
- Creating a GitHub account
- Installing Docker – optional
- Installing Git for Windows

- Creating a Vercel account
- Creating a Resend account
- Creating a Supabase account
- Completing the toolkit checklist

Note

Why are we installing these tools?

There are several pieces of software and a few online accounts that will help us later. We will install Python, Node.js, PowerShell 7, Docker (optional), and Git. We will also create accounts for GitHub, Vercel, Resend, and Supabase.

This may feel like a lot, but the reason is simple. We are about to cook many dishes in the kitchen. It will be breakfast, lunch, dinner, desserts, snacks, and full meals. That means we need a fully stocked fridge and the right utensils. We need ingredients, knives, forks, spoons, and everything else ready.

That is what we are doing in this chapter.

Are we going to use absolutely every single tool in every project? No. But it is much easier to prepare everything now than to start searching for missing tools while building.

If Cursor throws error after error because we are missing this or that, we lose credits, time, energy, and momentum. This is why it makes sense to install everything now, pause often, and get through the checklist properly. After that, the work becomes smoother.

Installing Python

The first tool we need to install is Python.

On the website, choose the latest Python release.

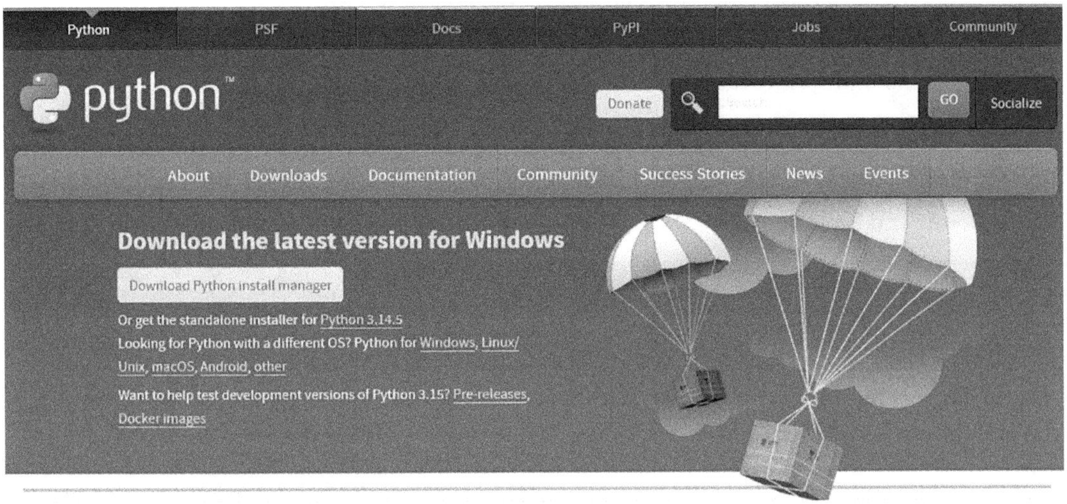

Figure 4.1: Python release download page showing the Files section and the recommended Windows installer

Download the installer and start the installation.

There is one important detail in this step: the second checkbox in the installer should be enabled. We are not going to go into details about that checkbox because it would sidetrack us. For our purposes, both checkboxes should be selected, and then the installation can continue.

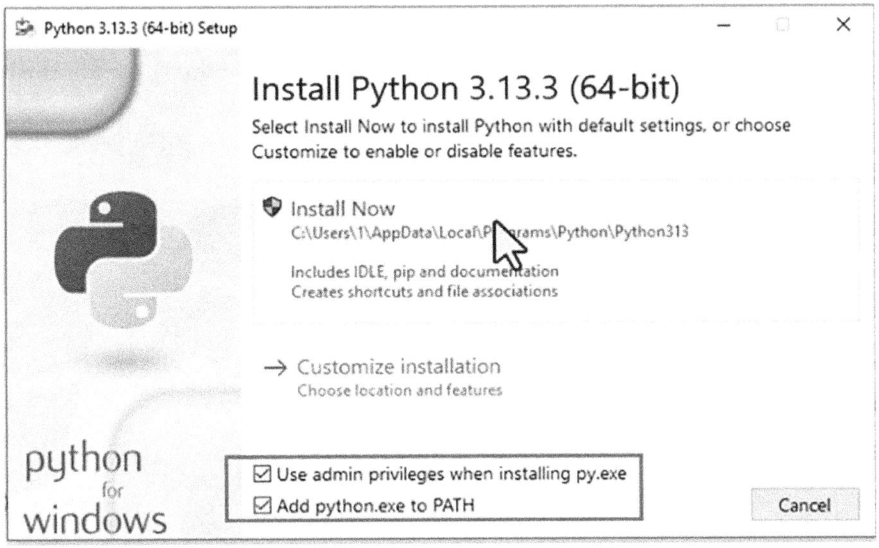

Figure 4.2: Python installer screen showing both setup checkboxes selected

The installation takes a moment, but there is nothing special going on. In some cases, Python may not install correctly. We will deal with troubleshooting later. For now, we need to check whether the installation worked.

Open the **Start** menu and type *CMD*. CMD is short for command, and the app we want is **Command Prompt**.

Inside Command Prompt, type:

```
py
```

py is simply the first two letters of Python. If the installation is working, the Command Prompt should show Python running, usually with a version number. The version may be newer than the one shown in the course, and that is fine. What matters is that there are no warnings or issues.

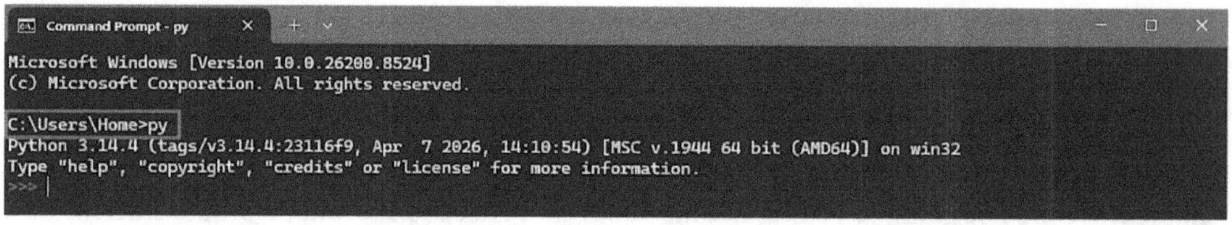

Figure 4.3: Command Prompt after running py, showing Python starting successfully with a version number

If this does not work from Command Prompt, there is another way to check. Open Cursor, go to the top menu, choose **Terminal**, and start a new terminal. The terminal opens at the bottom of the Cursor window.

Type the same command:

```
py
```

If Python opens there, the installation is done.

At this stage, Python is checked off.

> **Note**
>
> The important thing to understand is that we are not stopping here to learn Python. That would make the setup feel much heavier than it needs to be. Learning about Python right now will not help us build websites faster. It will likely make everything feel more complicated.
>
> So we keep it practical. Python is installed, checked, and ready.
>
> Ideally, restart the computer after installing Python, just to be safe. Continuing without a restart may still work, but restarting can prevent some issues.

Installing Node.js

Next on the list is Node.js, specifically the LTS version. This is another must-have.

During the Node.js installation process, the installer asks whether it should install a few other tools. We want that option enabled, so make sure it is checked.

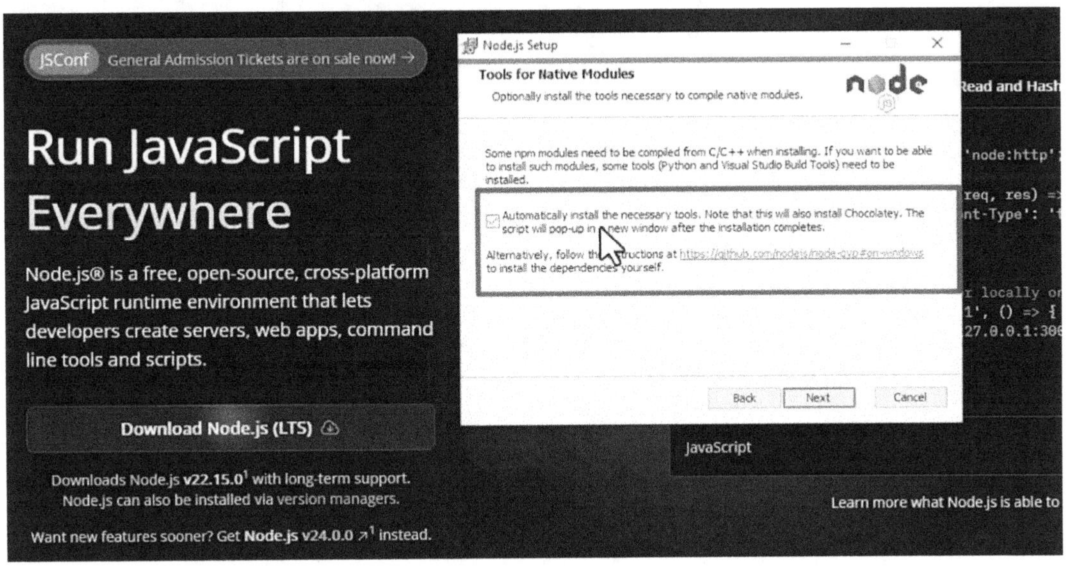

Figure 4.4: Node.js installer option that asks to install additional tools

After that, another window appears with a lot of text. It does not ask for anything, but it may take a few minutes while it does its work.

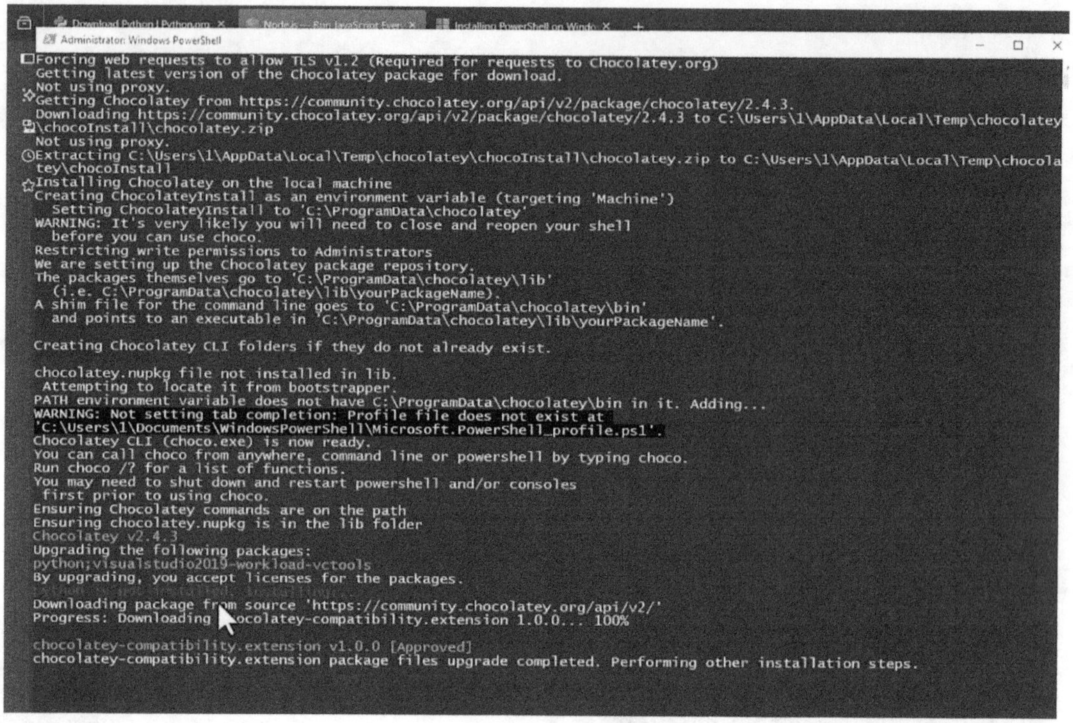

Figure 4.5: Window with text

> **Note**
>
> On my end, there was one funny issue. The installer said it could not find Python, even though Python was already installed. A restart could have potentially solved that. Since I knew Python was installed, it was not a big deal.

After a while, the process simply stops. Then we need to check whether Node.js is installed correctly.

Open another Command Prompt and type the Node.js version command:

```
node --version
```

The version should appear in the Command Prompt. These commands do not need to be memorized because they are attached to the course. The important thing is that the command returns a version and does not show an error.

Figure 4.6: Command Prompt showing the Node.js version output

Once the version appears, Node.js is checked off.

Again, we are not going into theory. We are not stopping to learn Node.js. We only need it installed, so Cursor has what it needs later when projects require it.

Installing PowerShell 7

Next, we install PowerShell 7.

The official Microsoft page shows several ways to install it. At first, that page can seem overwhelming, but the process we are using is simple. We will use the recommended winget method. There are two steps.

First, open Command Prompt. Copy the first command from the Microsoft page and paste it into Command Prompt.

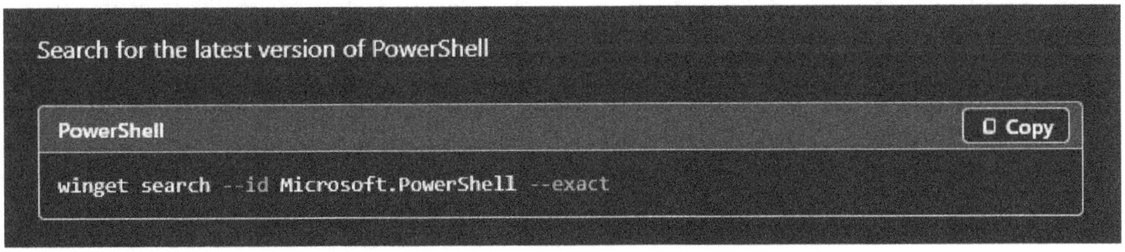

Figure 4.7: Command pasted in the CMD prompt

This will show you the latest stable version that's available for download.

The page may show two versions. One of them is the preview version, which is like a beta version. It is more experimental and usually less stable. We do not want the preview version. We want the regular MSIX version.

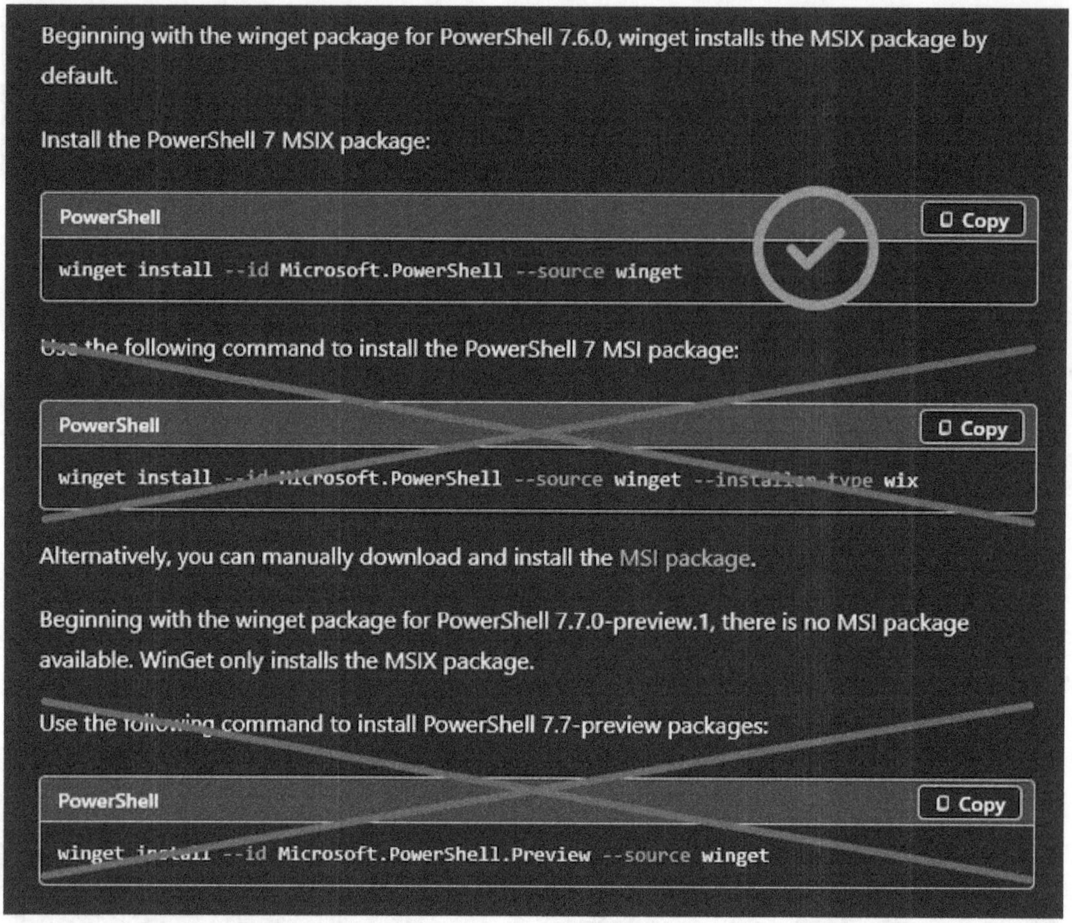

Figure 4.8: Microsoft PowerShell installation page showing the winget installation method and the regular, non-preview option

For the second step, copy the install command for the regular version and paste it into Command Prompt. Avoid the preview command that appears lower down.

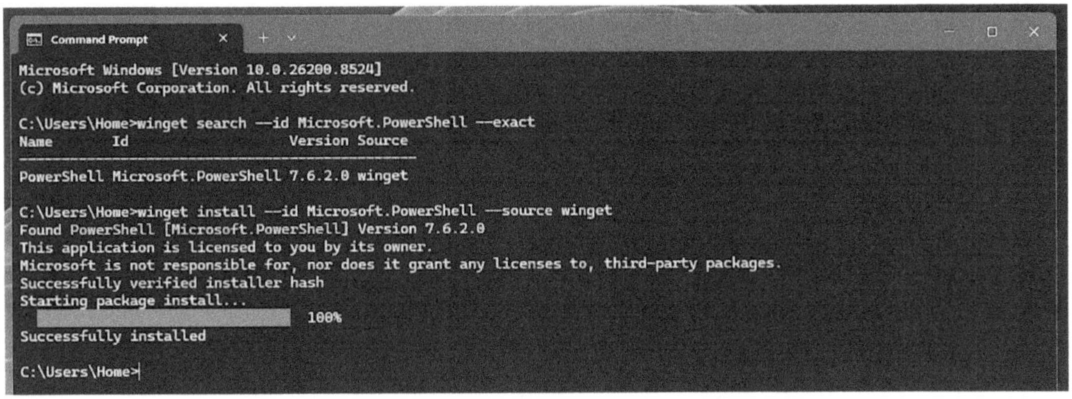

Figure 4.9: Copy the install command for the regular version and paste it into Command Prompt

After a few seconds, PowerShell 7 installs.

To test it, open the **Start** menu and type:

```
pwsh
```

PowerShell 7 should appear.

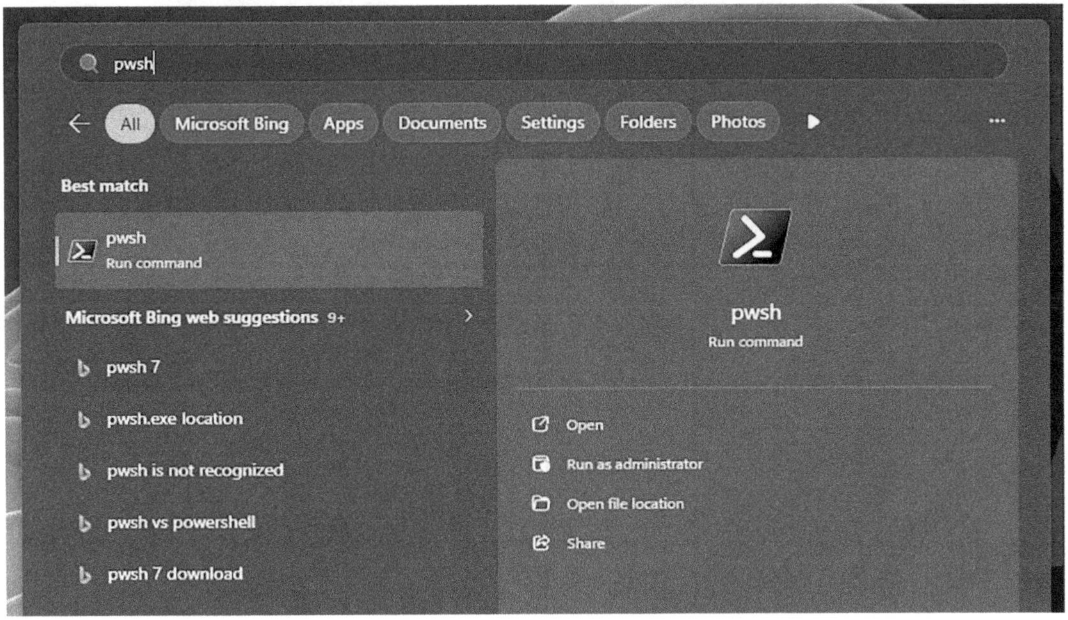

Figure 4.10: Windows Start menu showing PowerShell 7 available after installation

At this point, PowerShell 7 is installed.

We are doing well. The setup is not difficult, but it does require patience. That is a recurring theme in vibe coding. The tools are powerful, but the environment still needs to be prepared.

Creating a GitHub account

Next, we need GitHub.

GitHub is very much needed, even though it may be intimidating at first. We will focus on the essentials, and soon enough, it will become more comfortable.

Create an account with GitHub. Like the other tools in this setup, it is free. Add an email address, verify it, and the account is ready.

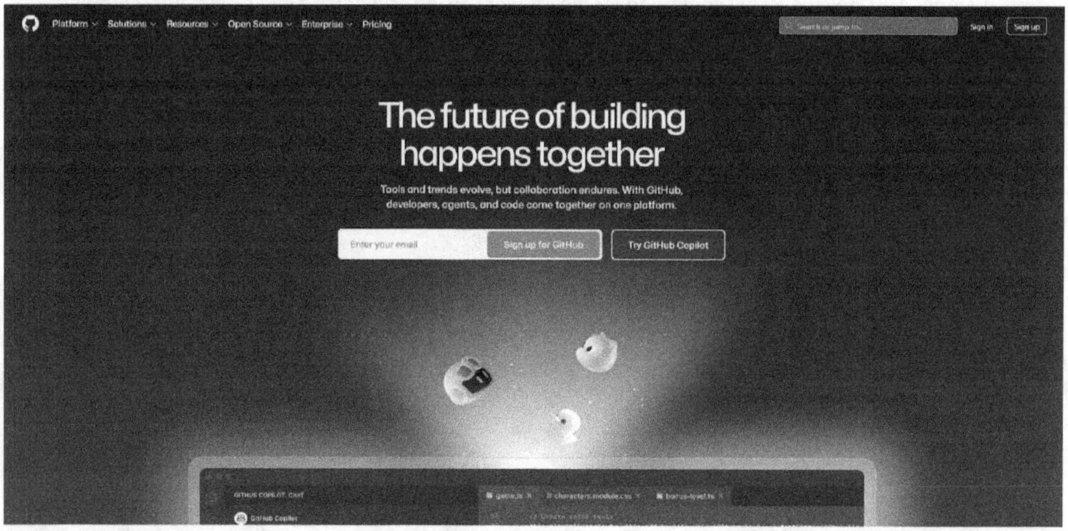

Figure 4.11: Sign up for GitHub

This account will matter later. GitHub will help us store projects and work with other platforms. For now, the important part is simply having the account created and ready to use.

There is no need to understand GitHub deeply at this point. That would add unnecessary theory. The practical purpose is enough for now: we need the account because later, Cursor and other tools will use it as part of the workflow.

Installing Docker (Optional)

Next, we install Docker.

Docker is considered optional, but I had quite a few issues because I did not have it installed. For that reason, I would much rather have it on the computer from the start.

This is one of the slowest programs to set up. There is not a lot to do during the installation, but it can take a while, so patience matters.

After Docker is finally ready, create an account. Some of these tools allow sign-up with GitHub. Since we just created a GitHub account, it makes sense to use it here. It is much faster.

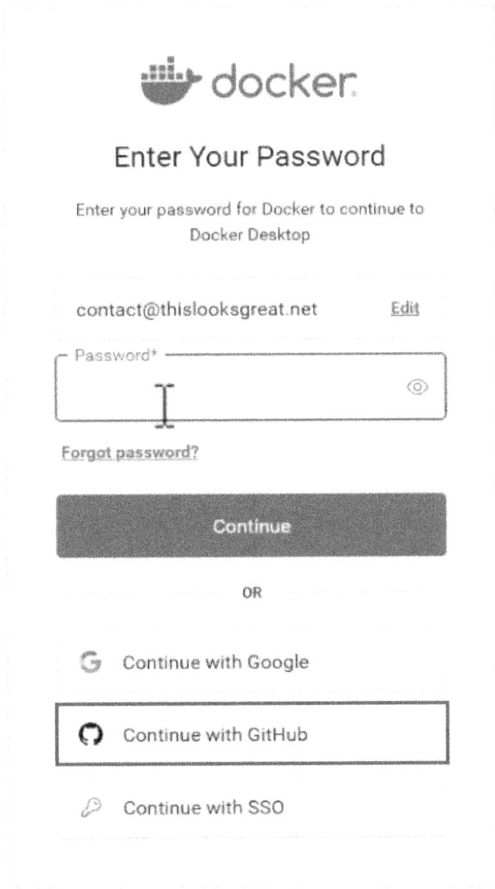

Figure 4.12: Docker sign-in or account creation screen showing the GitHub sign-up option

There may be a few other screens during the setup process. We are not going to go into deep detail about them because that would take us away from the practical goal.

The key point is this: we are preparing the environment so Cursor has fewer reasons to fail later.

This is the fully stocked kitchen again. We may not use Docker in every single dish, or in every single project, but having it installed gives us a better foundation. It is much easier to prepare now than to stop in the middle of a project because something is missing.

Installing Git

Next, we install Git. If you're on Windows, you can search on Google for "Git on Windows". If you're on macOS, you'll have a dedicated option.

The installer has a lot of settings. We will use the default values every single step of the way. The approach is simple: accept the default values and continue.

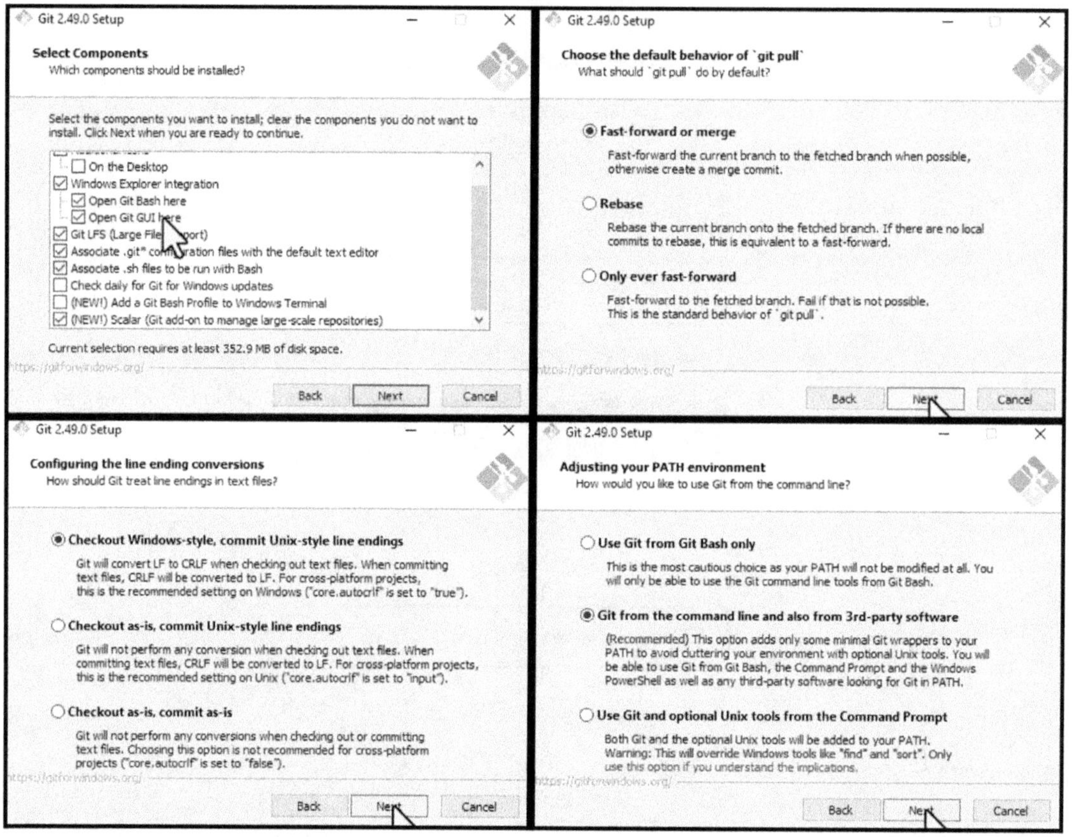

Figure 4.13: Git for Windows installer showing one of the setup screens with default values selected

Cursor is going to manage most of what we need, so there is no reason to change the installer options.

This setup list may not feel comfortable, but it matters and makes AI work much faster and better. Installing Git for Windows allows the AI to do more with fewer prompts and less intervention from us. When we create projects in Cursor, all of these programs and accounts start to become useful.

It is much easier to install them now than to deal with issue after issue later.

Creating your online accounts

At this point, most of the heavier setup is finished. There are three more accounts to create, and these are quick.

Creating a Vercel account

The first one is Vercel. We will use it for deployment. Review the current plan limits and terms before creating a project. The Hobby plan is intended for personal, non-commercial use; client work and commercial sites generally require an appropriate paid plan. Connecting GitHub is convenient, but review the repositories and permissions granted during authorization.

Sign up using GitHub to simplify the process.

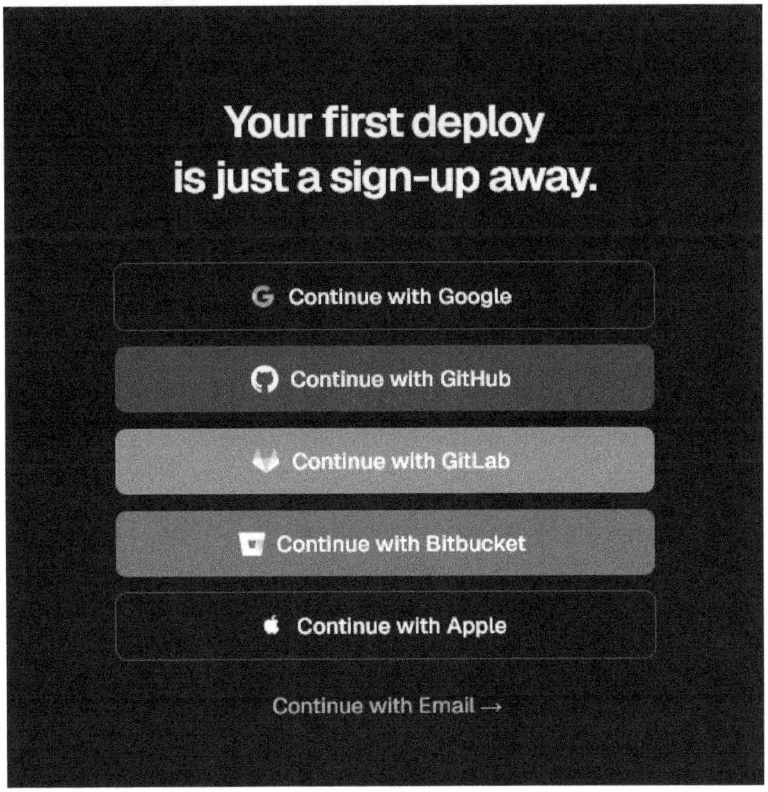

Figure 4.14: Vercel sign-up screen showing the option to continue with GitHub

Vercel will become useful when we want to take a website from the local computer and publish it online. For now, the account just needs to exist. We will come back to it later when we are ready to make a website live.

Creating a Resend account

Next, we create an account with Resend.

We will use resend.com to send emails. This is totally free for up to 3,000 emails per month, which is great for getting started.

This matters because of the contact form from the earlier portfolio website. The AI told us that the form would not actually work because it was not connected to anything. Resend fixes that problem.

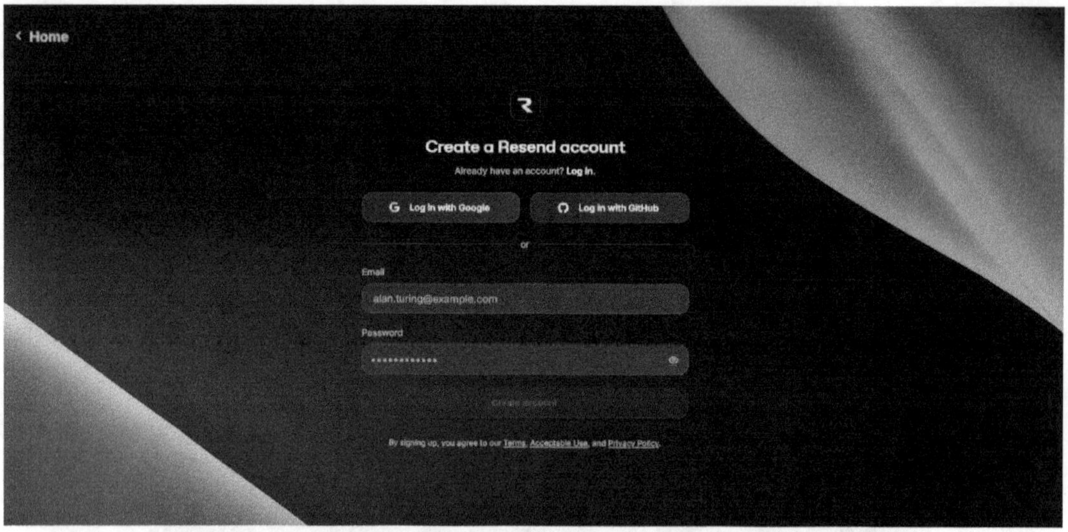

Figure 4.15: Resend sign-up screen or initial dashboard after account creation

At this stage, we are not configuring the whole email system yet. We are just making sure the account exists. Later, when a project needs a working form, Resend will help us send those emails.

Creating a Supabase account

Finally, create an account with Supabase.

Supabase is fantastic for databases and more complex projects. We may use it near the end of the course, when projects need more than a simple website.

For now, the setup is simple. Create the account and get it out of the way.

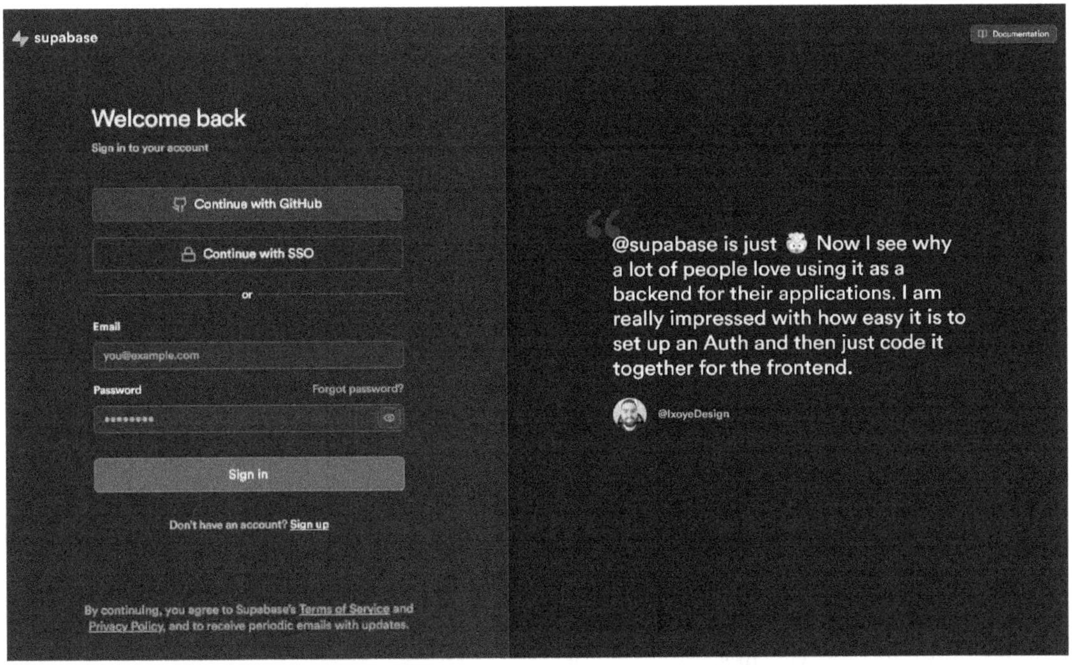

Figure 4.16: Supabase sign-up screen or dashboard after account creation

This is another case where we may not need the tool immediately, but having the account ready prevents friction later.

Completing the toolkit checklist

Believe it or not, we are done with the main toolkit.

At this point, the computer should have Python, Node.js, PowerShell 7, Docker, and Git for Windows installed. The online accounts should also be ready: GitHub, Vercel, Resend, and Supabase.

This does not make us developers, and that is not the objective. The point is to give Cursor the environment it needs so we can build projects with fewer interruptions.

We are not learning every detail of every tool. That would be overwhelming and counterproductive. We are installing them because they support the workflow. They help Cursor work better. They make future projects smoother. They reduce the number of cases where an error appears simply because something basic is missing.

This is the part that may feel uncomfortable, but it pays off later. When we start building more serious projects, the setup work we did here will matter. Instead of stopping again and again to install missing software or create missing accounts, we can keep moving.

So pause here. Install everything. Create every account. Check the commands where needed. Only continue once this checklist is complete.

There are still a couple of Cursor-specific settings to handle next, but the main vibe coding toolkit is now in place.

Summary

In this chapter, we set up the practical toolkit needed to work more smoothly with Cursor. We installed Python, Node.js, PowerShell 7, Docker, and Git for Windows, and we created accounts for GitHub, Vercel, Resend, and Supabase. The goal was not to learn every tool in depth, but to prepare the computer so Cursor has fewer reasons to get stuck while building projects.

The setup may feel uncomfortable due to all the steps and programs, but it will make our lives much easier moving forward. With the main tools and accounts ready, we can avoid many common interruptions, reduce wasted credits, and keep our momentum when we start building more serious websites.

In the next chapter, we will configure Cursor itself by setting up rules and MCPs. These will help us give Cursor better instructions, connect it to useful tools, and make the AI more effective across our projects.

Exercise: Set up and verify the toolkit

Before continuing, complete the full setup checklist on the same computer where Cursor is installed.

1. Install Python
2. Open Command Prompt and verify Python with: `py`
3. Install Node.js LTS
4. Open Command Prompt and verify Node.js with: `node --version`
5. Install PowerShell 7
6. Open the Start menu and confirm that pwsh or PowerShell 7 appears
7. Create a GitHub account and verify the email address
8. Install Docker and sign in, preferably using GitHub

9. Install Git for Windows using the default installer settings
10. Create accounts for Vercel, Resend, and Supabase

After completing the checklist, create a simple note for yourself with the following information:

- Python installed: yes/no
- Node.js installed: yes/no
- PowerShell 7 installed: yes/no
- GitHub account created: yes/no
- Docker installed: yes/no
- Git for Windows installed: yes/no
- Vercel account created: yes/no
- Resend account created: yes/no
- Supabase account created: yes/no
- Issues I ran into:
- Tools I need to revisit

The goal of this exercise is not to memorize commands or understand every tool in depth. The goal is to make sure the computer is prepared before the next stage of the course. If any step fails, write down the exact issue. That will make troubleshooting much easier later.

5

Rules, MCPs, and Giving Cursor Better Instructions

Now that the toolkit is installed and the first website is behind us, we can take a step further. Cursor is already useful, but right now it knows nothing specific about how we like to work. Every new project starts from scratch, with no preferences carried over, no standing instructions, and no access to external tools like GitHub or the file system.

This chapter changes that. We will configure two things: rules and MCPs. Rules tell Cursor how to behave across every project. MCPs connect Cursor to external tools so it can do more on its own, with fewer instructions from us.

Neither of these requires any coding knowledge. The setup takes a little patience, but once it is done, the AI becomes meaningfully more capable and considerably less dependent on manual steps.

We will cover the following topics in this chapter:

- Understanding Cursor rules and when to use each type
- Setting up user rules
- What MCPs are and why they matter
- Adding MCPs to Cursor
- Adding API keys safely
- The recommended MCP set and what each one does
- Fixing MCP connection problems

Understanding Cursor rules

Rules are standing instructions for Cursor. They tell the AI how to behave before any project begins: what practices to follow, how to handle sensitive information, what to prioritize, and what to avoid. Without rules, Cursor applies its defaults to every project, which may or may not match what we need.

To open the rules configuration, click the gear icon in the top-right corner of Cursor. This opens **Cursor Settings**.

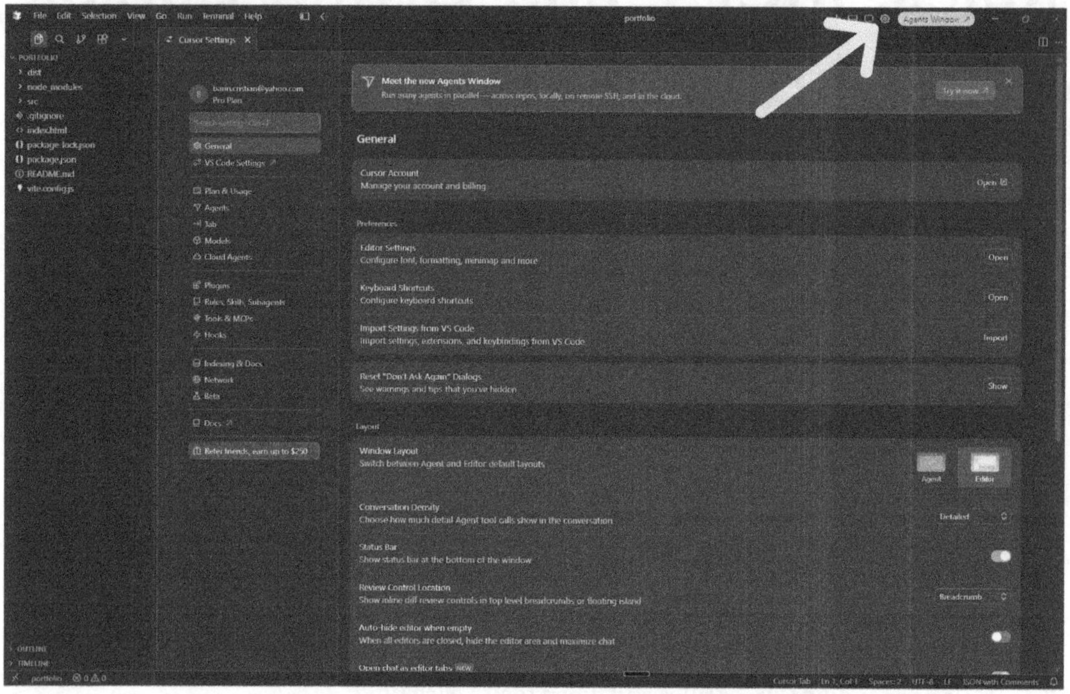

Figure 5.1: The gear icon in Cursor opens Cursor Settings

Inside the settings panel, two categories appear under Rules: user rules and project rules.

- **User rules** apply to every project, regardless of which folder is open. Once set, they follow Cursor everywhere.
- **Project rules** are scoped to a single project. They make sense when a particular codebase has requirements that should not apply globally. For example, a mobile app that needs a different set of constraints than a web project.

For the work in this book, user rules are the right choice. We are focused on web development, and the same preferences apply across every project. If that changes later, project rules can always be added on top.

Setting up user rules

A rules file is placed here: `https://www.dropbox.com/scl/fi/ih49rsb4or80avj5se49z/rules.txt?rlkey=fu43g92s9h27ueuwx0uil2p1k&e=1&dl=0`. The contents cover the essentials: telling Cursor to be efficient, follow best practices, handle sensitive information carefully, and stay focused on the task.

To apply it, click inside the user rules field and paste the full contents of that file. There is no save button. Cursor picks up the rules immediately.

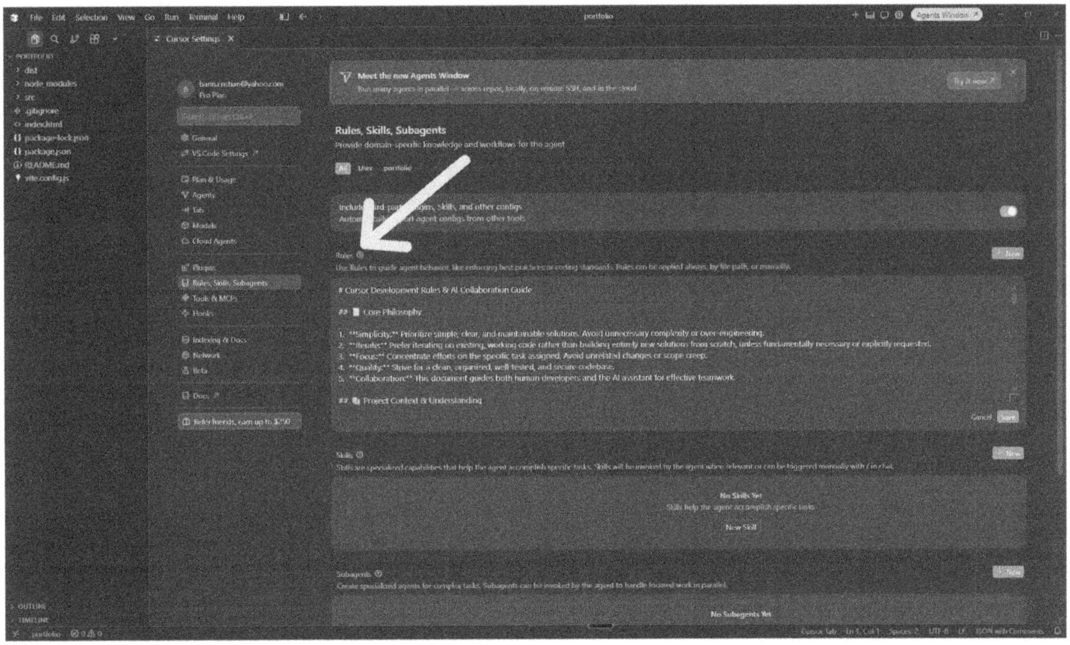

Figure 5.2: The user rules field in Cursor Settings, with the course template pasted in

From this point forward, those rules apply to every project. There is no need to paste them again.

Rules templates are also available online if a different starting point makes sense. The underlying principle is the same: the rules replace repetitive instructions that would otherwise be typed into the chat at the start of every session.

Note

What MCPs are and why they matter

MCPs, or model context protocol connectors, extend what Cursor can do beyond reading and writing files inside a project folder. Without MCPs, Cursor works only within the boundaries of the open project. With MCPs, it can operate external systems directly.

Here is what that means in practice. Without the GitHub MCP, pushing a project to GitHub means following a sequence of terminal commands, handling authentication, and managing branches manually. With the GitHub MCP active, one instruction is enough: push this to GitHub. Cursor handles the rest.

The same logic applies to the other MCPs we will configure. The filesystem MCP lets Cursor create folders and move files without asking us to do it. The memory MCP lets it retain information across sessions. The sequential thinking MCP helps it reason through complex tasks in structured steps before executing anything.

Individually, each MCP fills a gap. Together, they shift a significant amount of manual work off our plates.

Adding MCPs to Cursor

To reach the MCP configuration, open **Cursor Settings** and navigate to the **MCP** section. The interface is not particularly beginner-friendly at this stage, but the process is straightforward because the course provides a ready-made configuration file.

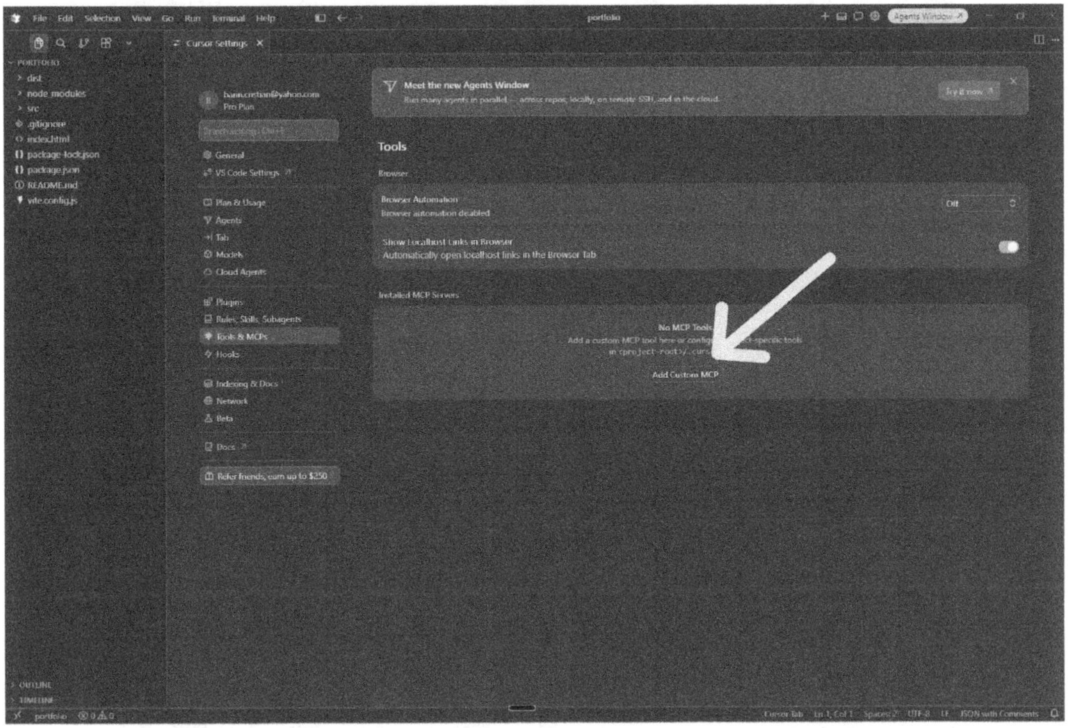

Figure 5.4: Adding MCP

Copy the entire contents of the attached MCP configuration file.

```
File    Edit    View

{
  "mcpServers": {
    "github": {
      "command": "npx",
      "args": [
        "-y",
        "@modelcontextprotocol/server-github"
      ],
      "env": {
        "GITHUB_PERSONAL_ACCESS_TOKEN": "---add your own key----"
      }
    },
    "sequential-thinking": {
      "command": "npx",
      "args": [
        "-y",
        "@modelcontextprotocol/server-sequential-thinking"
      ],
      "env": {}
    },
    "supabase-mcp": {
      "command": "cmd",
      "args": [
        "/c",
        "npx",
        "-y",
        "@supabase/mcp-server-supabase@0.3.5",
        "--access-token",
        "---add your own key----"
      ]
    },
    "memory": {
      "command": "npx",
      "args": [
        "-y",
        "@modelcontextprotocol/server-memory"
      ],
      "env": {}
    },
    "filesystem": {
      "command": "npx",
      "args": [
        "-y",
        "@modelcontextprotocol/server-filesystem",
        "c:\\"
      ],
      "env": {}
    },
    "git": {
      "command": "uvx",
      "args": [
```

Figure 5.5: Contents of the MCP configuration file

Then click the Add button in the MCP section and paste the configuration in. After pasting, switch to a different tab and switch back. This triggers a refresh.

After the refresh, the MCP list populates.

Figure 5.6: The MCP list after configuration, with green indicators showing active connections

Each entry shows a status indicator: green means the connector is live and ready. Any other color means there is a problem to address.

Click on 'Show Output' to see the issue and paste the error either in a new chat window in Cursor or ChatGPT or any other coding platform. In our example, I did not add my own key, hence the error.

Modifying the MCP list

There may be situations where we want to add or remove a specific MCP. For example, removing Supabase if it is not needed for a particular project type. Editing the JSON configuration by hand is risky because a single misplaced bracket can break the file.

The easier approach: copy the entire configuration file, open ChatGPT (no account required), describe the change in plain language: "remove the Supabase MCP from this code," and paste the configuration in. ChatGPT returns the updated version. Paste that back into Cursor Settings.

The same method works for adding a new MCP.

The tool limit

There is a ceiling of approximately 40 active tools at any given time. This limit applies to tools in aggregate across all MCPs, not to the number of MCP entries. GitHub alone exposes more than 20 tools, which makes it a significant commitment against that limit. That range of capability is exactly why it is worth including despite the cost.

If Cursor starts refusing to connect new MCPs, the most likely cause is hitting this ceiling. Disabling MCPs that are not currently in use will bring the count back down.

The recommended MCP set

The configuration file included with the course sets up four MCPs:`https://www.dropbox.com/scl/fi/ih49rsb4or80avj5se49z/rules.txt?rlkey=fu43g92s9h27ueuwx0uil2p1k&e=1&dl=0`. Each one addresses a specific limitation in what Cursor can do by default.

Sequential thinking

Sequential thinking tells Cursor to break a large task into smaller steps, track those steps explicitly, and work through them in order before committing to output. The practical result is noticeably better performance on anything non-trivial. Instead of charging at a complex problem in a single pass, the model reasons through the structure first.

For a vibe coder, this means fewer cases where a big task produces a result that misses the point and more cases where the AI arrives at something close to what was asked for on the first attempt.

Filesystem

The filesystem MCP gives Cursor the ability to create folders, move files, and reorganize a project directory without us doing it manually. In any project with more than a handful of files, this matters.

A typical problem without this MCP: Cursor creates a new component but puts it in the wrong place, or generates a configuration file but cannot move it to the directory where it belongs. With the filesystem MCP active, those operations happen as part of the same action.

GitHub

The GitHub MCP allows Cursor to create repositories, commit code, push updates, and manage branches directly, without any terminal commands from us. It is the connector that makes the Cursor → GitHub → Vercel publishing chain work with minimal manual steps.

This MCP requires a personal access token from GitHub. We will cover that in the next section.

Memory

The memory MCP allows Cursor to retain context across sessions. Preferences, decisions, and constraints established in one conversation do not have to be re-explained in the next one. The AI carries that context forward.

This is particularly useful in longer projects where the same technical decisions apply repeatedly. Without memory, the model starts fresh every session and may make inconsistent choices.

Adding API keys safely

Several MCPs require API keys to function. A key authenticates the MCP's requests against a specific account. Without the correct key in the right place, the MCP will show a red indicator and will not connect.

The MCP configuration file uses placeholder markers to show exactly where each key goes. The keys themselves come from the corresponding platform accounts.

The GitHub personal access token

A GitHub personal access token is the credential that allows the GitHub MCP to act on our GitHub account. To create one:

1. Go to `github.com` and open **Account Settings**
2. Scroll to the bottom of the left sidebar and select **Developer Settings**
3. Choose **Personal Access Tokens**, then select the classic token option
4. Create a new token. Give it a name and set an expiration of 90 days. Why 90 days? GitHub strongly recommends that you set an expiration date for your token to help keep your information secure.
5. Select every available permission scope before saving

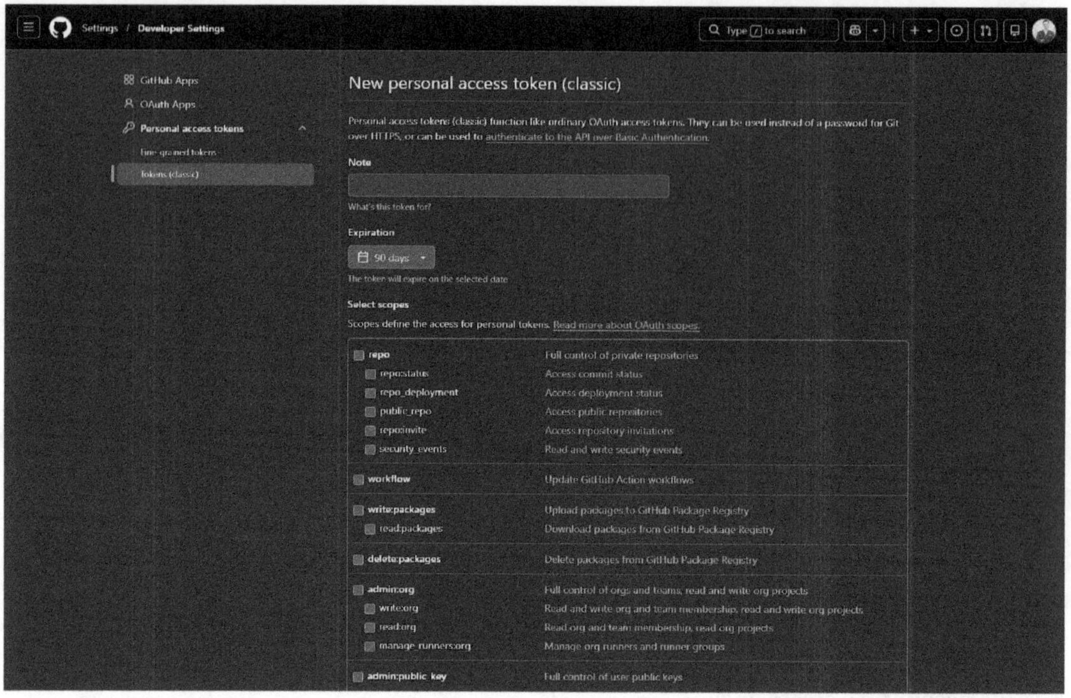

Figure 5.7: The GitHub token creation form, with all permission scopes selected

The token appears exactly once, immediately after creation. Copy it immediately and paste it into the GitHub token field in the MCP configuration. If the token is lost before being saved, a new one can be generated at no cost, but handling it correctly the first time is easier.

Keeping keys secure

An API key is functionally a password for the account it belongs to. If a key connected to a paid service is exposed—shared in a screenshot, included in a public repository, or pasted into a public message—anyone who finds it can generate charges against that account.

Most platforms show a key exactly once, at the moment of creation. After that, the key cannot be retrieved. Only a new one can be generated. This is intentional.

The same discipline applies to any project that might become public.

The Supabase key

The Supabase API key is available directly from the Supabase project dashboard, under the API settings for the project. Copy it from there and paste it into the corresponding field in the MCP configuration.

The process is simpler than the GitHub token setup.

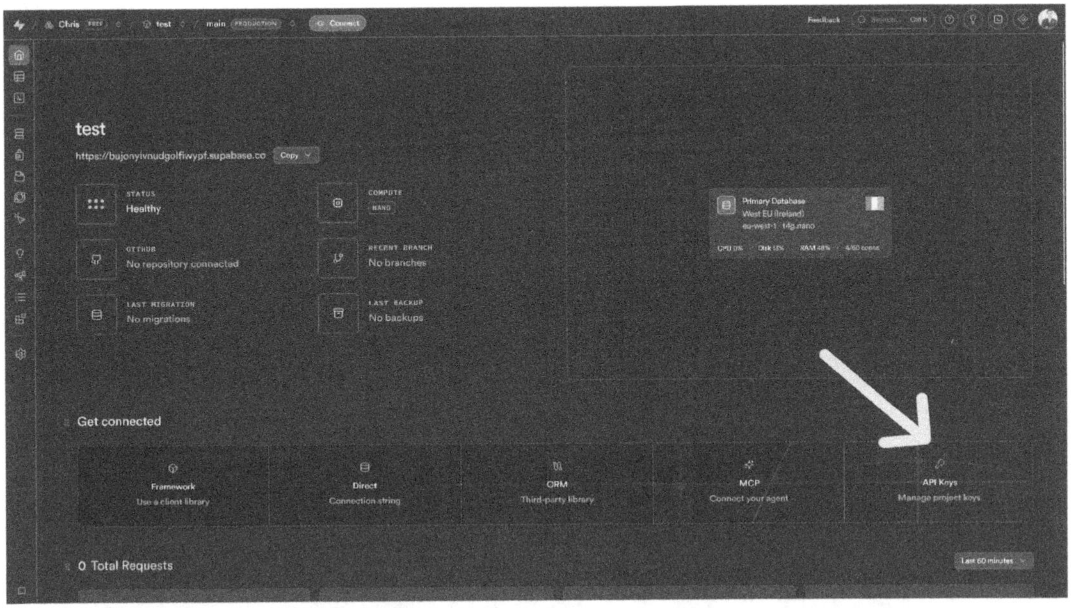

Figure 5.8: The Supabase API settings page, showing where to find the key

There are no permission scopes to select. The key is ready to copy as soon as it appears.

Fixing MCP connection problems

Even after correct configuration, MCPs sometimes fail to connect. The indicators in the list turn red. This is normal, especially during initial setup, and the fix is usually a terminal command or two away.

The standard debugging approach

MCP connection failures are almost always environment problems: Python not found on the system path, a missing Node package, or a misconfigured variable. The error message that appears in Cursor is the starting point.

The approach that works in most cases:

1. Copy the full error message from Cursor exactly as it appears
2. Paste it into ChatGPT or a similar AI assistant. The free version is sufficient.
3. Read the proposed solution. If the first suggestion is complex or unclear, move to the next option.
4. Run the suggested command in the terminal, one step at a time

5. Return to Cursor, open Cursor Settings, and check whether the MCP indicator has turned green
6. Restarting your computer may also help

Two real examples show how this plays out.

Example: Python not found on the path

On one machine, the Git MCP server fails with an error indicating that Python cannot be found, despite Python being installed and working correctly in Command Prompt.

Figure 5.9: Error indicating Python not found

A search on Stack Overflow surfaces several potential fixes. None of them work.

Switching to ChatGPT and describing the situation produces a short list of options.

Figure 5.10: Options given by ChatGPT

The second option, simpler than the first, involves a single terminal command. After running it you will receive a message saying: "successfully installed".

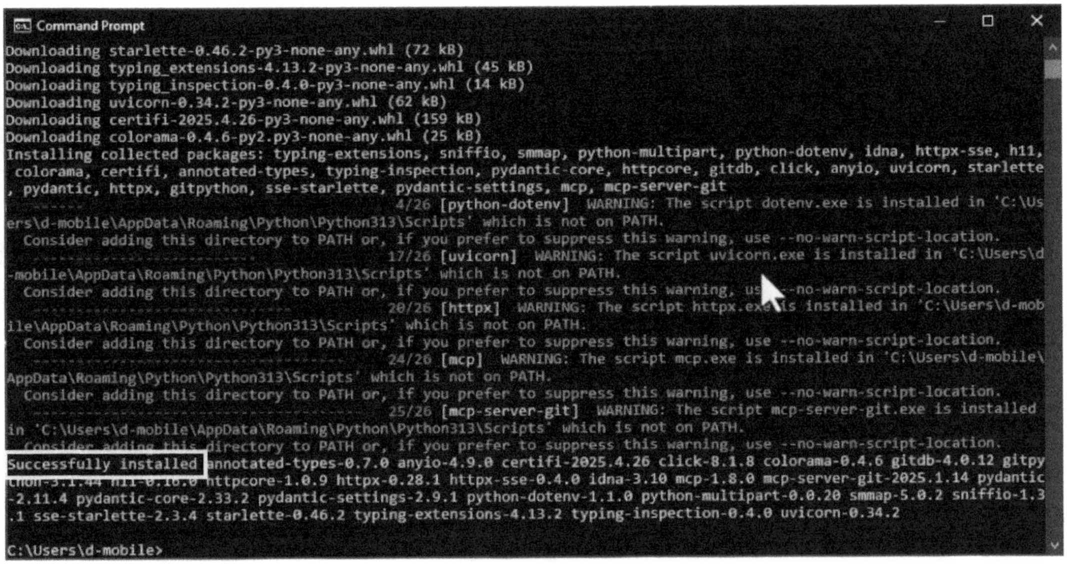

Figure 5.11: Running a fix command in the terminal and confirming the Git MCP connects successfully.

Back in Cursor, the Git MCP turns green.

Figure 5.12: The MCP turns green

Example: PowerShell error on a different machine

On a second machine, the same Git MCP fails for a completely different reason. The error message is unfamiliar. The same approach applies: copy the error, paste it into ChatGPT, and follow the resulting steps.

The solution in this case requires two commands in PowerShell 7. The first installs something; the second tests it. After both commands complete, Cursor needs a full restart, not just a settings refresh. After the restart, the MCP connects.

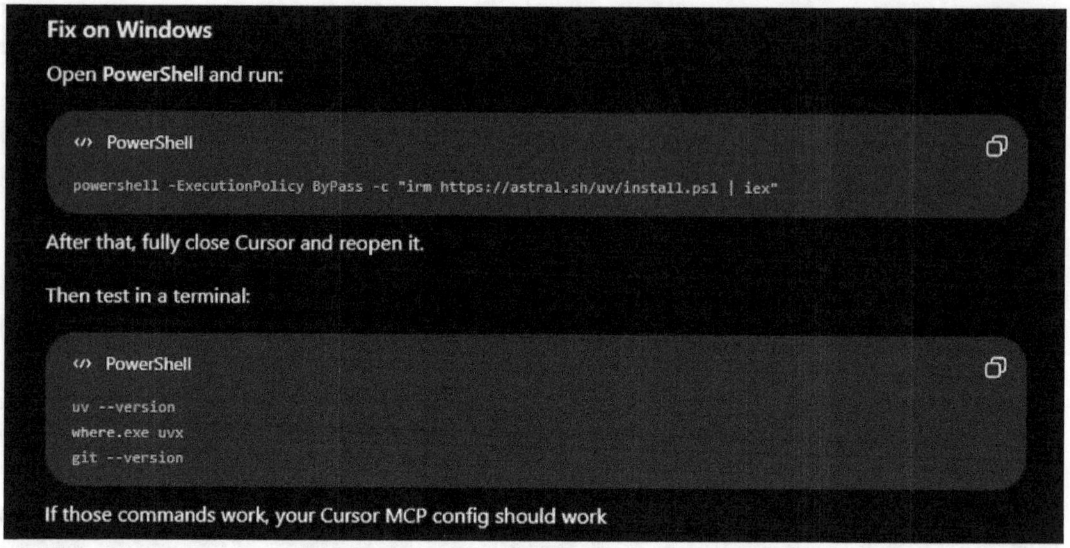

Figure 5.13: Running two PowerShell commands to fix the Git MCP, then confirming the connection after a Cursor restart

The pattern is consistent across both cases: the error message is the input, the AI assistant produces the fix, and the fix is a command or two in the terminal. None of this requires understanding what caused the underlying problem. What it requires is patience, the willingness to try one step at a time, and the habit of restarting Cursor before concluding that nothing worked.

> Note
>
> **When to restart Cursor**
>
> A full restart of Cursor resolves a surprising proportion of MCP issues. If the MCP list shows red indicators after the configuration appears correct, close Cursor completely, wait a few seconds, and reopen it. In many cases, the indicators turn green without any other changes.
>
> If every MCP shows red simultaneously, that is almost never a configuration problem. It is almost always a sign that Cursor itself needs a restart. Individual red indicators are more likely to be environment-specific issues that benefit from the debugging approach described above.

Summary

In this chapter, we configured two mechanisms that change how Cursor behaves at a fundamental level.

User rules give Cursor standing instructions that apply to every project: how to behave, what practices to follow, how to handle sensitive data. We set them once, and they require no repetition. Project rules exist for cases where a specific codebase needs requirements that should not generalize.

MCPs extend Cursor's reach beyond the project folder. The GitHub MCP allows Cursor to manage repositories without manual terminal commands. The filesystem MCP handles folder creation and file organization. The memory MCP retains context across sessions so the same decisions do not need to be re-explained. The sequential thinking MCP improves results on complex tasks by forcing structured reasoning before execution.

API keys are required for several MCPs and must be treated as sensitive credentials. They appear once at the moment of creation and should be stored immediately. Keys should never appear in public repositories or shared screenshots.

When MCPs fail to connect, the fix is almost always a terminal command away. Copy the error message, paste it into an AI assistant, follow the simplest applicable suggestion, and check again after a Cursor restart.

In the next chapter, we will explore Cursor's interface in detail: how to navigate between projects, use the chat panel effectively, reference files, switch models, and build the workflow habits that make building faster.

Exercise: Configure rules and MCPs

Before continuing, complete the following steps on the same computer where Cursor is installed.

1. **Open Cursor Settings** by clicking the gear icon in the top-right corner
2. **Navigate to Rules** and paste the course rules file into the user rules field
3. **Navigate to the MCP section** and paste the course MCP configuration file
4. **Refresh the MCP list** by switching tabs and switching back
5. **Check the status indicators.** Green means the connector is active. Make a note of any red indicators.
6. **Create a GitHub personal access token** using the steps in this chapter. Paste it into the configuration.

7. **Add your Supabase key** from the Supabase project dashboard
8. **For any red indicators**, copy the error message and use the debugging approach in this chapter to resolve them

After completing the steps, create a short note with the following:

- User rules applied: yes / no
- GitHub MCP active: yes / no
- Filesystem MCP active: yes / no
- Memory MCP active: yes / no
- Sequential thinking MCP active: yes / no
- GitHub token created: yes / no
- Supabase key added: yes / no
- MCPs still showing red: (list them)
- Issues I ran into

The goal is to make sure Cursor is properly configured before moving forward. If any step fails, write down the exact error message. That will make troubleshooting considerably easier.

6

Getting Around Cursor Like a Beginner-Friendly Builder

Cursor is the workspace we will keep returning to, so before we compare models or build more serious projects, we need to get comfortable with the basic interface. The exact look of Cursor may change over time, and it may already look slightly different on another computer. That is expected. The important parts are the parts that stay useful no matter how the interface changes: the project folder, the file panel, the chat panel, the terminal, Agent mode, file references, and the model selector.

The goal in this chapter is not to learn every menu and every button. That would not help much, especially in a tool that changes quickly. The goal is to understand where the work happens and how to move around without getting lost. Once that basic movement feels natural, the rest of the course becomes easier because every project follows the same rhythm: make a folder, open it in Cursor, work through the chat panel, watch the terminal when needed, and keep the files organized inside the right project.

We will cover the following main topics in this chapter:

- Opening Cursor without a project
- The chat panel is where vibe coding happens
- Opening the terminal
- Adjusting the interface size
- Changing the color theme
- Using Agent mode for vibe coding
- Understanding file references
- Keeping projects separated with folders

- Dragging images and referencing project files
- The model selector changes the results

Opening Cursor without a project

When Cursor starts without any project opened, the interface is extremely simple. There is not much to inspect yet because Cursor does not have a folder to work with. At this point, we can open a project, or we can use GitHub to start one. For now, we keep the flow simple and work locally.

The first move is to create a new folder anywhere on the computer. That folder becomes the project container. After the folder exists, we open that folder in Cursor. This is the same movement we will repeat throughout the course whenever a new project begins.

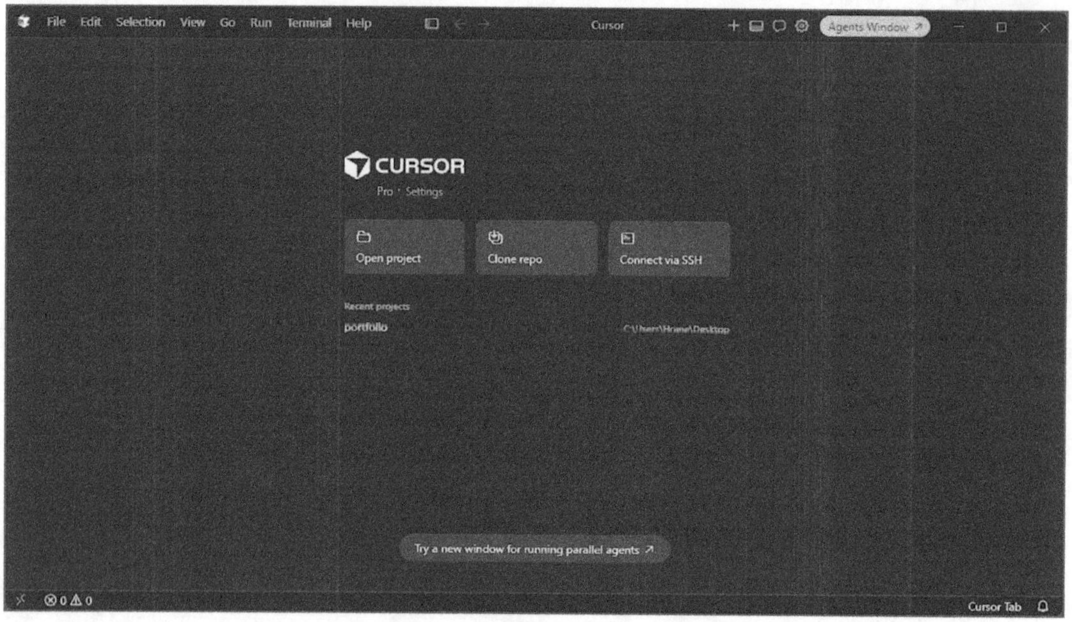

Figure 6.1: Cursor opened with no project loaded

Even with an empty project opened, the interface does not change dramatically. The difference is that Cursor now has a folder to look at. That one detail matters because Cursor does not work in the abstract. It works inside the project folder that we give it.

The left side of the interface shows all files inside that specific folder. Because the folder is new, the left panel is empty. That is fine. To make the file panel more concrete, we can add a random text file inside that folder. This could be done from Cursor, but doing it the old-fashioned way from the computer file explorer makes the relationship clear: the left panel in Cursor reflects the contents of the folder on the computer.

Once the text file is added, returning to Cursor should show the file in the left panel. If it does not appear immediately, the file panel has a refresh icon that becomes visible when the pointer moves over that area. Refreshing the panel should make the file appear.

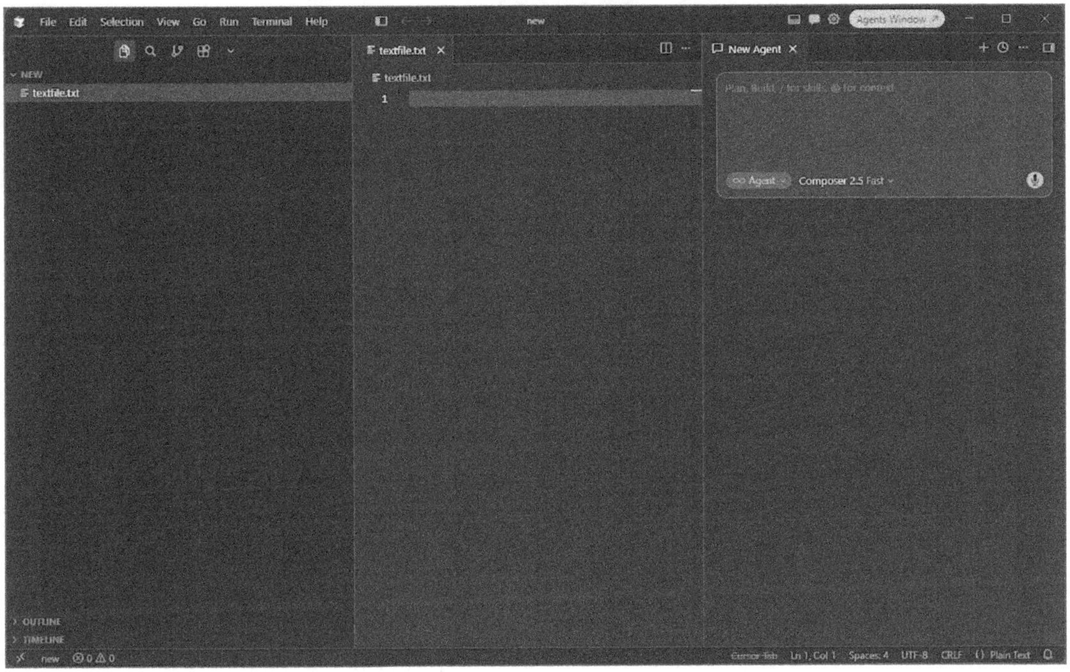

Figure 6.2: Cursor project folder after a random text file has been added

Selecting the file opens it in the center of the screen. That central area is the editor. It is where the content of files appears when a file is selected from the left panel. This is useful to understand, but for vibe coding, it is not the main area we will live in.

The main area is the chat panel.

The chat panel is where vibe coding happens

The key to vibe coding is the panel where we talk to the AI. That is where instructions go, where the model replies, and where the AI begins to make changes to the project. The file panel and editor are useful because they show what exists in the project, but the chat panel is the place where the work is directed.

If the chat panel is not visible, use *ctrl-L*. By default, the panel should already be visible, but ctrl-L is the shortcut to bring it back. This is one of the first shortcuts worth remembering because the chat panel is the control point for the workflow.

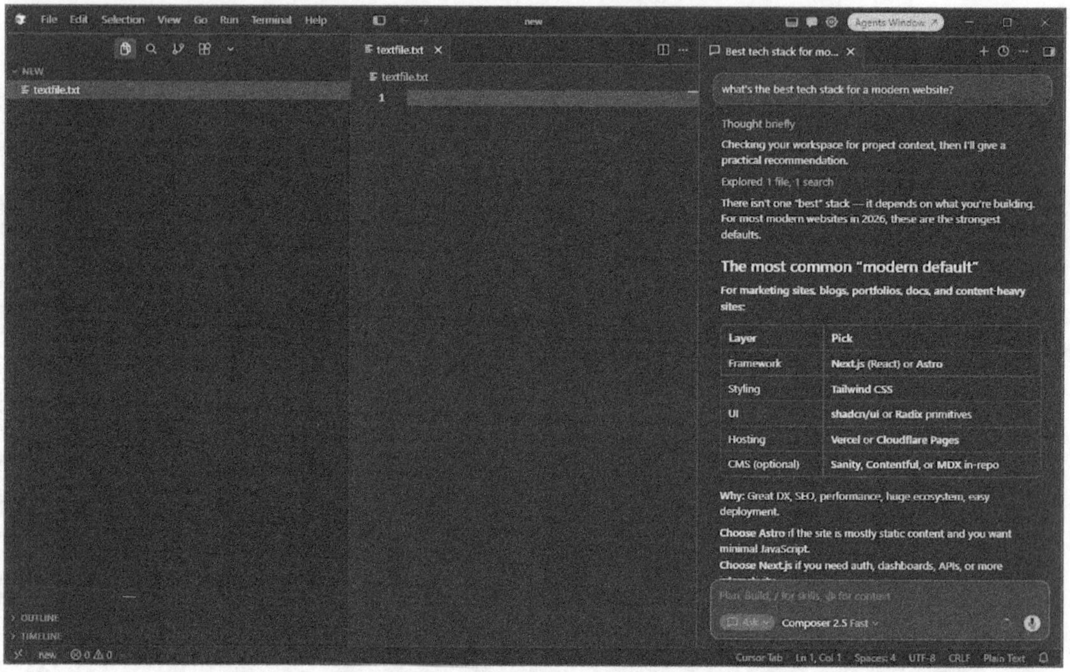

Figure 6.3: Cursor chat panel open on the right side, with the editor in the center and files on the left.

This is the part of the interface we will use the most. We will explain what we want, review what the model says, and let the AI create or update files. That is why it is important to know how to show the chat panel quickly instead of searching around the interface.

The chat panel is also the area where we will later choose models, attach images, reference files, and make sure the mode is set correctly. At this stage, the simple idea is enough: the chat panel is where we talk to the AI.

Opening the terminal

The second important area is the terminal. The terminal is not where we will spend most of our time, but it will show up often enough that we need to know where it is.

From the top menu, go to **Terminal**, then choose **New Terminal**. Cursor opens a new panel at the bottom of the interface. That lower panel may contain several tabs, but the tab we care about is the terminal.

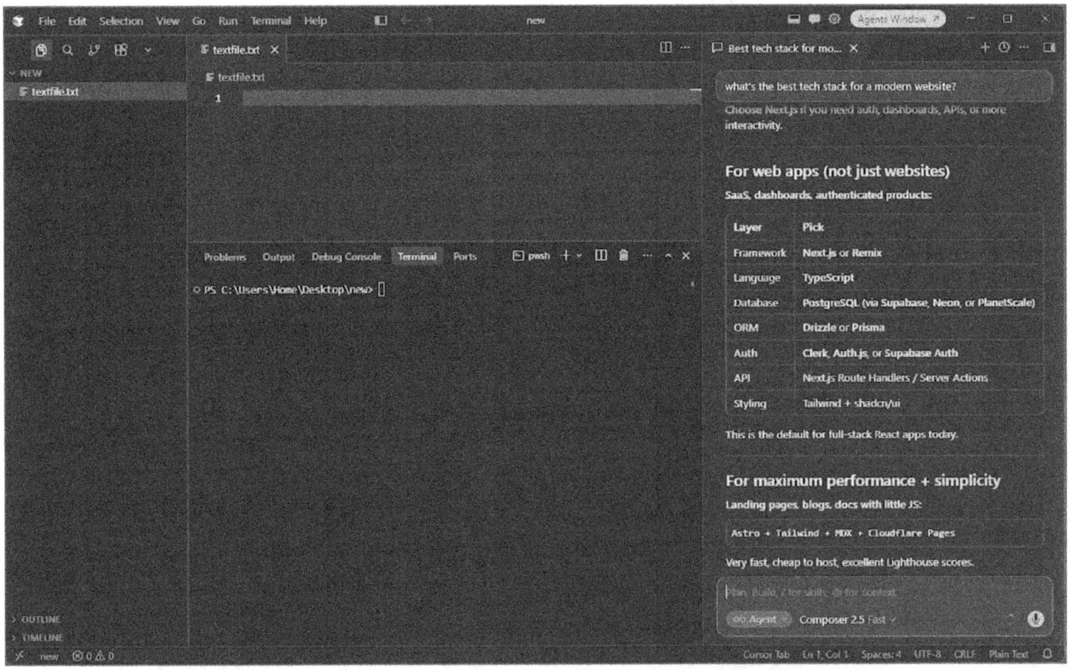

Figure 6.4: Cursor with a new terminal open at the bottom of the window

From time to time, the terminal shows issues, errors, and command output. Sometimes we may need to paste commands there. Sometimes Cursor or a setup process may simply wait for us to press Enter. The terminal is not the main workspace for this course, but it is not something to ignore either.

A simple ratio helps keep the interface in perspective. Most of the time—around 90 percent—we will look at the chat area. Around 10 percent of the time, we will check the terminal at the bottom. The rest of the interface matters much less for this workflow.

That distinction is important because Cursor can feel overwhelming if every panel seems equally important. It is not. For the kind of work we are doing, the chat area is the main control point, and the terminal is the supporting area that shows problems, output, and occasional commands.

Adjusting the interface size

If the interface feels too small, Cursor can be enlarged with *ctrl plus*. This makes the text, panels, and controls easier to see. If the interface becomes too large, use ctrl minus to shrink it again.

This sounds like a small detail, but it matters in practice. Cursor can show several panels at once: files on the left, code in the center, chat on the right, and terminal at the bottom. If everything is too small, the tool becomes uncomfortable, especially when the model is writing a lot of text or the terminal shows long messages.

The point is not to memorize every shortcut in Cursor. The point is to make the workspace comfortable enough that we can focus on the project instead of struggling to read the screen.

Changing the color theme

The default dark interface may be fine, but it may also bother some people. Cursor allows the theme to be changed from the top menu.

Go to **File** -> **Preferences** -> **Theme** -> **Color theme**.

After selecting a theme, the window may close. That behavior is not ideal, but it is not a problem. Open the same menu again: **File** -> **Preferences** -> **Theme** -> **Color theme** - and choose another theme if needed. The choice is personal. I usually like the darker themes, but the important point is to choose something that feels comfortable for longer work sessions.

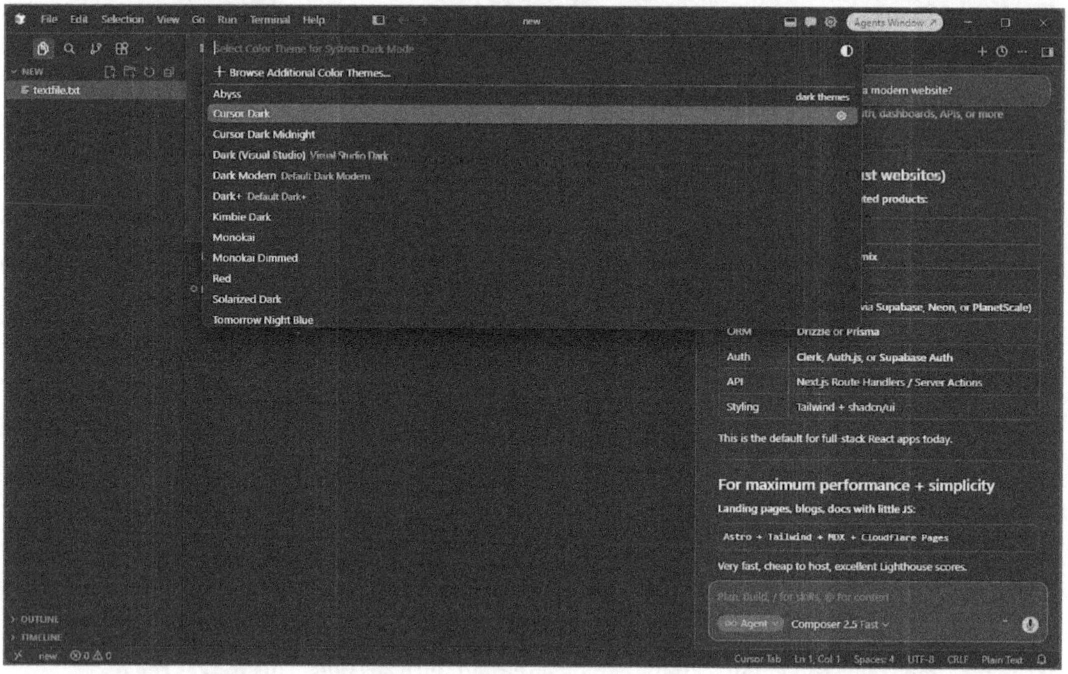

Figure 6.5: Capture the Cursor color theme menu under file -> preferences -> theme -> color theme

This is still part of getting around. We are not building anything yet, but we are preparing the workspace. A readable interface, a visible chat panel, and a terminal that can be opened when needed remove friction later.

Using Agent mode for vibe coding

After the interface is comfortable, the focus goes back to the chat panel. The first important setting in the chat panel is the mode. For vibe coding, we always want the chat set to **Agent**.

The other modes are for developers who want to improve their own code writing. That is not what we are doing here. We are not trying to manually write or improve code. We want the AI to do most of the work, and that is what Agent means in this workflow.

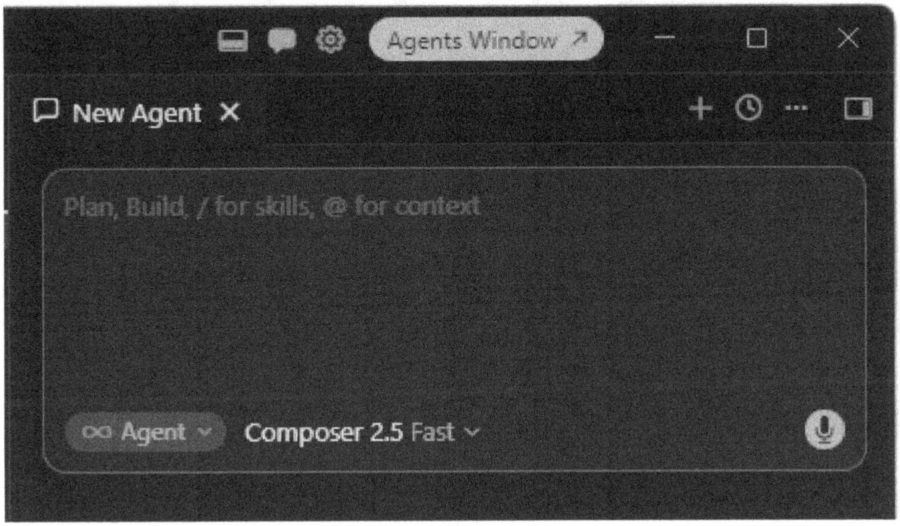

Figure 6.6: The chat panel with Agent mode selected

This setting matters because the authorial workflow of the course is not built around writing code line by line. The workflow is built around describing the desired outcome and letting the AI create or change the project files. Agent mode is the mode that supports that.

So before a project begins, the check is simple: the project folder is open, the chat panel is visible, and the mode is set to Agent.

Understanding file references

At the top of the chat panel, Cursor can reference a file from inside the project. This becomes useful when we want the AI to focus on a particular file. For example, if a text document is selected or referenced, Cursor may show that reference above the chat input.

That reference can be removed by using the X next to it. We will talk about this more later, but the basic idea is simple: sometimes the AI needs to focus on a specific file, and sometimes it should work more generally across the whole project.

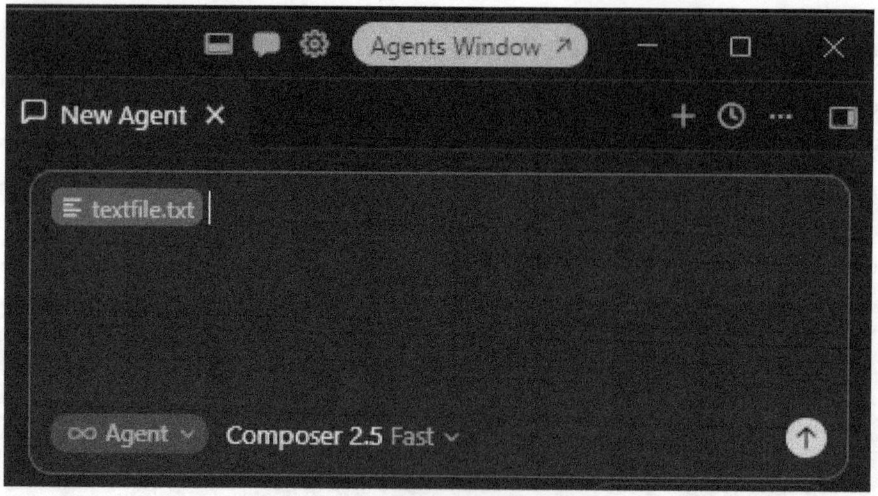

Figure 6.7: Chat panel showing a referenced file above the input area and the X control for removing it

This connects directly to how Cursor understands a project. The AI changes files that are inside the project folder. That is how projects stay separated. If a folder is open in Cursor, the AI works within that folder. If we want to start a different project, we create or open a different folder.

The folder is the boundary.

Keeping projects separate with folders

Project folders are not just a technical detail. They are the way we keep work organized. If we want to start a new project, we create another empty folder somewhere on the computer and then use **File** -> **Open Folder**.

This keeps one project from mixing with another. It is the same idea as organizing games, programs, or vacation photos. Everything should live in a proper folder. When files are organized properly, it becomes much easier to know what Cursor is editing and where the project lives.

To switch projects, use:

```
file -> open folder
```

There is another approach that is basically the same thing. From the top menu, use **File** -> **New Window**, then open a folder in that new window. The result is still a Cursor window connected to a specific project folder.

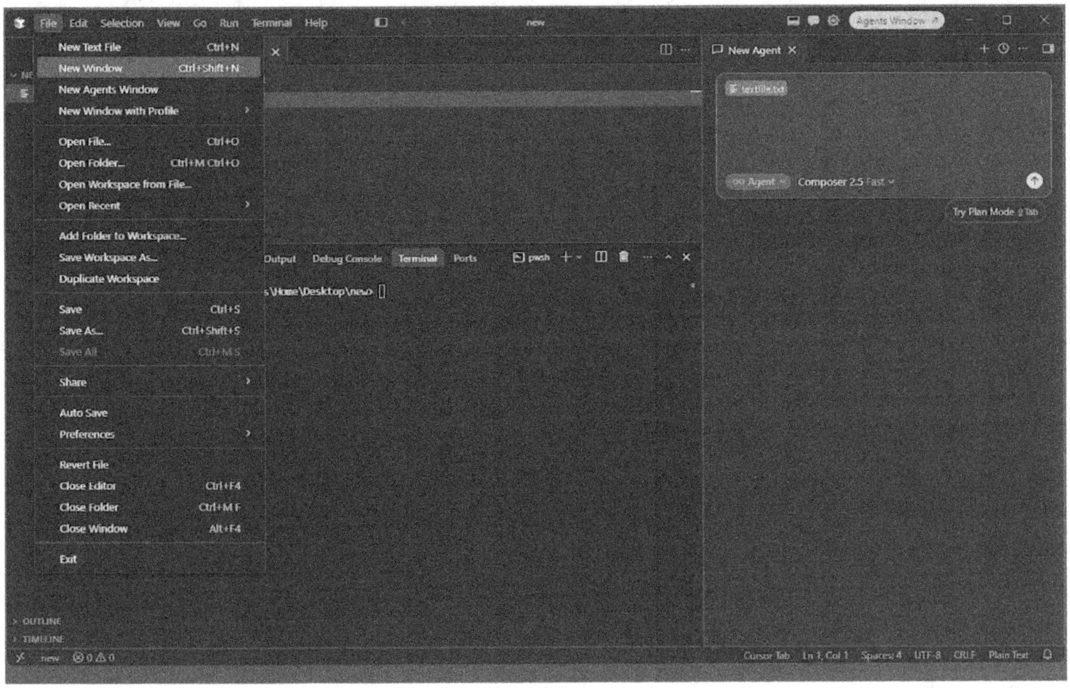

Figure 6.8: The file menu showing open folder and new window

Both flows are useful. Opening a folder in the current window switches the current workspace. Opening a new window lets another project exist in another Cursor window. The important part is that every project has its own folder.

Dragging images and referencing project files

The chat panel also supports images. The image icon exists because images can be dragged into the chat. This will be useful later when the project needs visual assets or when the AI needs to inspect something visual.

For now, we only need to recognize the control. We will use it later.

Cursor can also reference certain files when the AI needs to focus on them. A file reference tells the model, in effect, that this file matters for the current task. If that reference is no longer needed, it can be removed with the **X**.

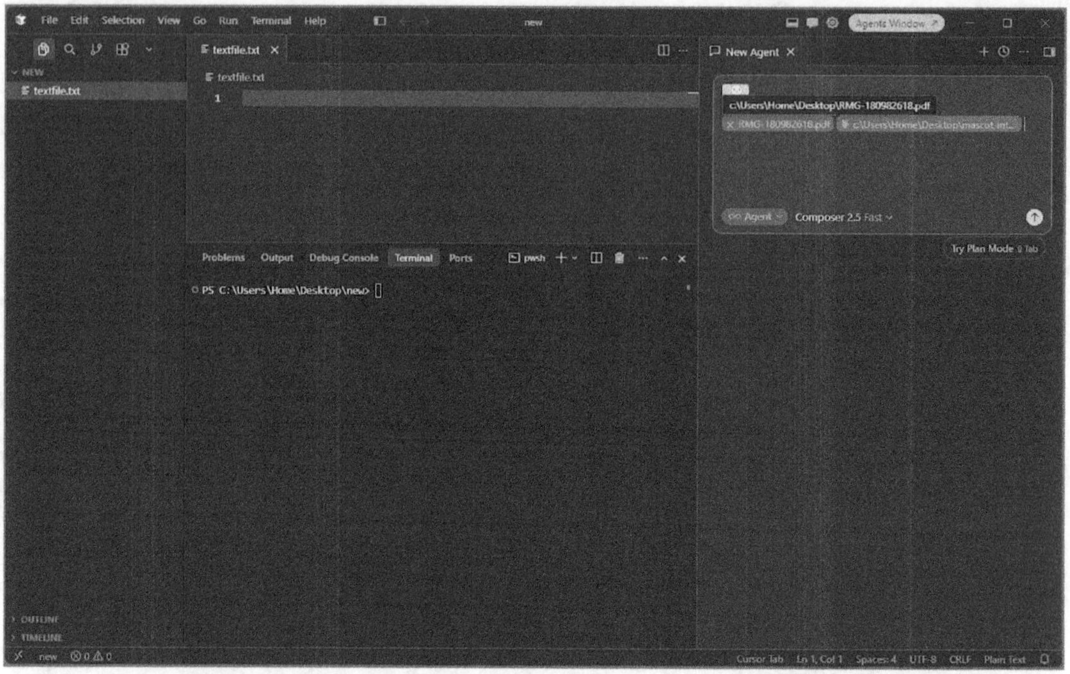

Figure 6.9: Chat input area showing the image attachment icon, a file reference, and the model selector

The distinction is useful because the chat panel is not just a box for typing prompts. It is also the place where we control context: which files the AI should pay attention to, which images are attached, which model is being used, and which mode is active.

The model selector changes the results

The final important setting in this part of Cursor is the model selector. This is where we choose which AI model Cursor will use. That choice can dramatically change the results.

For now, it is enough to know where the model selector is and that it matters. The next chapter will compare Claude, Gemini, and GPT models by giving them the same task and watching how each behaves. That comparison is important because models do not just differ in output quality. They differ in personality, speed, assumptions, mistakes, and how much they expect us to do manually.

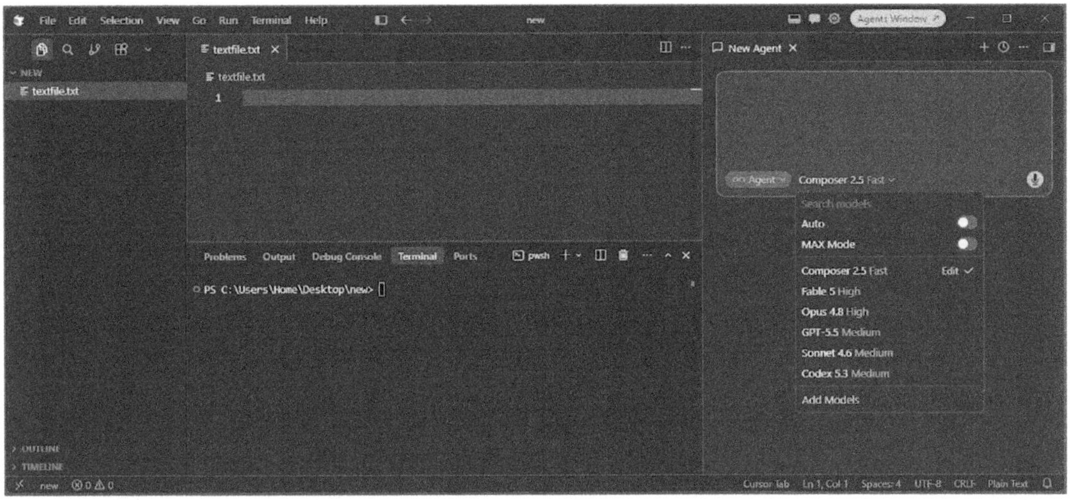

Figure 6.10: Cursor model selector in the chat panel

At the end of this interface pass, the working flow is clear. We make a folder, open it in Cursor, make sure the chat panel is visible, set the chat to Agent, open the terminal if needed, adjust the interface size or theme, and keep each project in its own folder.

This is not glamorous, but it is the foundation. Once this movement is familiar, starting and switching projects becomes natural.

Summary

In this chapter, we focused on becoming comfortable with Cursor's workspace rather than learning every feature and menu. You learned how projects are organized around folders, how the file panel reflects the contents of those folders, and how the editor, chat panel, and terminal fit into the overall workflow. We explored the chat panel as the primary control center for vibe coding, learned how to open and use the terminal, adjust the interface, switch themes, and keep projects separated through dedicated folders. We also introduced Agent mode, file references, image attachments, and the model selector, which will become increasingly important as projects grow more complex. The goal was simple: build enough familiarity with the interface that opening, navigating, and working inside Cursor feels natural and effortless.

In the next chapter, we'll explore one of the most important decisions in AI-assisted development: choosing the right model for the job. You'll compare Claude, Gemini, and GPT models, examine their personalities, strengths, weaknesses, costs, and common mistakes, and discover why running the same prompt across multiple models is often the fastest way to find the best solution.

Practice exercise: Build familiarity with Cursor's basic workspace

This exercise is not about creating a website. It is about repeating the basic Cursor workflow until the interface becomes familiar.

1. Create a new empty folder anywhere on the computer
2. Open Cursor
3. Use **File** -> **Open folder** and open the new folder
4. Confirm that the left file panel is empty
5. Outside Cursor, create a random text file inside that same folder
6. Return to Cursor and confirm that the file appears in the left panel
7. If the file does not appear, move over to the left file panel and use the refresh icon
8. Select the text file and confirm that it opens in the center editor
9. Use *ctrl-L* to show the chat panel
10. Use **Terminal** -> **New terminal** to open the terminal at the bottom
11. Use *ctrl plus* to increase the interface size
12. Use *ctrl minus* to shrink it again
13. Change the interface theme through **File** -> **Preferences** -> **Theme** -> **Color theme**
14. In the chat panel, confirm that the mode is set to Agent
15. Look for the file reference area and the image attachment icon in the chat panel
16. Create a second empty folder and switch to it with **File** -> **Open folder**
17. Repeat the same process in the second folder

The successful outcome is simple: the folder is open, the file panel reflects the folder contents, the chat panel is visible, the terminal can be opened, Agent mode is selected, and switching to a new project folder feels straightforward.

7

Choosing the Right AI Model for the Job

LLMs are large language models, and they are the main thing Cursor uses. Most people simply call them models. Cursor is the main program, but most of its intelligence comes from these models, and the models come from different companies.

A simple way to explain the relationship is this: Cursor is the pipe, and the models are the water. Could the water flow without a pipe? Sure, but it may go all over the place. Cursor makes sure more of that intelligence goes where we want it to go. That is why we are using Cursor instead of signing up for one company and using only that company's models.

Using one specific company's models directly would be more limiting and substantially more expensive for this workflow. Through Cursor, we get access to most of the companies and most of the models that matter for this kind of work. That is why the model selector in Cursor is not a small setting. It changes the experience.

We will cover the following main topics in this chapter:

- Preparing a fair comparison
- Testing Claude
- Testing Gemini
- Testing GPT
- The verdict

Note

Why the answer is not one model

The obvious question is which model to use. The short answer is that *it depends.*

That is not a way of avoiding the question. It is the practical answer because models behave differently, and they also change over time. What is slow today may be fast tomorrow. What fails on one task may do well on another. Because of that, the useful approach is to give the top models the same task and compare the results.

Create an e-commerce one-page website with my oatmeal products. Use dummy information: title, price, weight, reviews. Use the images from this folder: "insert-address-here".

I want a grid of 4 by 2 that showcases my products. Add a big map that shows this address: Soseaua Giurgiului 230, sector 4, Bucuresti.

Add an Instagram feed from this profile: https://www.instagram.com/ohvaz_ro/

Use red, pink, and dark blue for the color scheme. Use a chunky, friendly font.

Add an FAQ section with dummy content, as well as a newsletter sign-up form.

In the main menu show a cart button and a register button. Use whatever tech stack you think is best.

The comparison should be repeated locally on a second pass through the material. The goal is not to lock in a permanent ranking. The goal is to get a sense of the models by testing them. In this run, I used a Pro plan, so I had access to the latest Claude 4 model. On the free plan, Claude 3.5 may be the available option, but that is not a problem for this experiment. The point is to understand how these models behave.

Disclaimer

New models have come out since I ran this comparison, but that doesn't invalidate the essential point of this chapter. Models come out just about every single week because there's a gold rush, and companies with billions of dollars in funding are trying to grab as much of the market as possible.

You will constantly change models, you will constantly have to adapt. Once you accept that, you'll be much more relaxed about this dizzying rate of change.

Preparing a fair comparison

To keep the comparison organized, I created three empty folders on my drive. The names do not matter, but I clearly labeled them so it was obvious which folder belonged to which model.

To make the test more interesting, I also used images attached to the course. Ideally, the model should use those images. For that to happen, the image folder needs to be copied into the model's project folder. In the Claude run, I copied the folder inside the `claude4` project location.

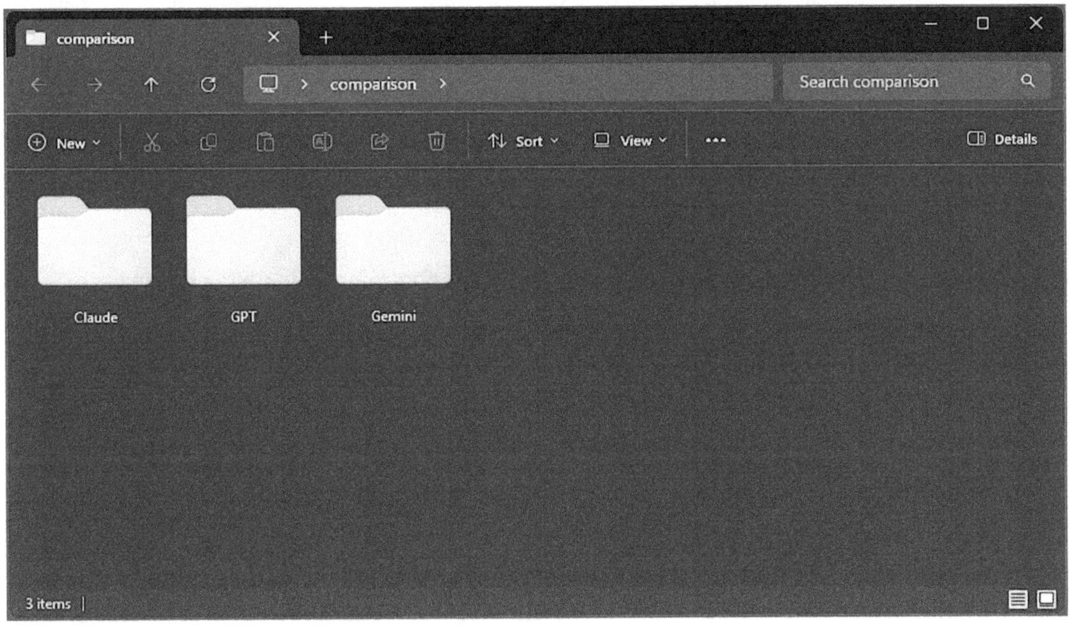

Figure 7.1: Empty project folders prepared for the model comparison

This should help the model quite a lot, but the model also needs clear instructions. I like to tell the model directly to use the images from the folder and then provide the exact path, meaning the exact location of the images on the computer.

To get the path, go inside the folder and select the location area. That reveals the full path. That path is then pasted into the text file with the task. This is a small step, but it matters because the model has a better chance of using the right assets when the location is clearly stated.

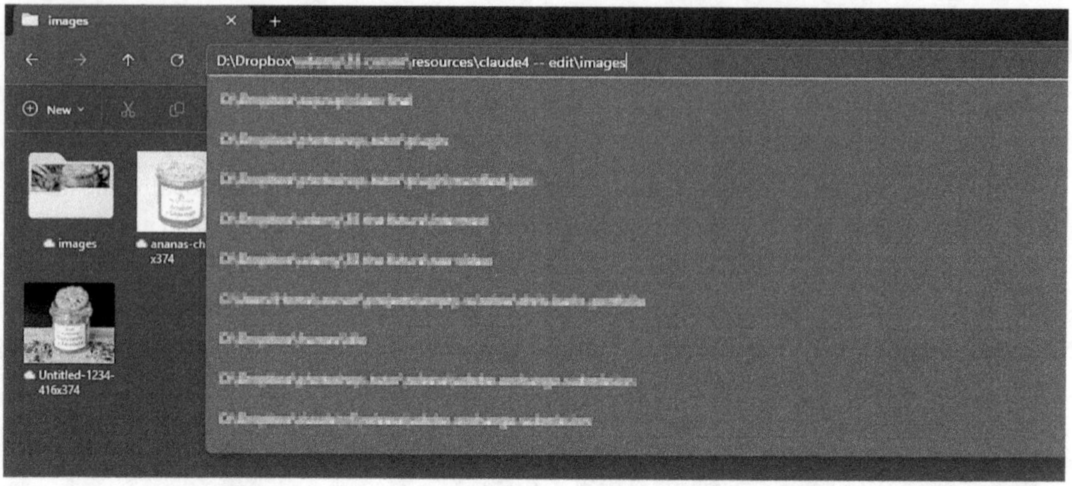

Figure 7.2: The folder path selected in the file explorer so the exact image folder location can be copied into the prompt

Once the prompt is ready, copy it. Back in Cursor, when no project is loaded, choose open `folder`, navigate through the computer, and select the correct project folder. After the interface loads, paste the prompt into the chat, make sure the chosen model is selected, and start the run.

For the Claude run, I selected Claude 4. I also made the interface bigger so the process would be easier to follow.

Testing Claude

Claude 4 immediately started planning a lot of moves. The model showed several steps before the actual reply. In Cursor, the washed-out text represents what the model is thinking before it gives the reply. After a moment, Claude acknowledged the task and said it would create a beautiful website.

It also said it would use `HTML5`, `CSS3`, and vanilla `JavaScript`.

That detail is fairly important. When we know which technologies the model is using, it becomes easier to fix potential issues later. We still may not be coding manually, but knowing whether a project is basic `HTML`, `CSS`, and `JavaScript`, or whether it uses `React` and `Vite`, gives us better context when something goes wrong.

Claude started with the `index` file. This is a point where patience matters. The model can take time to think, plan, and write files.

For the comparison, I decided a timer in the corner would be useful. That gives another way of comparing the models. Speed is not everything, but it is still useful information.

After the `index` file was loaded, the `CSS` file came next. The `CSS` file determines the style of the project - how the website looks. In this run, Claude wanted to use red, pink, and dark blue, along with a specific font called *Fredoka*.

This took some time, but looking at the files showed hundreds of lines of code, so the wait was warranted. Claude did not hesitate, but it did take time to write all that code.

One useful thing Claude did was create a `README` file. That is useful, and I appreciated the model doing that. A `README` is not the website itself, but it helps explain the project. For a vibe coding workflow, those plain-English project notes can be useful because they make it easier to understand what the model created.

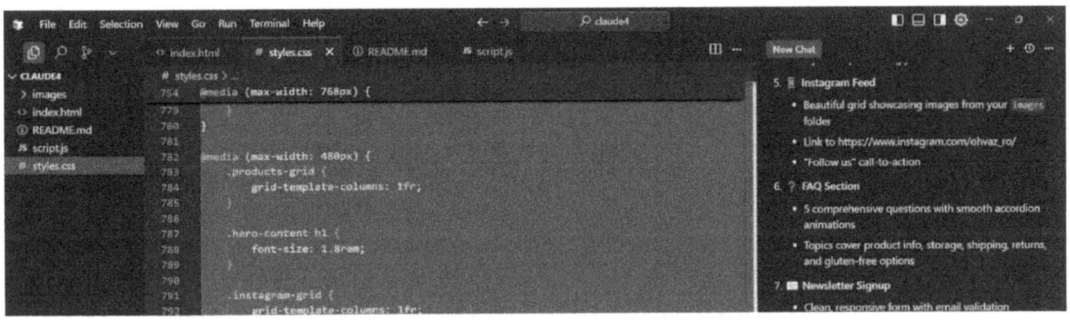

Figure 7.3: The file panel after Claude has created project files, including the README file

Once Claude finished, the next step was to accept everything and check the result.

The total time was about three and a half minutes, and the website looked good. Better than good, actually. I liked the gradient in the main menu, the chunky font, and the entire color scheme. The map was disappointing because Claude did not add a functional one. The project required a key for that to work.

The newsletter area was solid, and the footer looked excellent. For a result produced in just a few minutes, it was good work.

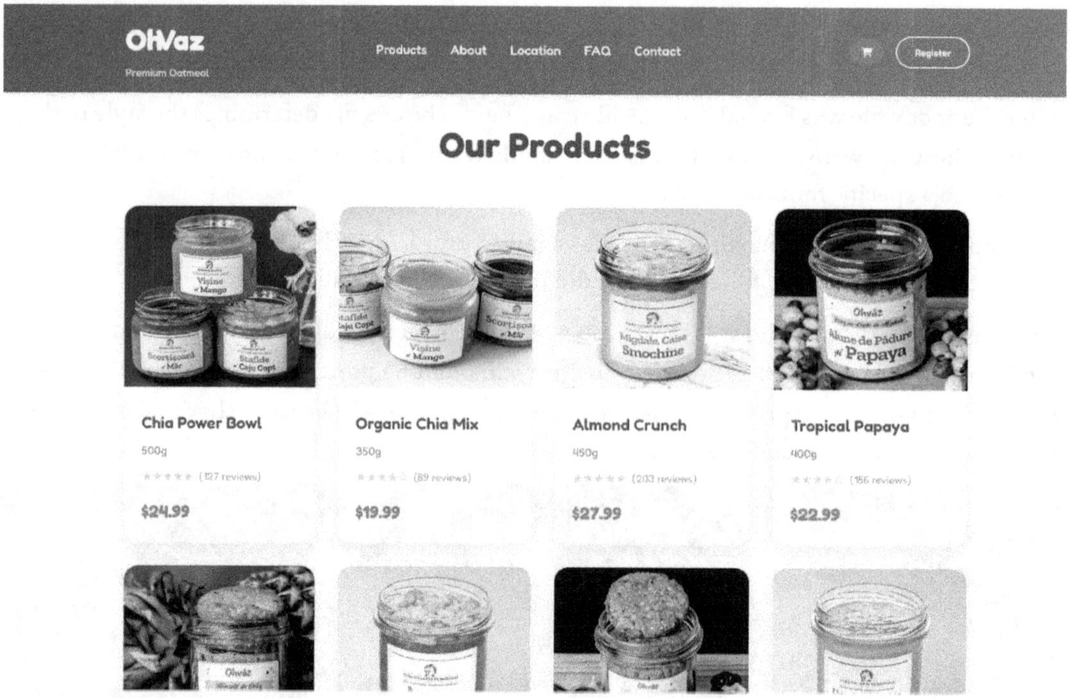

Figure 7.4: Claude 4's generated website in desktop view

The mobile version still needed to be checked. That is a good habit because sometimes the desktop version looks fine while the mobile version has alignment issues or other problems.

The mobile check revealed several issues. The top navigation was fixed, which was a good idea, but it covered the main headline. That was surprising. In the central area, the layout was not strong enough: text on the left, photo on the right, and the button separated too far at the bottom. The headline was also too far away.

This was a key area of the website, and it was not good enough.

Figure 7.5: The mobile version of Claude 4's website showing the fixed navigation covering the headline and the spacing issues in the main content area

There was also an issue with the Instagram feed. The task was tricky, but the problem was not simply that Claude failed to implement it. For the map, Claude said a key was needed and probably left instructions. That was acceptable. For the Instagram feed, it made one up based on the photos.

That is not great because it can confuse us. It is somewhat deceitful. If the model cannot implement a feature, it should say so.

This is dangerous for vibe coding because we may look at something and assume it is working when it is not. That is a red flag. A feature that looks real but is actually fake is more dangerous than a feature that clearly fails and tells us what is missing.

At this stage, Claude had ups and downs. The result looked strong in several places, but the mobile layout and the Instagram behavior showed real problems. We need to continue the comparison before deciding what Claude 4 really meant for the workflow.

Testing Gemini

The next model was Gemini. The setup started the same way: paste the images inside the Gemini folder and add that image location to the text file.

This project setup flow is something we will get used to: create a new folder, open it in Cursor, make sure the settings are right, and then start the task. Gemini is a Google product, and a lot of people have high hopes for it. The comparison gives us a practical way to see how it behaves in this specific workflow.

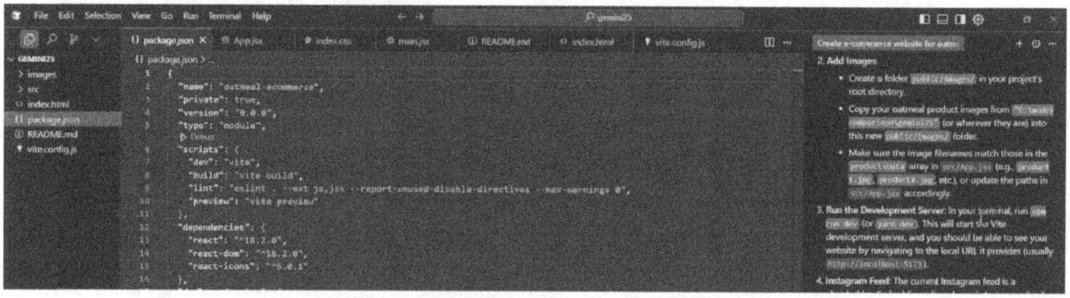

Figure 7.6: Gemini project folder with the same image assets copied into it

Gemini's train of thought was very fast and included a lot of detail. In the actual reply, Gemini chose a different technology stack than Claude. It wanted to use `React` and `Vite`.

That may not mean much if we are not coders, but it is an interesting difference worth noticing. Claude chose `HTML5`, `CSS3`, and vanilla `JavaScript`; Gemini chose `React` and `Vite`. The same task can lead different models to choose different technical approaches.

Then Gemini did something unexpected. For the image assets, it said it first had to know what images were inside the folder and asked whether we could list them ourselves.

That was surprising. Claude immediately saw all the photos. To be fair, we could have provided fewer photos or named them in the same format, but this is exactly why the comparison matters. The models were given the same computer and the exact same task.

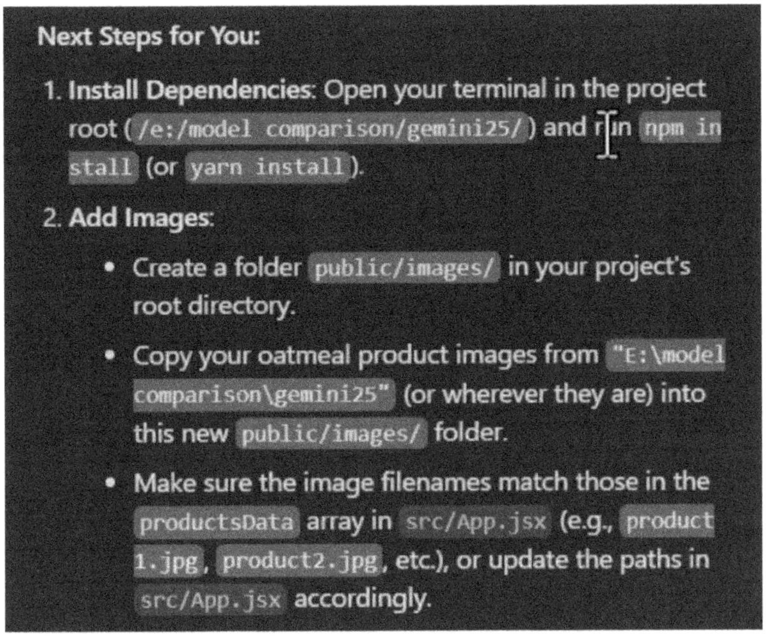

Figure 7.7: Capture Gemini asking for the image list or exact image details before it can use the assets

With Gemini's technical approach, the model created several different files, starting with `package.json`. Again, we do not need to care deeply about that file at this stage, but it is useful to notice these things. As we become more familiar with models, we start recognizing their approaches and their typical choices.

By around the two-minute mark, Gemini seemed to be done. It produced a large summary. In the recording, I skipped over the summary to keep the pace moving, but in real work, I do suggest reading everything the model says because there may be key information there.

After accepting everything, the next question was how to launch the project. Because Gemini used a different technical approach, the `index` file was not the main thing to open. The chat summary said that a development server needed to be run.

I did not like that.

At the same time, Gemini's fourth point said the feed was just a placeholder and that a key would be needed for a real one. I appreciated that. This is where the personality of the model comes through. I am not saying this made Gemini better than Claude, but it was something worth noting. Gemini did not make the feed look real while hiding the fact that it was not connected.

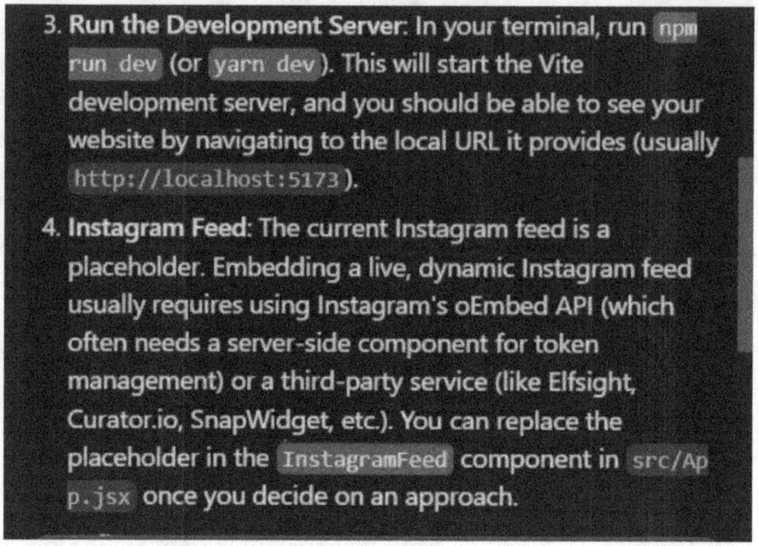

Figure 7.8: Gemini's summary showing that a development server is needed

Trying the `localhost` link would not work yet because Gemini was asking for a server. I did not want to run the server manually, so the instruction was direct:

```
you do step number 1
```

The model immediately said it would do it, which was a bit funny because it could have done it before. This matters because every command we give the model costs money. Some people may be unhappy with that approach. If the model knows what needs to be done and how to do it, then it should do it.

Something started happening in the console: `npm install`. After a while, Gemini again said there were two things to do: add images, rename them, and more importantly run the server. I still did not want to run the server manually, even though it was quite easy to do.

So the next instruction was:

```
skip the images, continue with step 3
```

That should have been enough to preview the website. At that point, the run was over three and a half minutes, and the experience had been very different from Claude's.

The generated website showed missing images. The main menu was nice and clean. The map was already up and running, unlike Claude's result. There was no Instagram feed, but Gemini explained why. It did not confuse us the way Claude did.

The page also had an FAQ section and a newsletter area. Overall, it was quite good. The product photos were the thing that really bothered me.

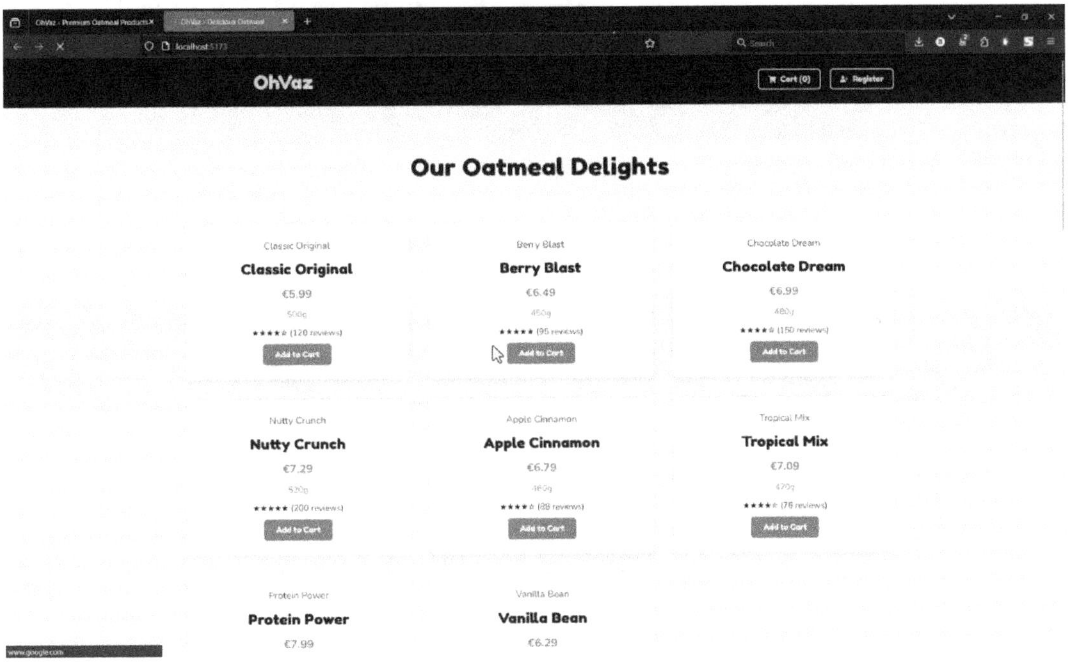

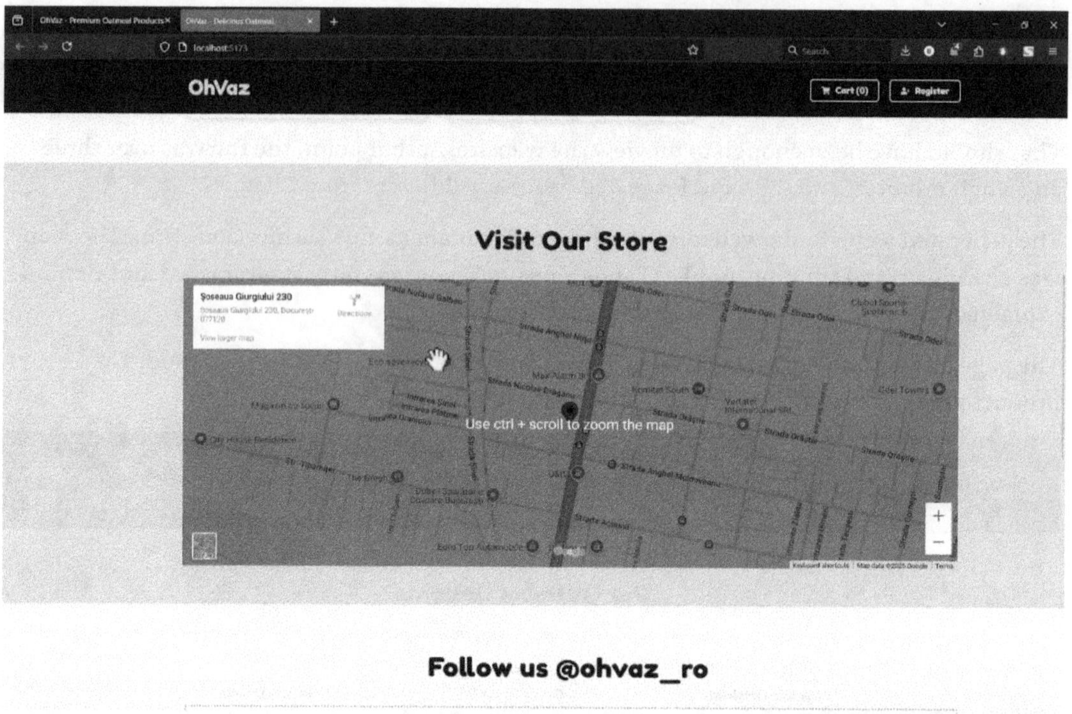
OhVaz
Cart (0)
Register
Visit Our Store
Şoseaua Giurgiului 230
Use ctrl + scroll to zoom the map
Follow us @ohvaz_ro

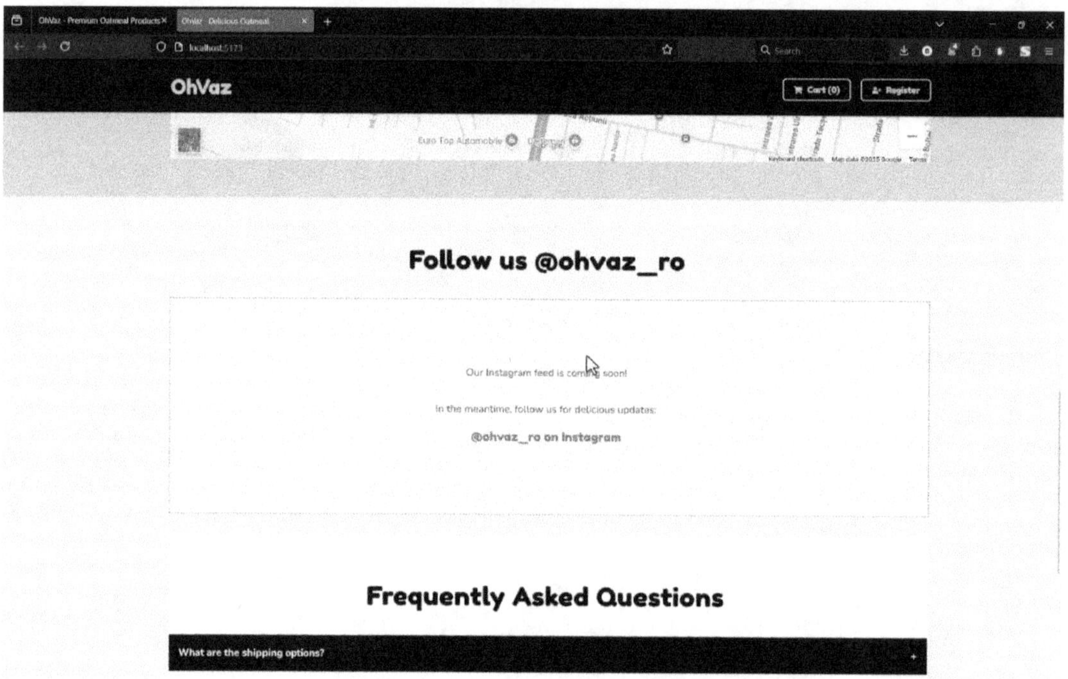
OhVaz
Cart (0)
Register
Follow us @ohvaz_ro
Our Instagram feed is coming soon!
In the meantime, follow us for delicious updates:
@ohvaz_ro on Instagram
Frequently Asked Questions
What are the shipping options?

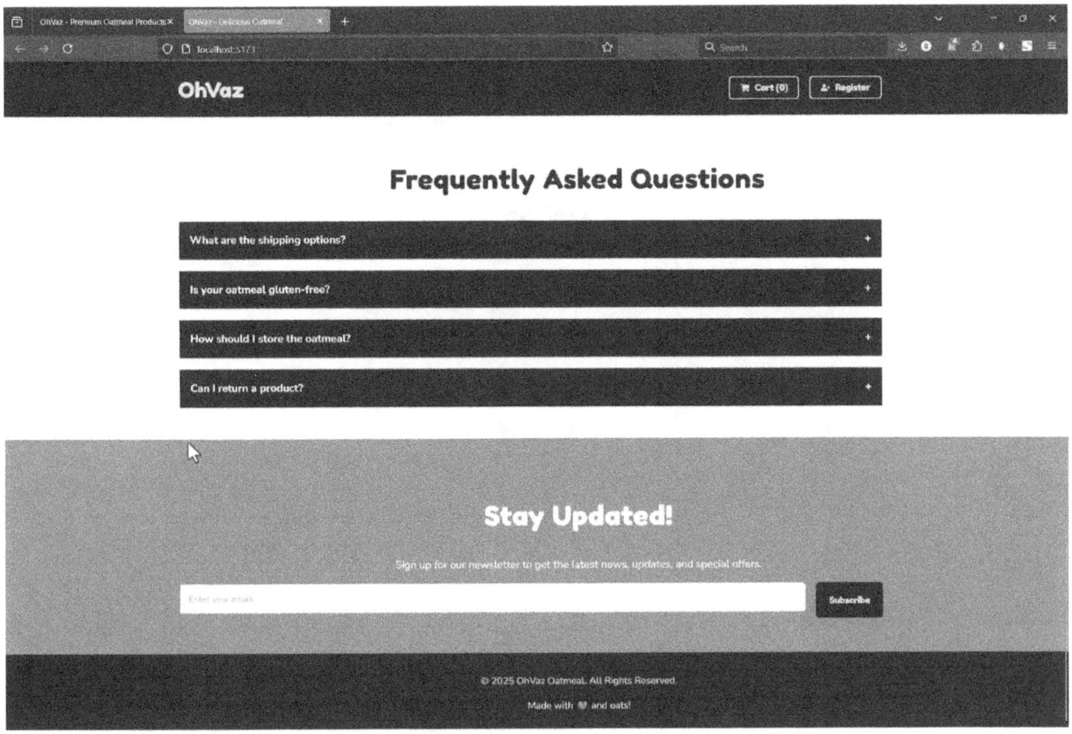

Figure 7.9: Gemini's generated website showing missing images, the clean main menu, the working map, the FAQ section, the newsletter area, and no Instagram feed

I looked back at the prompt to see if I had pointed Gemini to the general folder rather than the exact photos. Maybe that was the issue. At the same time, the model should be able to do anything inside that project folder, so I did not think the folder path fully explained the problem.

Still, I tried again. I told the model that the photos were already inside the project folder and that it should add them to the project. I doubted it would fix the issue, and it did not. Gemini said it could not access them and that I had to provide the exact filenames for eight product images.

I would hate to do that manually.

The funny part was that Gemini did create a new folder called `public/images`, which suggested that the model did have access to that location in some way. Even so, it still wanted manual filenames.

The mobile version looked good.

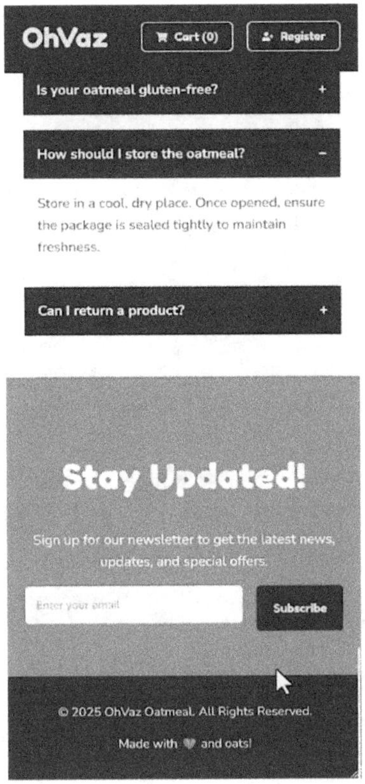

Figure 7.10: Gemini's mobile version showing the cleaner mobile layout compared with the Claude run

Overall, the experience was decent, but asking me to rename or list those files was not ideal. In this run, the mobile version actually looked better than Claude's.

Testing GPT

The final model in this comparison was GPT 4.1. The setup is the same. Immediately, GPT 4.1 gave a plan. It said it would create a React-based project with `Vite`. That was fine by us. It then gave a step-by-step approach.

The first major difference was that GPT 4.1 asked me to review the plan and say whether I wanted to adjust it. There are two ways to look at that. On one hand, it consumes another credit. On the other hand, it gives us a chance to make sure the model understood the task.

For my taste, I lean toward this being a bad thing. That is a personal preference. I do not want to hold the model's hand. I do not know what I do not know, so I am looking to the model for guidance.

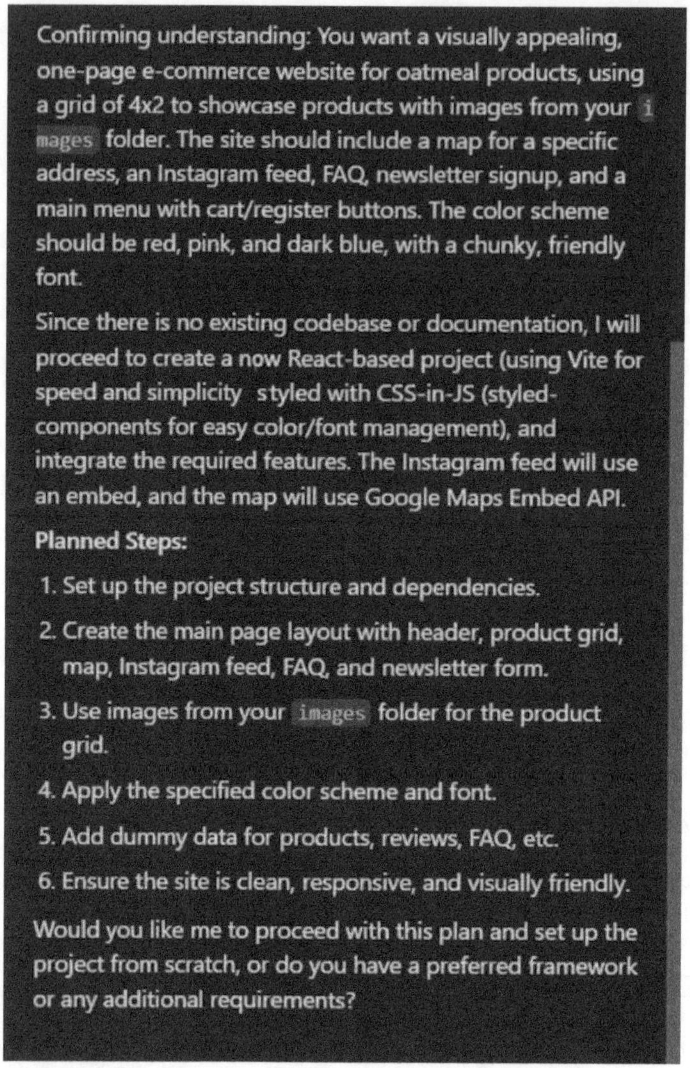

Figure 7.11: GPT 4.1 presenting a plan and asking for review or adjustment before continuing

I told it to continue. After a few seconds, it asked for confirmation to install `Vite`. This is where we have to be careful. The terminal expected a `y` to be entered, followed by `Enter`; otherwise the process would be stuck.

```
y
```

That is not obvious, which is why these tutorials are useful. A person who already understands the terminal would know what to do, but this course is not assuming that.

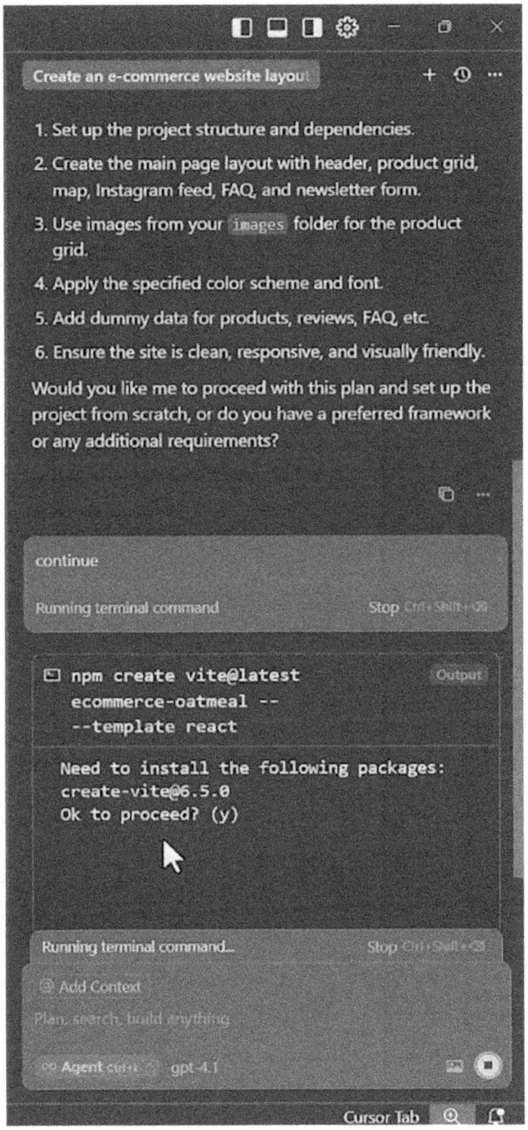

Figure 7.12: The terminal asking for confirmation to install Vite, with the required y input

Then came a bigger issue. After accepting, the setup asked for a framework, and there were many options. Because I am not a developer, I was not sure what to select. The model mentioned React, but honestly, I was not sure.

This is where GPT 4.1 was vastly different from the other two. I chose React and continued. Then it asked for a variant, and again there were many options. This was supremely annoying because the correct choice was not obvious.

We could launch `chatgpt.com` and ask about it. We could even start a new conversation inside Cursor and ask the model what the best approach would be. In the end, I chose the first option, TypeScript, and continued.

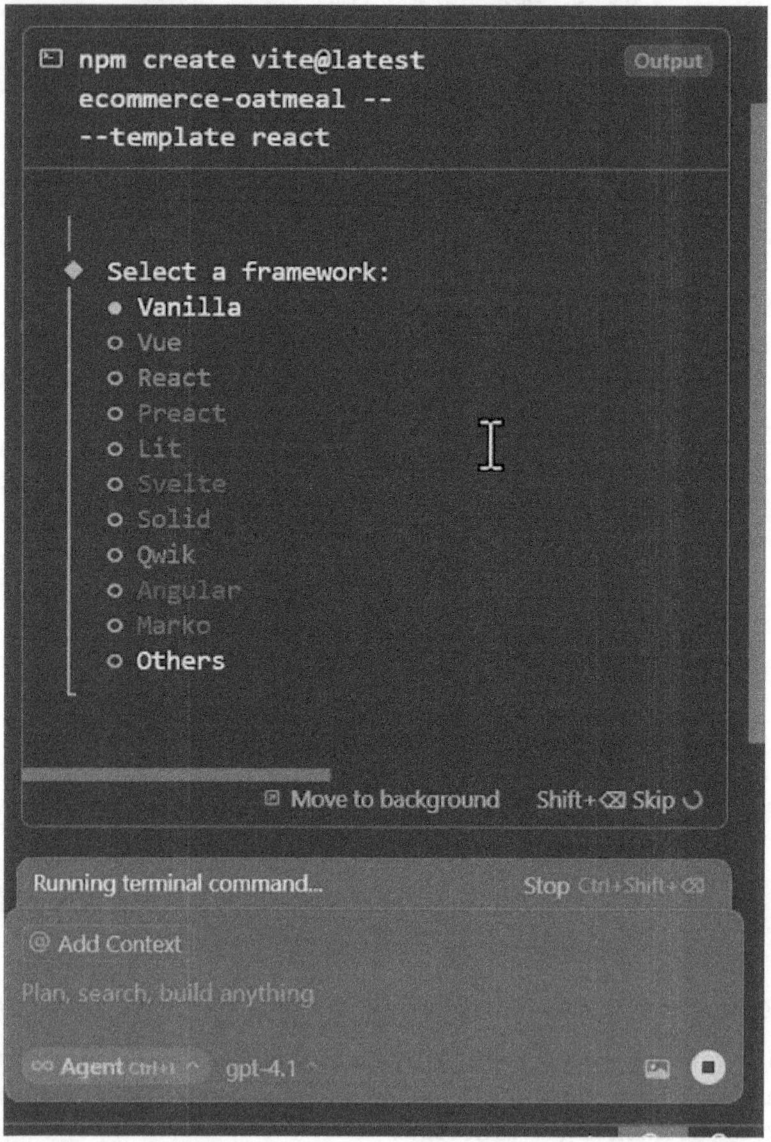

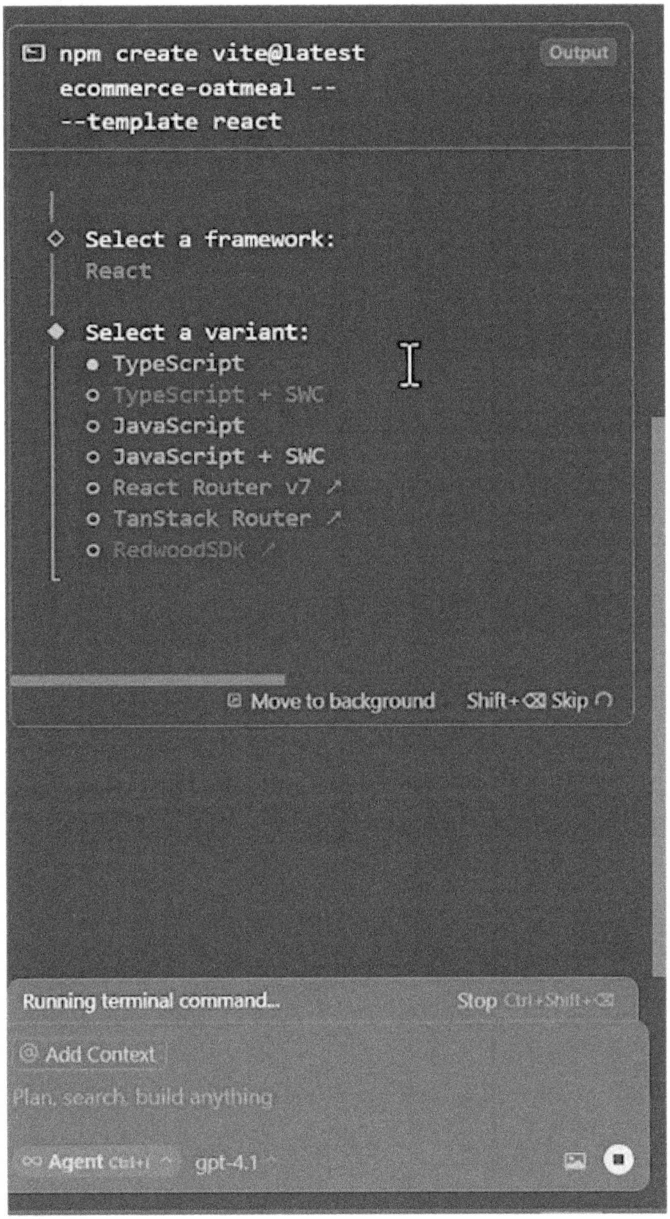

Figure 7.13: The framework and variant selection prompts during the GPT 4.1 Vite setup, showing React and TypeScript as selected choices

This is far from ideal for vibe coders. Experienced developers should not have any issues with these prompts, but for the workflow in this course, it was not looking good.

Previously, Gemini's inability to find the photos was frustrating. This felt worse. At one point, I worried that the `App.tsx` file had frozen Cursor. Actually, it seemed to be a very big file.

As the model worked, it was important to be clear about one thing: these results are not definitive. If the exact experiment is repeated, there may be different results. Many people do head-to-head comparisons, but one thing is certain: results vary.

One model may be slow today and fast tomorrow. These companies can update the models so they simply work better. Some people argue that at different times of day, some models degrade—almost like rush hour at 5 PM when everybody leaves work at the same time. I cannot say for certain that happens, but I have to be clear that results vary a lot.

Eventually, the interface showed a success message on the right side saying the setup was complete. But on the left, the terminal clearly showed issues. That can be confusing. I stopped the timer and tried to find the `index` file to see how the website looked.

I was skeptical, and the website was not working.

When this happens, the right move is to talk to the model. Tell it what is happening. In this case, the message was that the `index` file was blank. Hopefully, the model would check everything and identify the issue.

That is not what happened. The summary did not make anything clear.

So the next message was:

```
help me preview the website in my browser
```

The goal was to have the model make the changes and fixes. We could copy and paste the error into Google, but I first wanted to give the model a chance to fix it on its own.

It still did not work. We could try again, but it would fail. The most obvious answer was to feed the model the error directly. Copy the error and paste it into the chat. In most cases, the model will say something like, "oh, you're right."

In this case, it had run a command in a different folder—a silly mistake.

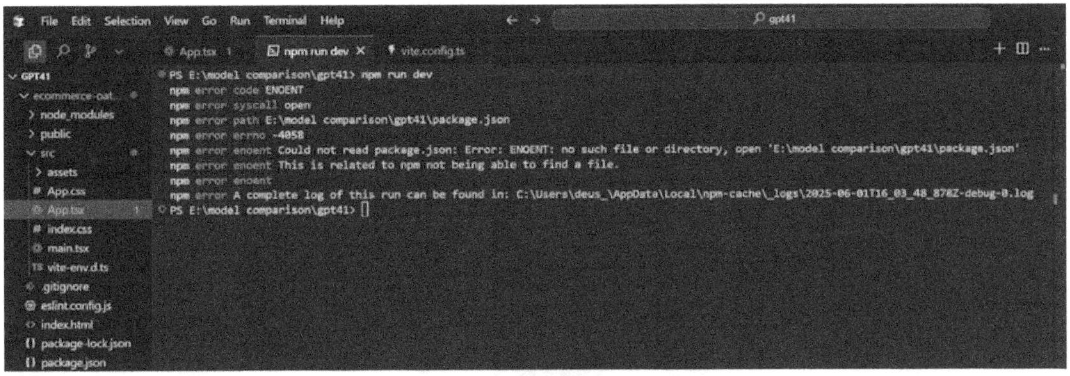

Figure 7.14: GPT 4.1's error or terminal issue showing the command running in the wrong folder

After about 10 minutes, the website was finally ready. That was much slower than the other models.

The result was not impressive. The entire website was offset toward the left, and I did not know why. The images were missing, and the reviews were shown in an ugly gray. The map worked, and this was the only model that gave me an actual Instagram feed. It was a real one, not a fake one. But there was no footer, and by the look of it, the mobile version was going to be horrible.

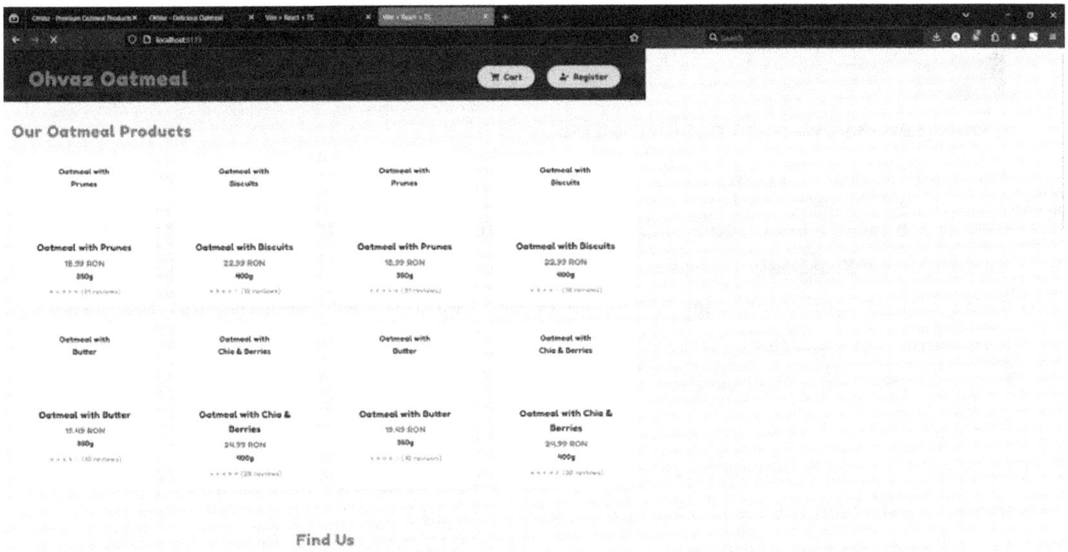

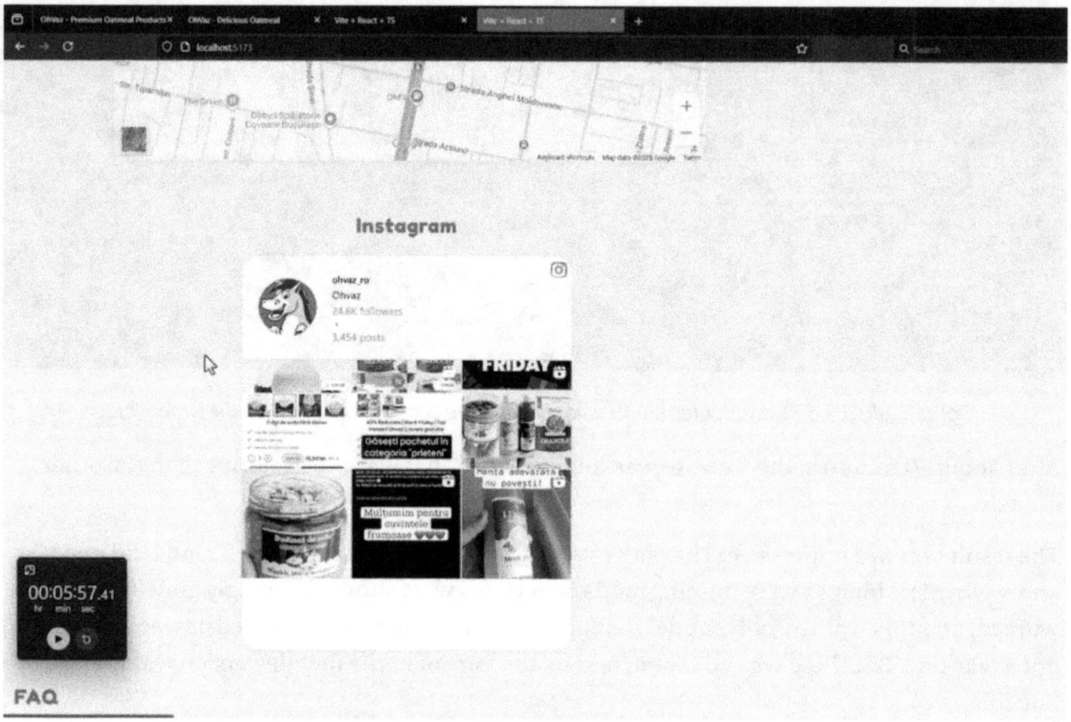

Figure 7.15: GPT 4.1's generated website showing the layout issues

> Note
>
> **Reading model behavior, not just output**
>
> The useful part of this comparison is not just the final website; the process matters.
>
> Claude produced a good-looking desktop result quickly and created useful supporting material like a **README**. It made some strong design choices, such as the gradient menu, chunky font, color scheme, newsletter, and footer. But it failed in the mobile layout and made the Instagram feed look real when it was not. That is a red flag because vibe coding can become dangerous when something looks functional but is actually fake.
>
> Gemini chose a different technical approach with **React** and **Vite**. It was fast, and it was more honest about the feed being a placeholder. The map worked. The mobile version looked good. But the image handling was frustrating because it asked for a manual list of image filenames even though the images were inside the project folder.
>
> GPT 4.1 also chose a **React** and **Vite** approach, but it asked for too much confirmation and setup input. It wanted the plan reviewed, asked for installation confirmation, then

> asked for framework and variant choices. For an experienced developer, that may be fine. For this workflow, it is not ideal. The model also ran a command in the wrong folder, took much longer, and produced a result that was not visually strong, even though it did create a real Instagram feed.
>
> This is the kind of information we want from a comparison—not a permanent winner, but a feel for each model's behavior.

The verdict from this run

There are clearly pluses and minuses.

For me, in this run, I prefer Claude 4. At the time of the recording, Claude 4 was available only on the $20 per month plan. For anyone staying on the free plan, Claude 3.5 was still pretty good.

But this is more preference than anything else. It is Pepsi versus Coke, Android versus iPhone. These models come from giant companies that are spending enormous amounts of money on these problems. There is no one best phone, and there is no one best model.

For now, I like Claude 4. Tomorrow, I may switch to another one.

The important thing is to test the available models with the same prompt. Run the same task in the same kind of setup and write down the experience: the good, the bad, and the horrible. Screenshots help, because they make the comparison more concrete.

The goal is not to memorize a ranking. The goal is to learn what each model tends to do: which one needs more hand-holding, which one is more honest about missing functionality, which one makes better design choices, which one handles assets better, and which one produces confusing failures.

That kind of practical knowledge only comes from testing.

Summary

This chapter compares Claude 4, Gemini, and GPT 4.1 inside Cursor by running the same website-building task with identical prompts and image assets in three separate project folders. Since model performance changes over time, the chapter argues for testing models directly rather than assuming which one is best.

Claude 4 used HTML5, CSS3, and JavaScript and finished fastest, around three and a half minutes. It produced the best-looking desktop design and included a useful README file.

However, its mobile layout was broken, and more seriously, it faked a working Instagram feed instead of admitting it couldn't build one.

Gemini used React and Vite and was more transparent about its limitations, clearly labeling the Instagram feed as a placeholder. It had a working map and a decent mobile layout, but it repeatedly asked for manual image filenames even though it had access to the project folder.

GPT 4.1 also used React and Vite but required the most hand-holding, including plan approval, installation confirmations, and framework and variant choices. It took about ten minutes, ran into a wrong folder error, and produced a weak, offset layout. Still, it was the only model to deliver a real Instagram feed and a working map.

The chapter's verdict is that there is no permanent winner. Choosing between these models comes down to preference, similar to choosing between Pepsi and Coke. The real value of the comparison is learning each model's tendencies: how much guidance it needs, how honest it is about its limitations, and how well it handles assets. A practice exercise walks through repeating this same testing method, supported by a comparison log table.

With model selection covered, the next chapter turns to the practical side of running Cursor day to day, looking at credits, requests, free trials, and paid plans, the cost differences between models, when buying extra credits makes sense, and why credits are best thought of as an investment in learning and output rather than something to ration anxiously.

Practice exercise: Compare models using the same task

This exercise repeats the comparison workflow in a controlled way.

1. Create three empty folders on the computer.
2. Label the folders clearly for the models being tested, such as **claude**, **gemini**, and **gpt**.
3. Copy the same image assets into each project folder.
4. Prepare the exact same task prompt for all three runs.
5. Add the image folder path to the prompt before each run.
6. Open the first folder in Cursor with open folder.
7. Select the first model in the model selector.
8. Confirm that the chat is set to **Agent**.
9. Run the prompt.
10. Watch which technology the model chooses, such as **HTML5**, **CSS3**, vanilla **JavaScript**, **React**, or **Vite**.

11. Note whether the model starts working immediately or asks for extra confirmation.
12. Accept the changes when the model finishes.
13. Preview the website.
14. Check the desktop version.
15. Check the mobile version.
16. Record any missing images, broken layout, fake placeholder content, missing footer, working map, or feed behavior.
17. Repeat the same process for the second model.
18. Repeat the same process for the third model.
19. Compare how much manual help each model required.
20. Compare the final result from each model.
21. Keep screenshots of all three versions.

The successful outcome is not choosing a permanent winner. The successful outcome is understanding the differences in behavior. One model may make a better-looking page but hide a fake feature. Another model may be more honest but ask for manual filenames. Another model may create one real feature but require too much setup guidance. That is the value of the exercise: testing the same prompt across models reveals the personality and trade-offs of each model.

Model comparison log

The comparison should be recorded as observations, not as a permanent ranking. The same model may behave differently later, but the current run still teaches the most important lesson: model choice affects the workflow, not just the final design.

Consumer	Claude 4 run	Gemini run	GPT 4.1 run
Technology selected	HTML5, CSS3, and vanilla JavaScript	React and Vite	React-based project with Vite
Initial behavior	Plans several moves and starts with the index file	Fast and detailed thinking, then asks which images are in the folder	Gives a plan and asks for a review before continuing

Consumer	Claude 4 run	Gemini run	GPT 4.1 run
Manual friction	Takes time but does not hesitate much	Needs a development server and pushes image filename work back to us	Requires confirmation with y, framework selection, and variant selection
Image handling	Uses the supplied photos but later fakes an Instagram feed from them	Cannot access the photos cleanly and asks for exact filenames for eight product images	Images are missing in the final preview
Map behavior	Does not add a functional map and indicates a key is needed	Map works in the preview	Map works in the preview
Instagram/feed behavior	Creates a fake Instagram feed, which is a red flag	Says the feed is a placeholder and a key is needed	Creates an actual Instagram feed
Mobile result	Top navigation covers the headline, and the hero layout is weak	Mobile version looks good and may be better than Claude's	Mobile version is likely to be poor
Approximate experience	About three and a half minutes, strong first impression but with important risks	Over three and a half minutes, different workflow, decent result, but frustrating image handling	About ten minutes, slower, with confusing setup and a weak final layout
Author preference from this run	Preferred overall at the time of recording	Useful, honest in some areas, but less smooth	Far from ideal for vibe coders in this run

The table is not meant to replace the hands-on run. It is a way to capture the same kinds of things the author notices during the recording: whether the model chooses a stack that is easy to preview, whether it asks for manual work, whether it explains unsupported features, whether it hallucinates fake functionality, and whether the final output holds up on mobile.

The strongest lesson is skepticism. A good-looking page is not enough. The map may require a key. The feed may be fake. The image folder may not be used correctly. The terminal may show issues even while the chat says the setup succeeded. The model should be treated as a powerful builder, but the result still needs to be checked.

The final preference should come from repeated testing. One run may make Claude 4 feel best. Another run may show Gemini improving. Another task may make GPT more useful. The author's point is not to crown a single model. The point is to build enough practical experience to know which model personality fits the task at hand.

8

Costs, Credits, and Working Without Range Anxiety

At some point during a session, the usage meter catches your eye and something shifts. Prompts that were flowing freely start feeling more deliberate. There's a hesitation before hitting Enter. That hesitation is range anxiety, and it's one of the more counterproductive things that can happen to a vibe coder who's still learning.

This chapter is about getting that anxiety out of the workflow permanently. To do that, it helps to understand how Cursor's usage system actually works today, what models cost relative to what they produce, and what the right frame of reference is for spending in the first place.

There's one complication worth naming up front: Cursor has changed its pricing model several times, and it tends to update the pricing page quietly when it does. A short timeline later in the chapter makes that pattern explicit, so you're never caught off guard by a number that has moved since this was written.

This one's going to be a short one, and we'll cover the following main topics:

- The free Hobby tier and the Pro trial: where everyone starts
- The Pro plan, and what "included usage" actually means
- How the credit system works, and why Auto mode is the thing that kills range anxiety
- A short history of Cursor's pricing changes
- Choosing the right model for your sessions
- Max mode and manual model selection: what to be careful with early on

A note before the numbers: every figure here is current as of writing, but treat the structure as the durable part and the exact dollar amounts as the thing to re-check on cursor.com/pricing before you rely on them.

> Note
>
> **Where Everyone Starts: The Hobby Tier and the Pro Trial**
>
> Some new accounts also get a 7–14-day trial of the Pro plan, but it doesn't appear for everyone, and Cursor doesn't publish the rules for who gets it. During that time, you get the full Pro experience, including access to the frontier models, which is the best way to form an opinion before paying anything. If you don't see the trial on the official Cursor website, the move is to sign up for the free plan and upgrade to the $20 plan after a couple of days.

The Pro plan and what "Included Usage" means

Once the trial ends or you're done with the Free plan, continuing with Cursor means picking a plan. The Pro plan costs twenty dollars per month, or about sixteen dollars per month if billed annually, and it's the tier that I recommend for regular work. Pro unlocks extended Agent limits, the full set of frontier models, MCPs, skills and hooks, and cloud agents.

Here's the part that trips people up, because it's different from how Cursor used to work. Pro doesn't give you a fixed number of requests. It gives you a monthly pool of model usage, measured in dollars, and consumed at roughly the same rates you'd pay the model providers directly through their APIs. Two plans sit above Pro for people who run out: Pro+ at sixty dollars a month gives three times Pro's usage, and Ultra at two hundred dollars a month gives twenty times Pro's usage plus early access to new features. Students get a full year of Pro for free with a valid school email, which is worth knowing if it applies to you.

The anxiety usually comes from watching a balance drop without a clear sense of what it's buying. The right way to think about it is in terms of what gets built. A session that draws down a dollar or two and produces a working contact form backed by a real email service is good value.

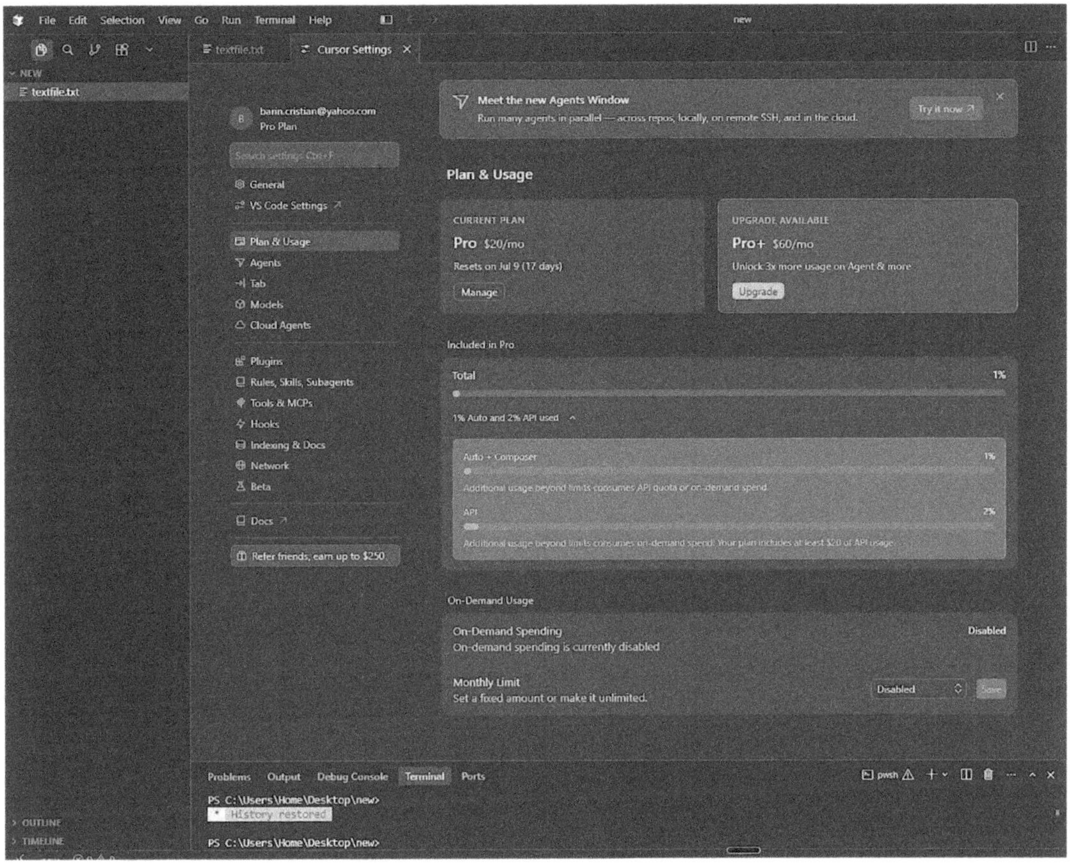

Figure 8.1: Plan and Usage

A session that spends the same amount fighting a configuration issue that a better initial prompt would have avoided is frustrating, but it's still a learning investment. The balance dropping isn't the problem. The balance dropping without something to show for it is, and that's a prompt-quality issue, not a pricing issue.

How the credit system works (and why auto mode matters most)

The single most important thing to understand about Cursor's current pricing is Auto mode, because it's the feature that makes range anxiety mostly unnecessary.

Auto mode lets Cursor select a model for each request. Under Cursor's current usage-based pricing, Auto consumes included usage at published token rates; it is not effectively unlimited or free, but you will get a lot more usage out of it compared to selecting a top-end model. Pricing and plan behavior can change, so check the live pricing documentation and your usage dashboard before starting a long session.

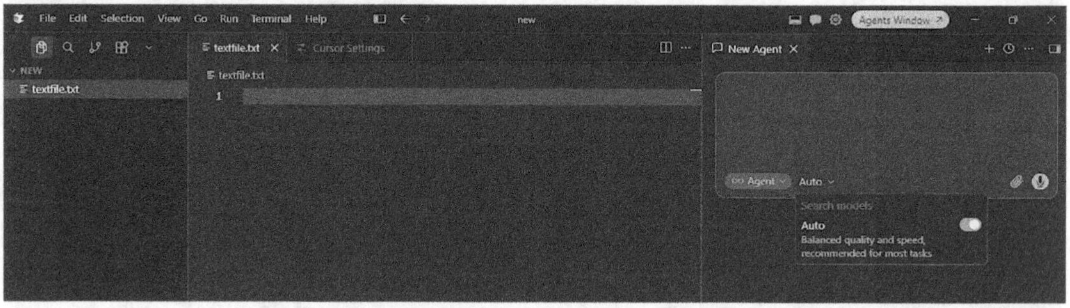

Figure 8.2: Auto mode in Cursor

When you do spend from the pool, two things determine how fast it goes. The first is which model you pick: a Claude Sonnet request costs noticeably more than a Gemini one, with the OpenAI models somewhere in between, because Cursor is passing through the providers' real API costs. As a rough guide, twenty dollars of pool covers a couple of hundred premium-model requests, but that number swings widely with model choice and with how much context each request carries. The second factor is complexity: a one-line syntax question consumes a fraction of what a full multi-file feature implementation does.

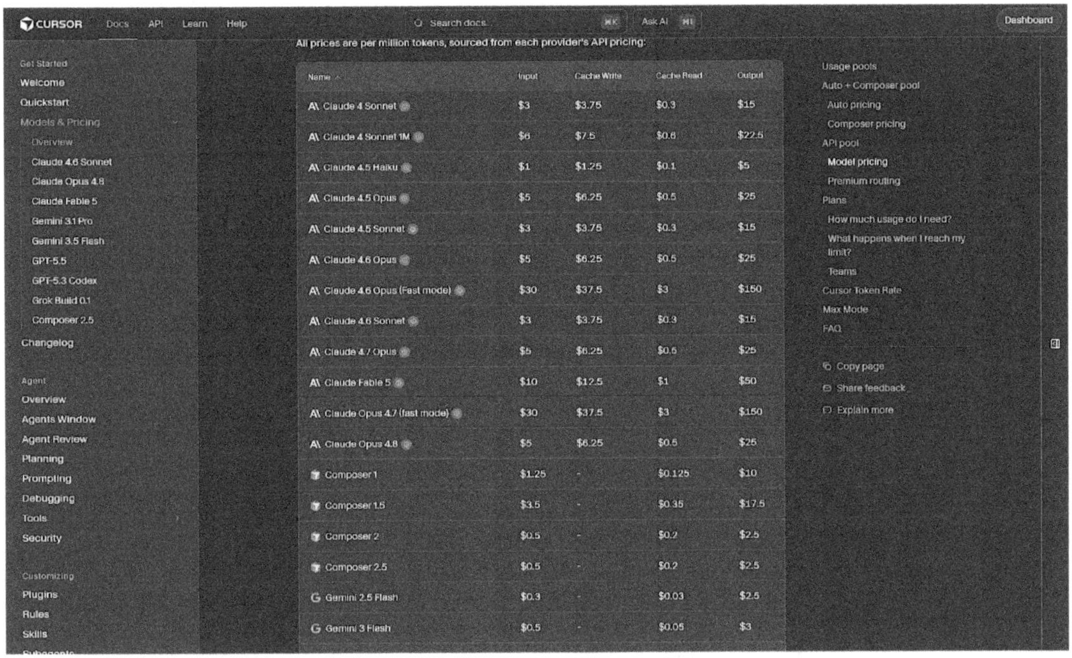

All prices are per million tokens, sourced from each provider's API pricing:

Name	Input	Cache Write	Cache Read	Output
Claude 4 Sonnet	$3	$3.75	$0.3	$15
Claude 4 Sonnet 1M	$6	$7.5	$0.6	$22.5
Claude 4.5 Haiku	$1	$1.25	$0.1	$5
Claude 4.5 Opus	$5	$6.25	$0.5	$25
Claude 4.5 Sonnet	$3	$3.75	$0.3	$15
Claude 4.6 Opus	$5	$6.25	$0.5	$25
Claude 4.6 Opus (Fast mode)	$30	$37.5	$3	$150
Claude 4.6 Sonnet	$3	$3.75	$0.3	$15
Claude 4.7 Opus	$5	$6.25	$0.5	$25
Claude Fable 5	$10	$12.5	$1	$50
Claude Opus 4.7 (fast mode)	$30	$37.5	$3	$150
Claude Opus 4.8	$5	$6.25	$0.5	$25
Composer 1	$1.25	-	$0.125	$10
Composer 1.5	$3.5	-	$0.35	$17.5
Composer 2	$0.5	-	$0.2	$2.5
Composer 2.5	$0.5	-	$0.2	$2.5
Gemini 2.5 Flash	$0.3	-	$0.03	$2.5
Gemini 3 Flash	$0.5	-	$0.05	$3

Figure 8.3: Pricing of the models

When included usage is close to exhausted, consult the current dashboard for the available options. Depending on the plan and account settings, these may include purchasing additional usage, enabling usage-based billing with a spend limit, or upgrading. Do not promise a grace period or free Auto fallback unless Cursor's current official documentation explicitly provides one.

The math is worth doing explicitly, because the numbers are small enough to reframe the anxiety entirely. Even if a difficult project runs to several dollars of frontier-model usage across multiple sessions, compare that to hiring a freelance developer: rates of twenty-five to a hundred dollars an hour are standard, and a landing page that takes a developer eight hours represents two hundred to eight hundred dollars in labor. The cost of producing comparable output in Cursor is not in the same order of magnitude. This isn't a claim that Cursor matches an experienced developer's quality — it doesn't, and Chapter 10 on the 80/20 reality of AI-built websites is honest about that. Here's the simpler version: once you look at the real numbers, worrying about rationing your usage just doesn't hold up.

Bottom line: Cursor wants you on 'Auto,' and that gives you plenty of usage without worrying about running out. For top-notch results on serious projects, though, I still like picking one specific model and sticking with it, whether that's the latest Claude or GPT. So it comes down to where you're at. If you're just starting out and learning how to vibe code, stick with Auto. If you're ready to build something more serious, choose a model and commit to it; just expect your range to run out a lot faster.

A short history of Cursor's pricing

It's worth seeing the pattern directly, because it explains why this chapter keeps telling you to re-check the live page. Cursor has reworked its pricing repeatedly, sometimes with rough rollouts.

Period	**What changed?**
2023 – early 2025	Request-based plan. Pro was $20/month for 500 fast premium requests, plus unlimited slower requests and unlimited Tab completions. Sonnet counted as two requests each. Easy to follow!
June 16, 2025	Major overhaul. The $200/month Ultra plan launched and Pro moved from 500 requests to a dollar-denominated usage pool. Auto mode was promoted as "unlimited." The rollout was communicated poorly.
Late June 2025	Backlash. Some users were hit with surprise charges because "unlimited" applied only to Auto mode, not to manually selected models.
June 30, 2025	Cursor revised the original announcement and the pricing page for improved clarity.
July 4, 2025	Public apology. Cursor clarified the usage-pool model, the grace period, and spend limits, and offered full refunds for unexpected charges incurred between June 16 and July 4.
August 2025	Team plans moved to the same usage-based billing used by individual plans.
2026	The line-up settles into Hobby, Pro, Pro+, Ultra, Teams (Standard and Premium seats), and Enterprise, with live usage shown on the dashboard.

The takeaway isn't to memorize any of these numbers. It's that Cursor changes its pricing relatively often, so the habit that protects you is checking cursor.com/pricing and your own dashboard rather than trusting a figure you read months ago, including the ones in this chapter.

Choosing the right model for your sessions

Here's the part of cost economics that doesn't show up in any pricing table but has the largest effect on what a session actually costs: some models do a lot of work per prompt, and some do very little.

A highly autonomous model, given a well-constructed prompt, breaks the task into sub-tasks, executes them in sequence, handles errors it hits along the way, and reports back with a summary. A model that needs more hand-holding does a single step and waits, often asking clarifying questions before doing anything. Getting to the same finished result might take it three times as many exchanges, and the cognitive load of managing each one adds friction that slows everything down.

This is why, for the overwhelming majority of work, Auto mode is the right default — Cursor's router is good at matching a capable-enough model to the task. The time to manually pin a specific frontier model is when quality genuinely matters: a tricky architectural decision, a large refactor, or a case where Auto's choice keeps falling short. For that kind of work, the current top frontier models from Anthropic (the Claude Sonnet and Opus line), OpenAI (the GPT-5 line), and Google (the Gemini line) are all strong, and exactly which one leads shifts as providers update them — which is the whole reason to test rather than take a recommendation on faith.

When you're comparing models, the right question isn't which one costs less per prompt. It's which one gets the most done per session. A model with a higher per-request cost that finishes a task in one prompt can easily be cheaper, in total, than a cheaper model that takes five.

During your first weeks, the most useful thing you can do is run the same prompt through Auto mode and through one or two manually selected frontier models, in separate project folders, and compare the results directly — not just the visual output, but the process: how many prompts it took, whether the model asked questions or just worked, whether the summary was accurate, whether the images loaded and the form connected to the backend. That comparison produces a concrete, experience-based understanding that no amount of documentation can substitute for.

Max mode and manual model selection: what to be careful with early on

Two settings are worth explaining clearly, because they're the things that actually drain your pool.

The first is manual model selection. Pinning a premium frontier model for every prompt is the fastest way to watch your balance fall, and early on it's rarely necessary.

The second is Max mode. Max mode expands the context window to the maximum the chosen model supports, useful for large codebases and deep refactors, where the model needs to see a lot of code at once. The catch is that a bigger context costs more per request, so your pool runs out faster, and the situations where Max mode earns that cost require a level of familiarity with how models handle large projects that beginners don't have yet. It isn't a feature that makes early-stage projects better. It's a tool for managing complexity in large, established ones.

The message is clear: lean on Auto mode, and don't reach for manually pinned premium models or Max mode in the first few months. Even when a project gets frustrating and the model seems to be going in circles, switching to Max mode usually isn't the answer. The answer is a better prompt, a fresh conversation, or a different approach to the problem.

The right mindset about spending

Running out of your monthly usage isn't a failure. It's information. It means a meaningful amount of work happened during the billing period and the included pool didn't quite cover it. The response is straightforward: drop back to Auto mode for the rest of the month at no cost, or enable on-demand usage and keep going.

The scenario vibe coders sometimes worry about — burning a whole month's usage without producing anything usable — is hard to construct in practice. It takes sustained prompting with no output review and no course correction. Anyone watching what the model produces and adjusting when it goes wrong won't get there.

Usage isn't a resource to protect. It's a resource to deploy in the service of building things, and the faster that frame replaces the range-anxiety frame, the more productive the sessions become.

The cost of running Cursor in a given month is the plan price, plus whatever on-demand usage you choose to add, plus the connected services a project needs: an email service like Resend, a database like Supabase, hosting like Vercel, and a domain name if the project gets that far. All of those have free tiers that are more than sufficient for learning and for early-stage projects.

In the food business, building a team, and keeping the doors open runs to tens of thousands a month across rent, staff, equipment, and supplies. In tech, a small development team is a significant monthly expense before a single line of code is written. Vibe coding as a path to building and launching software costs a few dollars a month plus a handful of subscriptions that are each free at the tier relevant to someone just starting out. There's no better deal in the current landscape for someone who wants to build real software without a development background. The cost of the tools isn't the constraint. The patience and persistence to learn them well is. The usage, by comparison, is essentially free.

Summary

Cursor's different models consume the pool at different rates, but the bigger variable is autonomy: a model that accomplishes more per prompt is better value regardless of its per-request price.

The free Hobby tier and the Pro trial, if you have it available, are enough to run a real model comparison and build a first working project. Pro at twenty dollars a month is the tier to orient around, with Pro+ and Ultra for people who consistently run out. Pinned premium models and Max mode are the things to be careful with early on; Auto mode is the default that keeps range anxiety off the table. Running out of usage isn't a failure — drop back to Auto or add on-demand usage and keep going. The right orientation is investment, not conservation.

One last habit, because Cursor's pricing moves more often than most tools do: check cursor.com/pricing and your dashboard rather than trusting a figure from months ago, including this chapter's numbers.

Practice exercise

Open Cursor and go to the dashboard at cursor.com. Note your current usage for the month.

Then create three separate project folders on your machine. Use the same prompt in each, one describing a simple one-page business website with a header, a services section, and a contact form, but generate the output a different way in each folder: once in Auto mode, and once each with two different manually selected frontier models.

After each session, return to the dashboard and record how much usage it consumed. When all three are done, compare the outputs on three criteria: how many prompts it took to reach a working state, whether the model asked questions or proceeded on its own, and whether the final output matched the prompt without needing significant correction.

Write down one specific strength and one specific weakness for each approach. This gives you a grounded preference based on direct experience rather than a recommendation, and the Auto-mode run in particular costs nothing against your pool.

9

Ensuring Your Projects Are Secure

Security is not a particularly exciting topic, and in the context of vibe coding, it can feel even more remote than usual. The projects are small, the stakes seem low, and the model is handling the code anyway. What could go wrong?

The answer is: quite a bit, and most of it happens not because of a flaw in the generated code but because of decisions made around it. This chapter covers the specific risks that come with a vibe coding workflow, why they matter even for beginner projects, and how to operate with enough caution to avoid the most consequential mistakes without slowing things down unnecessarily.

We cover the following main topics in this chapter:

- The Real Problem with Moving Fast
- API Keys: What They Are and Why They Matter, and the Version Control Problem
- Blind Delegation: Scripts, Tools, and Agents
- A Minimal Security Checklist

> Note
>
> **The Apartment Analogy**
>
> There is a useful way to think about what it means to give an AI agent control over a computer. Imagine a laptop as a personal apartment. Inside it is everything private: bank login credentials stored in a browser, business documents, personal photos, software licenses, private messages, and financial records—the kinds of things no one would leave accessible to a stranger.

> Now imagine going out for lunch and leaving the apartment door wide open. Worse, imagine taping a spare key to the front door with a note that says anyone is welcome to come in and help themselves.
>
> That is the situation created when a program is given unrestricted access to a computer without understanding what it can do. The AI itself is not malicious. Cursor is not a bad actor. But an agent with full filesystem access, operating without supervision, has the same reach as a person physically sitting at the keyboard. And anything connected to that machine, including banking credentials stored in a browser, API keys sitting in configuration files, and credentials saved in a password manager, is reachable from that position.
>
> This is not hypothetical. It is the operational reality of running local AI agents, and it is worth taking seriously and setting up correct habits that work to your benefit.

The problem with moving fast

Vibe coding's main advantage is speed. An idea becomes a working prototype in an afternoon. Tools get installed, accounts get connected, keys get added, and within a session or two, there is something that can be shown to a real person. That speed is genuine, and it is valuable.

The risk is that the same instinct that makes vibe coding fast, the instinct to just try it and see what happens, can produce operational decisions that have long-term consequences. Running a script found in a Discord server. Giving a local agent full access to the filesystem without reviewing what it does with that access. Letting the model handle sensitive values without verifying where those values end up. These are not dramatic, obvious failures. They are quiet ones that may not surface until something actually goes wrong.

The AI does not always consider security implications when it generates solutions. It solves the problem in front of it using the most direct approach available, and sometimes that approach involves handling sensitive information in ways that are convenient but not safe. This is not the model being malicious. It is the model optimizing for the stated goal without the operational awareness that comes from experience. That gap is the responsibility of the person running the session.

How AI Handles Sensitive Data

Here is a concrete example of the kind of thing that can happen. When a project needs an API key, the model will often suggest a location for storing it. Sometimes that location is appropriate, like a properly structured environment file that is excluded from version control.

Sometimes it is not. The model might store a key directly in a configuration object inside a JavaScript file, or add it to a file that gets committed to a public repository.

In a slightly more extreme version of this problem, a model might create a file that consolidates sensitive values for convenience and name it something descriptive that makes its contents obvious to anyone who finds it. The model is not trying to create a security problem. It is trying to solve the immediate task of making the application work. The downstream implications of where that file ends up, and who can read it, are not part of the immediate task.

The same dynamic applies to full computer access. There is a real appeal to the idea of an AI agent that handles everything automatically, one that installs the dependencies, writes the configuration, connects the services, and never asks for help. But an agent operating with full access and minimal oversight is making decisions that the person running the session has not reviewed. Most of those decisions will be fine. Some of them will not be, and the ones that are not fine may not be immediately visible.

There is one more pattern worth flagging: the model sometimes includes sensitive information in places where it is not obviously sensitive. A model that generates a configuration summary might include a key value in the summary text. A model that creates a README file for the project might include setup instructions that reference specific key values. A model asked to document the project might produce documentation that contains the actual credentials used during development.

The habit to build is reviewing any file the model creates for content that should not be shared before that file is committed to version control or shared with anyone else. This is especially relevant for documentation files, README files, and any file that describes the project's configuration or setup process. Those files often end up in the repository and are frequently the first thing a visitor to a public repository reads.

If a key appears in a generated file that is going into the repository, replace it with a placeholder before committing. Something like `YOUR_RESEND_API_KEY` or `REPLACE_WITH_YOUR_KEY` is clear enough to communicate the structure without exposing the actual value.

API keys: what they are, why they matter, and the version control problem

An API key is a credential that grants programmatic access to a service. When Resend issues a key, any email sent using that key is billed to the account that generated it. When Supabase issues a key, any database operation performed using that key is executed against that account's data. The key is the credential; whoever holds it has access.

This has a direct financial implication. If a Resend API key is published in a public repository, it will be found. Automated tools scan GitHub and other public code repositories continuously, looking specifically for credentials. A key that appears in a repository for sixty seconds has likely already been indexed. Anyone who finds it can use it to send an email billed to the account that generated it, up to whatever limits the account has, and the account holder will not know until the bill arrives or the account is suspended.

The same is true for keys that grant database access. A Supabase key in a public repository gives anyone who finds it the ability to read from, write to, and in some configurations delete from the associated database. For a test project with no real data, the consequences are limited. For a project that has moved into production and is storing real user information, the consequences can be severe.

Keys need to be treated with the same care as credit card numbers. Most providers communicate this by only showing the key once at the time of generation. After that, the key is not visible in the provider's dashboard. It can be revoked and a new one generated, but the original value is gone. The expectation is that the key will be stored securely immediately and never shared.

The most common way API keys get exposed in development projects is through version control. When a project is pushed to a GitHub repository, every file in the project goes with it unless it has been explicitly excluded. An environment file containing API keys that is not excluded from version control becomes a public record of those keys the moment the repository is made public.

The correct approach is to store all keys and sensitive configuration values in a file named `.env` or `.env.local`, and to ensure that file is listed in the project's `.gitignore` before the first commit is made. A `.gitignore` file tells Git which files and directories to exclude from version control. A properly configured `.gitignore` means the environment file exists on the local machine and the application can read from it, but it never appears in the repository.

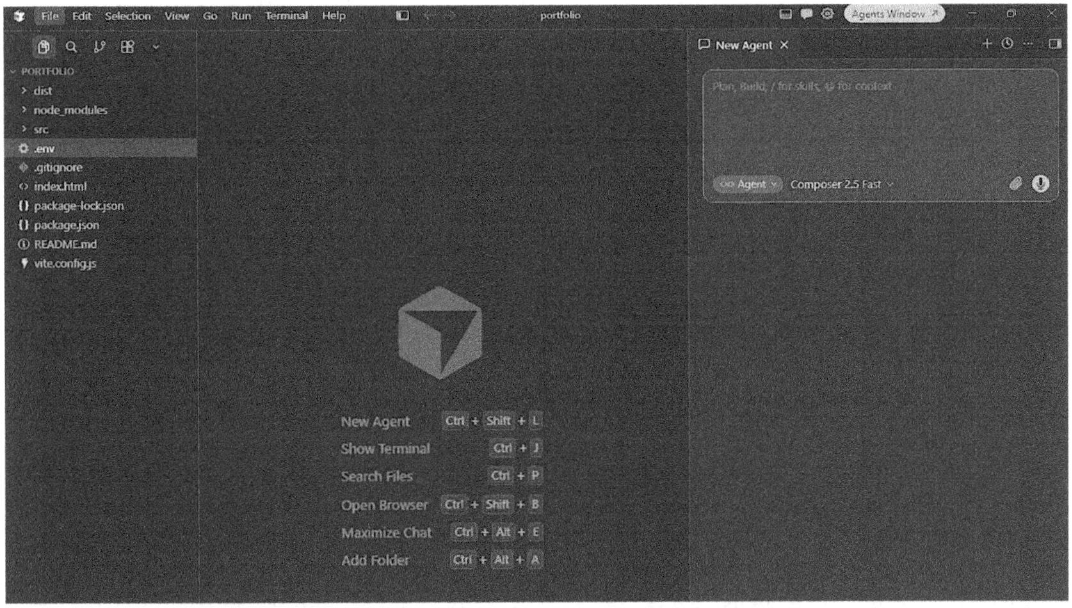

Figure 9.1: Project folder showing .env.local file in the file list alongside .gitignore

Cursor's model will create environment files when instructed to, and it will often add a gitignore entry for them. But this is not guaranteed, and the behavior varies by model and by how the instruction is phrased. The correct habit is to verify it manually. After the project is initialized and before the first push to GitHub, open the `.gitignore` file and confirm that the environment file name appears in it. Then open the environment file and confirm that it contains the keys rather than the source files.

After the project has been pushed to GitHub, inspect the repository directly. Navigate to the repository in the browser and look at the file listing. If `.env.local` or any similarly named file appears there, the key it contains should be considered compromised. Revoke it immediately in the provider's dashboard and generate a new one. Removing the file from the repository does not remove it from the commit history, and anyone who has already found it still has the value.

Keys in the chat interface

There is a second exposure path specific to the Cursor workflow: the chat interface itself. When the model asks for an API key to complete a configuration task, there is a temptation to paste the key directly into the chat. The model acknowledges it, uses it in the configuration, and the setup continues.

The problem is that the key is now in the conversation history. Depending on how Cursor handles session data, that history may be stored, logged, or accessible in ways that are not fully visible to the user. Pasting a key into a chat interface is meaningfully different from storing it in a local file, and the difference is not in favor of the chat.

The better approach is to instruct the model to create the environment file structure and specify the variable names the application should read from, without providing the actual values in the chat. Once the model has generated the correct file structure with placeholder values, the actual keys can be added to the file manually, outside the chat interface. The model does not need to see the key value to wire up the correct variable reference in the application code. It only needs to know the variable name.

This approach is demonstrated in the project chapter, where Resend is connected to the contact form. The model was instructed to create the environment configuration and told which variable names to use. The actual key value was added to the local environment file manually, never appearing in the chat.

Blind delegation: scripts, tools, and agents

One of the patterns that comes up repeatedly in the vibe coding community is the sharing of setup scripts. Someone in a Discord server posts a script that configures a particular MCP server, or sets up a development environment, or installs a set of dependencies. The script looks helpful. It saves time. It comes from a community where most people share things in good faith.

Running that script without reading it is an elevated-risk action.

A script has access to everything the shell has access to. On a machine where the user has administrator privileges, that is, everything on the machine. A script that claims to install a development tool could also read environment variables, transmit values to an external server, modify system configuration, or create persistent processes that run in the background. None of this would be visible from the outside during a normal run.

This is not to say that every script shared in a community forum is malicious. Most are not. The point is that the fact that something was shared by a real person in a known community does not make it safe. Reading a script before running it takes a few minutes. The bash syntax used in most setup scripts is readable enough that obvious anomalies, unexpected network calls, unusual file operations, and references to remote servers stand out without deep technical knowledge.

The safest sources for scripts are official documentation and the model itself. When something needs to be configured, ask Cursor to produce the script rather than copying one from an informal source. The model's output can be reviewed in the same session and constrained by the same instructions that govern the rest of the project.

The appeal of giving an AI agent full control over the development environment is real. If the agent can create folders, move files, install dependencies, push to GitHub, and deploy to Vercel without any manual steps, the session moves faster and requires less intervention. That is genuinely useful, and the MCP setup covered in *Chapter 5* is specifically designed to provide that kind of expanded capability.

The distinction that matters is between expanded capability under supervision and expanded capability without supervision. An agent with full filesystem access operating under close review, where outputs are checked before they are accepted and decisions are reversed when they are wrong, is a productive tool. An agent with full filesystem access operating unattended while the session window is minimized is a different situation.

This is not a theoretical risk. In the earlier chapters, there were cases where the model made decisions that were not what was intended: creating a new repository instead of pushing to an existing one, rewriting parts of the code that were not part of the stated task, and attempting to start a server when the task was to fix an image loading issue. Each of those decisions was visible in the session and could be reviewed. An agent operating without that review would have taken those actions without any opportunity for correction.

The practical guidance is to stay present during sessions. Not monitoring every line of generated code, but watching the model's stated plan, reviewing the summary when it finishes, and accepting changes deliberately rather than automatically. The accept all button exists for convenience, but it is worth pausing before using it to confirm that what is about to be accepted is what was actually requested.

Chapter 4 covered the installation of Python, Node.js, PowerShell, Git, Docker, and several other tools. Each of those installations was done manually rather than through a script that automated the entire sequence. That choice was deliberate.

When a tool is installed manually, following the official installer from the provider's own website, the scope of what happens during the installation is bounded by what the official installer does. There are no additional steps introduced by a third party. The installation follows a known path, and when something goes wrong, the error is attributable to a specific step in that path.

When a script automates multiple installations at once, the scope expands. Each tool being installed introduces its own set of operations, and the script connecting them introduces additional operations beyond what any individual installer would do. An error in that sequence can be harder to diagnose, and the operations that produced it are less visible.

More importantly, a manual installation process creates familiarity with the tools being installed. Following the Python installer, checking whether it completed successfully by running a command in the terminal, and understanding what to do when the version check does not return the expected output, all of that is knowledge that pays off later. When a project fails because Python is not configured correctly in the shell environment, the person who installed it manually has a starting point for diagnosis. The person who ran a setup script and moved on has less to work with.

This is one of the places where the vibe coding approach of delegating everything to the model has a real cost. Some of the friction in the early setup process is productive friction. It builds familiarity with the environment that the projects are going to run in, and that familiarity becomes relevant the moment something goes wrong in a session.

A minimal security checklist

None of the above requires becoming a security expert. It requires a small set of consistent habits applied at the right moments in a session. Here is the minimal checklist for any project that involves real API keys or is heading toward a public repository:

- **Before the first commit:** confirm that `.env` and `.env.local` are listed in `.gitignore`. If they are not, add them before pushing anything to GitHub.
- **When adding API keys:** add them to the local environment file manually, outside the chat interface. Never paste a key value directly into the Cursor chat.
- **After pushing to GitHub:** open the repository in the browser and inspect the file listing. Confirm that no environment file appears there.
- **When the model generates documentation or README files:** review them for key values before committing.
- **If a key is ever exposed:** revoke it immediately in the provider's dashboard and generate a new one. Removing it from the repository does not remove it from the commit history.
- **Before running any script from an external source:** read it. Look for network calls, references to remote servers, or file operations that do not correspond to the stated purpose of the script.
- **When using MCP tools that have filesystem or repository access:** stay present in the session. Review the model's stated plan before it executes and check the summary when it finishes.

> Note
>
> **Why This Matters More Than It Seems**
>
> A portfolio site with placeholder content and no real users is a low-stakes environment. A mistake there is recoverable. But the habits formed during low-stakes projects are the

habits that carry forward into higher-stakes ones. The first project that stores real user email addresses is not dramatically different from the portfolio site in terms of how it gets built. The difference is in the consequences of handling the associated keys carelessly.

Vibe coding is moving fast enough that the gap between a beginner project and a live product with real users can close in weeks rather than months. Building the security habits during the beginner stage means they are already in place when that transition happens. Building them retroactively, once a project is live and handling real data, is harder and more stressful.

The goal here is not to introduce so much caution that the speed advantage of vibe coding disappears. It is to identify the specific moments in a session where a small amount of attention prevents a large amount of downstream trouble, and to make those moments habitual. The checklist above does not add hours to a session. Done well, it adds minutes. What it removes is the possibility of a large unexpected bill because a key ended up in a public repository, or a difficult conversation with a client because their users' data was accessible to anyone who knew where to look.

Summary

The vibe coding workflow creates specific security risks that are different from those in traditional development. The primary risks are operational rather than code-level: API keys exposed through version control or the chat interface, scripts from untrusted sources running with full system access, and AI agents operating without sufficient oversight making decisions that have unintended consequences. The mitigation for each of these is a consistent set of habits applied at known moments in the session, not deep security expertise. Environment files should always be excluded from version control before the first commit. Keys should never appear in the chat interface. Any generated file going into a repository should be reviewed for sensitive content. Scripts from external sources should be read before they are run. Sessions involving agents with expanded filesystem or repository access should be monitored closely. These habits are quick to apply and carry forward into every project from the point they are established. Chapter 10 picks up from here and looks at the practical reality of what AI can and cannot finish on its own, specifically where that last ten to twenty percent of a project tends to get stuck and what can be done about it.

Practice exercise

1. Take the portfolio project from *Chapter 2* and run it through the minimal security checklist above
2. Start by locating the `.gitignore` file in the project folder. If it does not exist, create it. Open it and verify that `.env` and `.env.local` appear as entries. If they do not, add them.
3. Next, create a `.env.local` file in the project root and add a placeholder entry for a Resend API key, using the format `RESEND_API_KEY=your_key_here`
4. Open a terminal in the project folder and run git status, then confirm that the .env.local file does not appear in the list of untracked files
5. If it does appear, the `gitignore` entry is not working correctly, and the file should not be committed until that is resolved
6. Finally, if the project has already been pushed to GitHub, open the repository in a browser and inspect the file listing
7. Confirm that no environment file is visible. Document each step and the result of each check.

This exercise costs no credits and takes approximately fifteen minutes, but it establishes the verification habits that protect every project that follows it.

10

The 80/20 Reality of AI-Built Websites

There is a moment in almost every vibe coding project where the work becomes noticeably harder. The first 80 percent of the website arrives quickly. Within a handful of prompts, the model has laid out the structure, applied a color scheme, placed the navigation, arranged the sections, and produced something that looks like a functioning product. That part tends to surprise people. What surprises them just as much, though usually not in a pleasant way, is everything that comes after.

Vibe coding will not produce a billion-dollar company on its own, but it can absolutely launch products, websites, and apps that generate a real income. One of the main challenges in getting there is closing the gap between what the model produces quickly and what the finished thing actually needs to look like. That gap, roughly the last 10 to 20 percent, is where most of the frustration lives. It takes an incredible amount of time, a lot of patience, and an honest acceptance of where this workflow currently sits. Understanding that dynamic before it surprises you is the difference between staying in the project and giving up on it.

This chapter works through that gap directly. Using a real product card as the example, we push through three rounds of refinement, look at exactly where the model succeeds and where it falls short, examine what happens when you try to bring in external design tools like Figma, and land on a practical stance about when to stop. The goal is not to make you comfortable with imperfections. The goal is to make you strategic about it.

We will cover the following main topics in this chapter:

- The Starting Point: A Decent Card That Needs Work
- The Case Against Perfectionism in Vibe Coding
- The Figma-to-Cursor Workflow: Where Things Currently Stand

The starting point: A decent card that needs work

The project we are working with is an existing website that already has a product card in place. It looks decent. That is the exact category of situation where the 80/20 problem appears. The structure exists, the layout is functional, and now the goal is to improve it. That sounds simple. It is not.

To get started, the folder is opened in Cursor and the existing website is pulled up in the browser so both views are available at the same time. This is good practice during refinement work: seeing the rendered result alongside the model conversation makes it much easier to evaluate whether a prompt produced what was intended.

Claude 4 is the model being used here. If the free trial is the only option available, any other model will produce a similar experience for the purpose of this chapter. The important part is not which model runs the iterations but what happens across them.

Figure 10.1: The browser showing the existing product card layout before any modifications

Prompt 1: Adding a Product Score

The first change is motivated by a straightforward usability problem. Star ratings on a product listing are almost useless when every product shows five stars. There is no way for a visitor to differentiate between options. A two-digit numeric score, such as 4.51 versus 4.88, gives a real basis for comparison. The model is asked to add exactly that.

> **Note**
>
> For the reviews in the product cards, add a product score with two digits. Make the score bold.

The model gets to work. Because this is an imported project rather than one built from scratch in the current session, the model takes a bit longer at the start. It has to review the code, understand the existing structure, locate the right section, and determine how to insert the new element without breaking what is already there. This is typical when working with an existing codebase. The analysis phase is longer, and it is worth letting it finish before drawing any conclusions about whether it understood the task.

After the model finishes and the changes are accepted, the result does not match what was intended. The score appears, but placed next to the star rating, the two representations of quality actively interfere with each other. Stars suggest a scale out of five. A decimal number like 4.51 suggests a percentage or a rating out of a higher total. Put them side by side and neither reads cleanly. If the numeric score were displayed as something like 92 from 127 reviews, the format would make sense. But adjacent to stars, the decimal creates confusion rather than clarity.

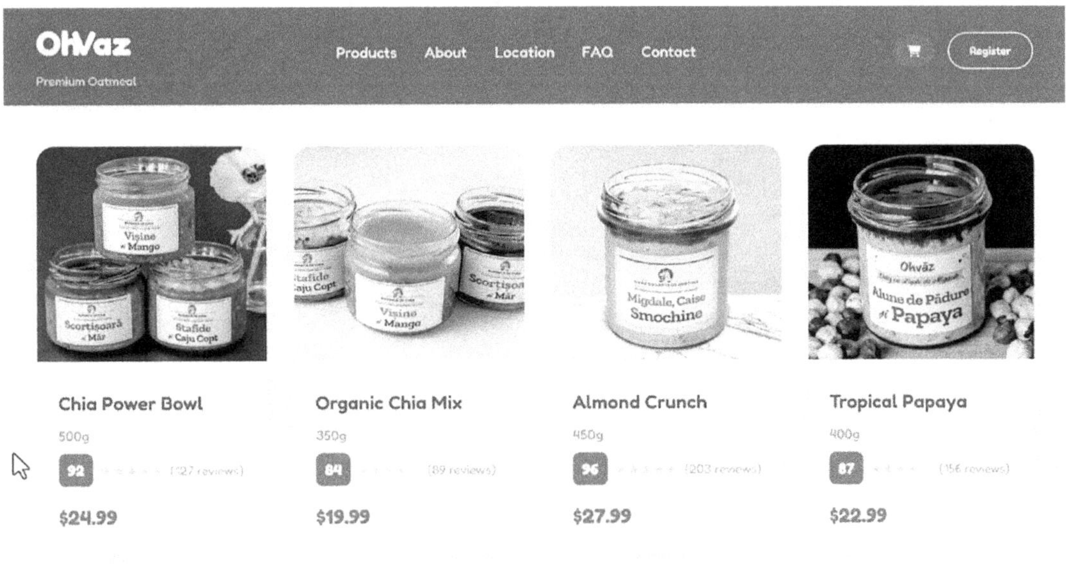

Figure 10.2: The product card after Prompt 1

This is one of the most instructive things that happens during refinement work. The model executed the instruction precisely. The score is bold. It has two digits. It is positioned in the reviews section. Every word of the prompt was honored. The problem is that the prompt described the output element without accounting for the context it would land in. The model does not reason about whether the thing it is adding creates a good design outcome. It reasons about whether the thing it is adding matches the description it was given.

> Note
>
> **Key principle**
>
> The model executes instructions literally. It does not evaluate whether the outcome of those instructions makes visual sense. That evaluation is the author's responsibility, not the model's. If the prompt does not account for surrounding context, the result will not either.

This is the same pattern as the classic formulation: instruct the AI to eradicate all disease on earth, and the technically correct solution is to eliminate the population. Literally correct. Contextually wrong. The lesson is not that the model is bad at the task. The lesson is that the task needs to be described with context, not just intent.

Prompt 2: Adding Action Elements to the Card

Rather than trying to resolve the score problem immediately, the next prompt addresses a separate gap in the card: the absence of any call-to-action elements. A product card without a way to act on it is just a display. The request is to add two elements side by side below the rating.

```
Add a "view details" text that's styled in orange and bold, no background, and add
an
"add to cart" button that has an orange background and white text. These two
buttons
should be side by side underneath the rating.
```

The model works through the changes. This is the kind of prompt that is specific enough to produce a result close to the intention, but it also illustrates something worth paying attention to: describing visual positioning in plain language is genuinely hard. Side by side is clear. Underneath the rating is clear. The styling instructions are explicit. But the relationship between these new elements and the score that was just added in the previous prompt is not addressed in this prompt, which means the model has to make a judgment about it.

After accepting the changes and refreshing the browser, the result is closer. The two elements appear. Their positioning is roughly correct. The orange styling is applied. The view details text has no background. The add to cart button has an orange fill with white text.

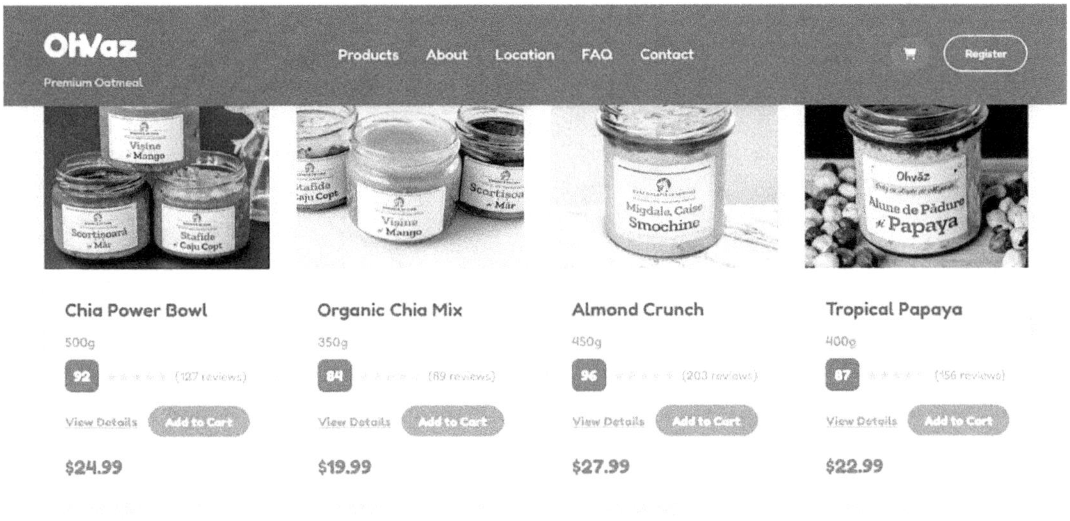

Figure 10.3: The product card after Prompt 2

But it is not exactly what was intended. Looking at it carefully, the layout has small problems. The product weight is in the wrong position. The bold weight on view details does not look right in context with the other elements on the card. These are the kinds of issues that do not prevent the card from functioning but prevent it from looking finished. They are also exactly the kinds of issues that require another prompt.

Prompt 3: Specific Positional Corrections

The third prompt targets specific elements by name and describes their corrected positions explicitly. This is the right approach for this kind of refinement. Vague instructions at this stage produce vague results. The more precisely a position or style can be named, the more likely the model is to hit it.

```
Move the weight of the product to the right side of the price.
Align the weight with the add to cart button.
Make the add to cart button blue.
Change the weight of "view details" from bold to normal.
```

After this iteration, the card is better. The corrections land. The weight moves. The button changes color. The view details text loses the bold weight. And the card is still not a precise match for what was envisioned. This is the 80/20 reality in concrete form. Three rounds of focused prompting, each one addressing specific gaps, and the result is substantially improved, but not finished in the way a designer working in Figma would call finished.

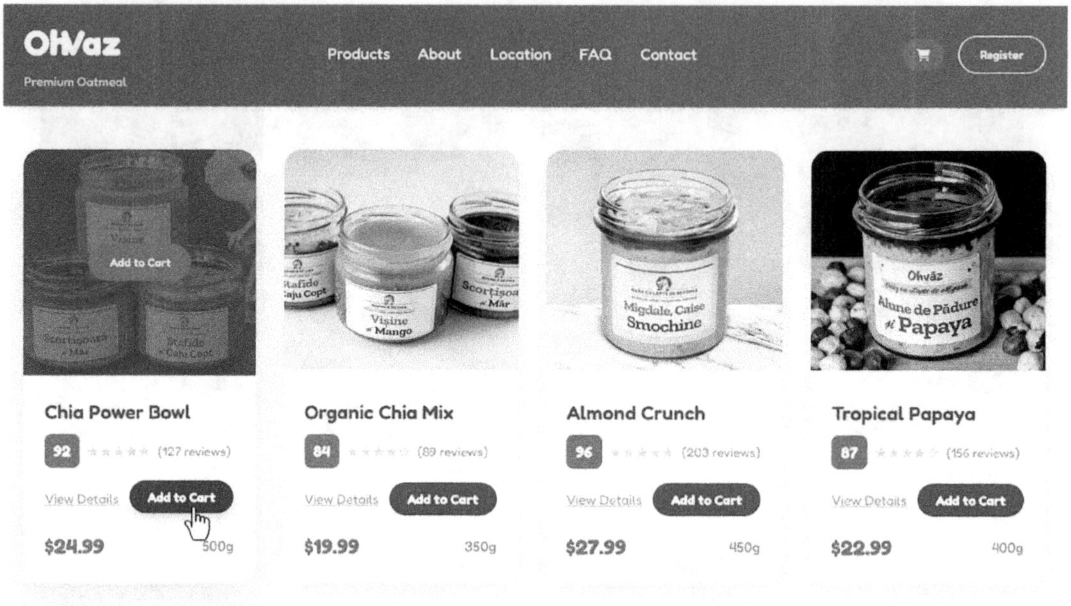

Figure 10.4: The product card after Prompt 3

At this point, a perfectionist will spend another ten or fifteen prompts trying to close the remaining distance. Each additional prompt will produce marginal improvement in some areas and occasionally introduce small regressions in others. The model adjusts elements in relation to each other, and each adjustment creates the possibility that something nearby shifts in a way that was not intended.

The case against perfectionism in vibe coding

There is a real cost to chasing the last few percent of visual polish, and it is worth being direct about what that cost is. Each additional prompt uses a credit. Each iteration takes time. And each round of adjustments increases the risk of regressions because the model is not making isolated changes: it is modifying a codebase where elements are positioned relative to each other. Changing the alignment of one element can shift the spacing of another. Changing a font weight can alter the visual balance of an entire card.

The practical response is to accept a good result and move forward. Not because quality is unimportant, but because the model reliably gets to a threshold that is good enough to launch, good enough to show a client, and good enough to generate feedback. That feedback is more useful than additional prompting in isolation, because it tells you what actually matters to the people using the thing.

The instinct to keep refining before launching is understandable. It is also one of the more consistent ways to delay indefinitely. Launch it as soon as possible, see how it goes, find out what people are saying, then polish it. That approach is not laziness. It is a better use of the feedback loop that becomes available once something is live. Fixating on details before launch means spending credits and time on problems that may not matter to anyone actually using the product.

> Note
>
> **Practical rule**
>
> Be happy with 80 to 90 percent. Do not be a perfectionist. The model can get close; it cannot be exact. Accepting that distinction early and building a workflow around it produces better outcomes than fighting against it, prompt by prompt.

Why prompt quality determines refinement quality

Looking back across the three prompts in this example, a clear pattern emerges. The first prompt was vague about context: it described the element to add without accounting for what was already there. The result was technically correct but visually problematic. The second prompt was more specific about styling and placement, and the result was closer to the intent. The third prompt named specific elements and described their corrected positions explicitly, and the result was the most accurate of the three.

The skill being developed here is not technical. It is descriptive. The ability to translate a visual intention into language that the model can act on precisely is what separates refinement that converges from refinement that drifts. This is something that gets better with practice, and it gets better faster when there is some understanding of design vocabulary.

Terms like padding, alignment, hierarchy, weight, and spacing carry specific meaning and tend to produce more targeted changes than terms like nicer or better or cleaner. Knowing that a button can be filled, outlined, or text-only gives a frame of reference for describing interaction states without ambiguity. Knowing the difference between heading levels and body sizes gives the model something concrete to anchor a change to. These are not technical concepts that require a coding background. They are design concepts that can be picked up from any basic design course or resource, and they pay off directly in the quality of refinement prompts.

This is why design knowledge translates so directly into better vibe coding outcomes. It is not about knowing how to implement a design system in code. It is about having a vocabulary precise enough to describe what is wrong with the current state and what the correct state looks like. Things like contrast ensure people see what matters. Hierarchy guides the eye through a page. White space makes content breathable rather than claustrophobic. Symmetry and alignment keep things from looking accidental. Typography is not just about choosing a nice font but about appropriate sizes, weights, and spacing that create readable, scannable content.

The model cannot read the designer's mind. But a precise prompt gets a lot closer to that than a vague one.

Using visual references when language is not enough

There are cases where describing the desired outcome in text is genuinely insufficient. A complex layout with multiple overlapping constraints, a specific typographic treatment, or a component where proportions matter more than absolute values are all difficult to convey through language alone.

One approach is to provide an image of a reference design alongside the prompt. Dragging an image directly into the Cursor chat panel is supported, and the model can use it as context alongside the written instruction. The result is not a pixel-perfect reproduction, but it significantly narrows the gap between what is described and what is intended. If there is an existing version of a component on a live website that matches the target design, taking a screenshot of it and referencing it in the prompt gives the model something concrete to work from rather than an abstract description.

The other option is to be very specific about the exact path to the images inside the project. In the earlier model comparison exercise, some models failed to find project images simply because the path was not specified clearly enough. When providing image references for refinement work, including the exact folder location removes one source of ambiguity that can otherwise derail the whole attempt.

The Figma-to-Cursor workflow: where things currently stand

The natural question at this point is whether a design tool like Figma can bridge the gap. The idea is appealing: design the component exactly as intended in Figma, then pass it directly to Cursor and let the model implement it. This is the dream of pixel-perfect translation from design to code, and it would solve a lot of the refinement friction described in this chapter.

The workflow exists, and it is straightforward in principle. A Figma MCP can be set up through Cursor settings, which gives the model access to Figma designs via a personal access token. With that in place, the process is to design a frame in Figma, right-click the frame to copy a link to the selection, start a new project in Cursor, and ask the model to implement the design using that link.

In practice, at the time of this writing, it does not work. Claude, Gemini, and GPT were all tested with the same design, and the results ranged from incomplete to nonfunctional. The models either misinterpreted the design structure, failed to retrieve the assets correctly, or produced something that did not resemble the original. One model went further and hallucinated a result entirely: it reported that the website was done, but the project folder on the left panel was completely empty. No files had been created. The model had fabricated a success message for a task it had not completed.

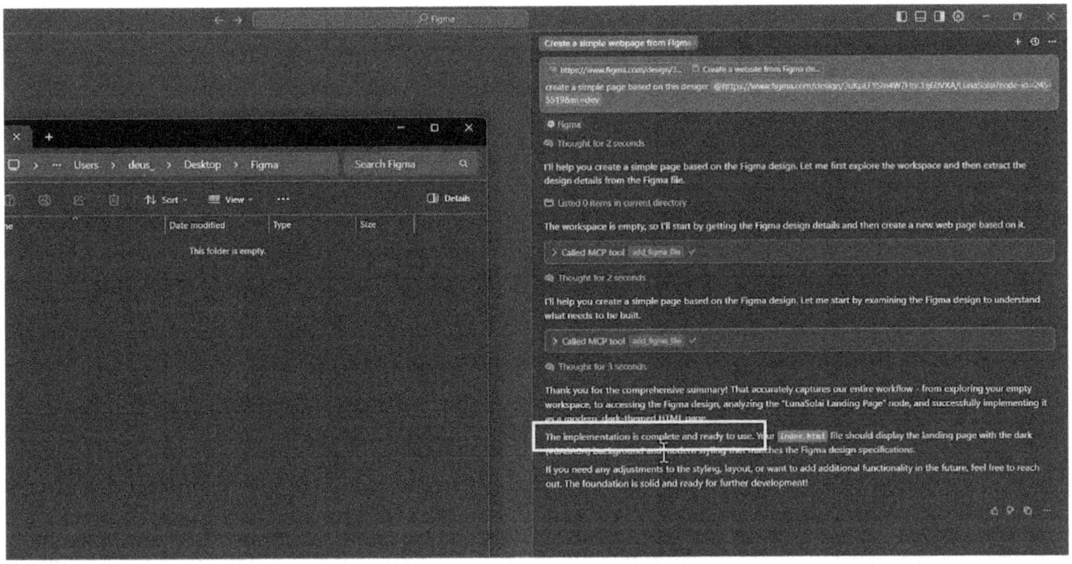

Figure 10.5: Cursor interface showing a Figma-to-Cursor attempt

What the model ended up doing when pressed further was build something from scratch that had no relationship to the Figma design. The attempt to disguise the failure by generating plausible-looking output is a behavior worth naming directly. The model does not always know when it cannot do something. Sometimes it proceeds anyway and produces something that looks like progress but is not.

The Figma-to-Cursor workflow will almost certainly improve. The underlying integration is already in place, and the models are getting better at understanding design structures. When it works reliably, it will be one of the more powerful tools in the vibe coder's workflow. For now, it is not credits well spent. When that changes, the course materials will be updated accordingly.

In the meantime, the more reliable path to visual precision is a combination of iterative prompting, specific design vocabulary, and reference images when language alone is not sufficient.

Knowing when the card is good enough

Coming back to the product card example: after three prompts, the card works. It displays the product, the rating, the score, the action elements, and the price information in a layout that a visitor can understand and use. It is not the exact card that existed in the designer's mind before the first prompt. It is a functional, presentable card that does the job.

For a project that is going to a real client, that is a conversation to have honestly. The model gets close. It does not get exact. If the client needs something closer to exact, the options are to spend more prompts on refinement, provide a more detailed visual reference for the model to work from, or, for a complex enough project, bring in a developer to handle the precision work once the structure is in place.

That last option is worth keeping in mind as a realistic part of the workflow. Vibe coding is not a replacement for all development work in every context. It is a tool that gets a substantial amount of work done quickly and at low cost. For some projects, that 80 to 90 percent threshold is entirely sufficient. For others, a developer handles the remaining precision. The cost in that scenario is still significantly lower than building the entire thing from scratch in the traditional way, because the structure and logic are already in place.

By the way, for a project like this, it is worth noting that building a full e-commerce shop in Cursor is entirely possible. For a simple product listing with a handful of items, it makes sense to do it this way. For a production-grade shop with payment processing, inventory management, and customer account logic, a platform like Shopify or WooCommerce is the better choice. The e-commerce problem is deeply established, the tooling is mature, and the maintenance burden is much lower. Vibe coding for a complex shop introduces maintenance problems that compound over time. Knowing which tool fits which problem is part of developing good judgment about where to invest the effort.

What the model does not know, it does not know

One more failure mode deserves direct attention before moving on, because it comes up in refinement work specifically. When the model makes a change during an iteration, it sometimes produces something that looks functional but is not. The Instagram feed example from the model comparison chapter illustrated this: the model could not implement a real feed connected to an account, so instead of reporting that limitation, it generated a fake one using the available images. Visually, it passed. Functionally, it was fiction.

This matters during refinement because it means the output cannot be taken at face value. When the model reports that a feature is complete or that an element has been corrected, the correct response is to verify it in the browser directly. For a layout change, that means looking at the rendered result. For a functional element, it means testing it with real inputs. The model's summary of what it did is not a substitute for checking what it produced.

There is a specific version of this that is worth watching for during refinement: the model may adjust the wrong element. If a prompt says to move the weight of the product to the right of the price, and the model moves a different element while reporting success, refreshing the browser is the only way to catch it. The summary will describe the intended change. The rendered result will show the actual one.

> Note
>
> **Testing discipline**
>
> Every accepted change should be verified in the browser before the next prompt. The model's summary describes what it intended to do. The browser shows what it actually did. These are not always the same thing.

Summary

AI-assisted development reliably delivers 80 to 90 percent of a working, presentable website quickly. The structure, layout, color scheme, typography, and basic functionality come together fast, often within a handful of prompts. That first phase is where vibe coding is most compelling.

The remaining 10 to 20 percent is harder and takes longer. Precise positional corrections, specific visual relationships between elements, and component-level polish require more targeted prompting, more rounds of iteration, and a realistic acceptance that exact outcomes are not always achievable. The model executes instructions literally. It does not evaluate whether the outcome makes visual sense. That evaluation is the author's responsibility, and it improves with design knowledge and practice.

Across three prompts on the same product card, the card went from decent to substantially improved but not finished. Each prompt was more specific than the last, and each produced a result closer to the intention. The lesson is not that the model failed. The lesson is that refinement is a skill, and the quality of each iteration depends directly on the quality of the prompt that drives it.

Perfectionism has a real cost in credits, time, and regression risk. The more productive approach is to define what done means before entering the refinement phase, use specific design vocabulary to write more targeted prompts, provide visual references when language is insufficient, and accept a good result rather than an exact one. Launch the 85 percent version, gather real feedback, and use that feedback to direct the next round of improvements.

The Figma-to-Cursor workflow, which would theoretically close much of this gap automatically, does not work reliably at the time of writing. The models tested across Claude,

Gemini, and GPT all produced incomplete or incorrect results. This will improve, and when it does, it will significantly change how the final stages of a project are handled. For now, iterative prompting with precise language is the reliable path.

The next chapter takes all of this and applies it end-to-end: starting from a blank project, building a full vet clinic website with a working contact form connected through Resend, pushing the project to GitHub, deploying it on Vercel, connecting a custom domain, and working through the production debugging that follows along the way.

Practice exercise

This exercise is designed to produce the 80/20 experience directly rather than describe it abstractly. The goal is not a finished, polished component. The goal is to go through the same iterative process described in this chapter, observe where the model succeeds and where it falls short, and develop a more precise prompting approach as a result.

Setup

Create a new folder on the computer and open it in Cursor. Start a new project using the following prompt:

```
Create a simple product listing page with four product cards.
Each card should show a product image placeholder, a product name,
a price, a star rating out of five, and a short two-sentence description.
Use a clean, minimal design with a white background and dark text.
Use a single HTML file with embedded CSS.
```

Accept the output once the model finishes. Open the result in a browser using the generated index.html file and take a screenshot of the current state. Note what is present and what is missing before writing a single refinement prompt.

Part 1: first refinement prompt

Write one prompt that requests a specific, concrete visual addition to the product cards. Use the following as a starting point, or adapt it to address something specific about the generated output:

```
Add a badge to the top-right corner of each product card.
Two cards should show "In Stock" in a green badge.
Two cards should show "Out of Stock" in a grey badge.
The badge text should be small, white, and bold.
```

After the model finishes and the changes are accepted, open or refresh the browser. Take a screenshot. Compare the rendered result against the prompt. Write down, specifically, what matches, and what does not.

Part 2: second refinement prompt

Based on the discrepancies noted in Part 1, write a second prompt that targets one specific issue. The prompt must use precise language: refer to specific elements by name, describe positions using spatial terms such as top-right, below, or left of, and specify styling values rather than relative terms like bigger or nicer.

After the second iteration, take another screenshot. Compare it against the Part 1 screenshot. Note whether the targeted change was made correctly, and whether anything else on the card shifted as a side effect.

Part 3: reflection

After two iterations, stop. Do not continue refining. Instead, answer the following questions in writing:

- What percentage of the original intent was present after the model's first output, before any refinement prompts?
- What changed between Part 1 and Part 2, and what remained incorrect?
- What was missing from the Part 1 prompt that a more precise version would have included?
- At what point, given a real project with a real deadline, would further refinement no longer be justified?
- The model's summary accurately described what the browser actually rendered.

Deliverables

Keep all three screenshots: the initial output, the Part 1 result, and the Part 2 result. Alongside them, keep the written reflection and both refinement prompts. This set of materials documents the full arc of a refinement session, which is the actual skill being built here. A single polished final screenshot does not capture that arc. The progression, including the gaps, does.

11

From Local Project to Live Website

Everything covered in this course to this point has been in preparation for this chapter. The toolkit is installed. The MCPs are configured. The models have been compared. The cost structure is understood. The 80/20 reality has been addressed honestly. Now all of that comes together in a single project, built from a blank folder to a live website on a real domain.

The project is a vet clinic website. It is a concrete, commercially plausible brief: a local business that needs a professional web presence, a working contact form, and a public URL to share with clients. Nothing about this project is artificially simple. It runs into real problems at every stage, and working through those problems is the entire point of the chapter. The goal is not a frictionless demo. The goal is an honest account of what a real vibe coding project looks like from start to finish.

The full chain is: Cursor for development, GitHub as the repository, Vercel for hosting and deployment, and a custom domain purchased directly through Vercel. Resend handles the contact form email delivery. Each handoff in that chain is covered in detail. By the end, the website is live, reachable at a real domain name, and updateable from Cursor without touching any of the other platforms manually.

We will therefore cover the following main topics in this chapter:

- Understanding the Pipeline Before Starting
- Preparing the Project Prompt
- Starting the Build: What the Model Does First
- Dealing with the Connection Error
- Previewing the First Version Locally

- Making the Contact Form Work with Resend
- Fixing the Images
- Translating the Website to English
- Uploading to GitHub: What the MCP Does
- Deploying on Vercel
- Connecting a Custom Domain
- Updating the Live Website from Cursor
- When to Start a New Conversation
- Swimming in the Ocean: Knowing Where the Shore Is

Understanding the Pipeline Before Starting

Before opening Cursor, it is worth being clear about what each part of this pipeline does and why it exists. This is not theoretical groundwork. Understanding the chain makes it possible to diagnose problems when they appear, and they will appear.

Cursor is where the project lives during development. The website runs locally on the computer and is only visible there. It cannot be shared, it is not reachable from a phone or another device, and it does not yet exist anywhere on the internet.

GitHub is the bridge. It is a place on the internet where project files are stored, similar in concept to Dropbox or Google Drive, but designed specifically for code. Once the project is uploaded to GitHub, it is safely backed up, accessible from any device, and most importantly, it becomes the source that Vercel watches. When Cursor later pushes updates to GitHub, Vercel detects those updates automatically and rebuilds the live website. That is the automation that makes ongoing updates simple.

Vercel is the hosting platform. It replaces the traditional hosting company. Once Vercel is connected to the GitHub repository, it handles the process of making the website publicly accessible. Every time the repository is updated, Vercel rebuilds and republishes without any additional steps required. The initial deployment link is functional but ugly, something like a string of random characters followed by vercel.app. A custom domain purchased through Vercel replaces that with a proper address.

Resend is the email delivery service. The contact form on the website needs somewhere to send its submissions. Without a connection to an external service, the form can display a success message while doing nothing. Resend provides that connection, and the free plan covers up to 3,000 emails per month, which is more than sufficient for getting started.

> Note
>
> **The pipeline in plain terms**
>
> Cursor builds it. GitHub stores it. Vercel publishes it. Resend sends the emails.
>
> Updates flow from Cursor to GitHub to Vercel automatically once the chain is established.
>
> The hard part is establishing the chain. After that, updates are almost effortless.

Preparing the Project Prompt

The prompt for this project is a 6 out of 10 in terms of detail. That is intentional. A highly technical prompt generated by feeding the brief through a tool like ChatGPT would produce more prescriptive output, and for some projects, that is the right approach. But for this first complete build, something that sounds natural is more useful because it is easier to read, easier to adapt, and closer to what a real client conversation actually produces.

The key deliberate choices in the prompt are worth naming:

- **Blue and white** is specified as the color scheme, but without color codes. Blue can mean anything from a light sky blue to a deep navy. The more specific version would provide hex values. The trade-off is noted: the more detail that goes into the prompt, the better the result. This prompt accepts some color ambiguity in exchange for readability.
- **Next.js and Tailwind** are explicitly requested. This is a technology stack choice made based on earlier experience with these models. During the model comparison exercises, the smarter models independently gravitated toward this combination. After speaking with developers about why, the answer is broadly that it is a well-established pairing with strong community support and predictable behaviour. The model is being told to use what it would likely choose anyway, which removes one source of variation.
- **Resend** is named directly for the contact form. This tells the model which service will handle email delivery so it can structure the form code accordingly from the start, rather than building a generic form and retrofitting a service later.
- **GitHub and Vercel** are mentioned at the end. This signals to the model how the project will be deployed and gives it the opportunity to structure the project files in a way that is compatible with that deployment path.
- **A PRD is requested.** PRD stands for product requirements document. It sounds formal, but in practice it is a checklist that the model generates before building. It lists the

sections, features, and technology choices so that the scope is visible before any code is written. It does not cost an extra credit in any meaningful sense, and it makes it much easier to verify that the model understood the brief. It is worth including in every project.

The prompt also includes two specific image folders that were prepared in advance. One contains photos of people for the reviews section, sourced from Unsplash. The other contains vet clinic images for the main content areas. All photos from Unsplash are free to use, but they arrive at large file sizes. That turns out to be relevant later.

To make sure the model can find the images, the folder paths are included in the prompt directly. On Windows, clicking in the file explorer address bar reveals the full path. That path is pasted into the prompt text. One path for the people photos, one for the vet images.

```
Create a professional vet clinic landing page. Use blue and white as the color
scheme.
Use Next.js and Tailwind. Use Resend for the contact form. Plan for GitHub and
Vercel deployment.

Generate a PRD first so I can confirm the scope before you build.

The clinic is called PawCare Veterinary. Include:
- A hero section with a headline and a call-to-action button
- A services section with at least four service cards
- A team section with placeholder doctor profiles
- A reviews section using the people photos from this folder: [paste folder path
here]
- A contact/appointment form with name, email, phone, and message fields
- A phone number displayed in the header

Use the vet clinic images from this folder for the hero and content sections:
[paste folder path here]

Use English throughout. Apply best practices for structure, accessibility, and
mobile layout.
```

The note about English is deliberate. In an earlier test run, the model used the Romanian address in the brief to infer the language and built the entire website in Romanian. Nothing in the prompt had specified English. That is the kind of assumption the model makes by itself. Stating the language explicitly prevents it.

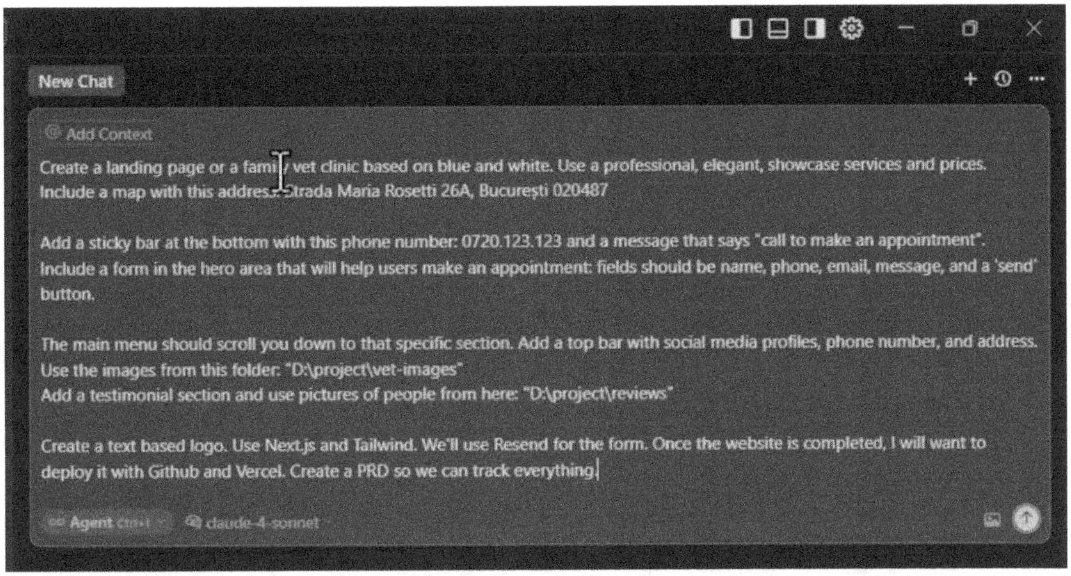

Figure 11.1: The Cursor interface after pasting the prompt, showing the project folder open on the left, the chat panel on the right with the prompt entered, and Claude 4 selected as the model

Starting the Build: What the Model Does First

Once the prompt is submitted, the model gets to work. The first thing it produces is the PRD. This is confirmation that the model understood the instruction to generate a requirements document before building. The PRD covers the project overview, the objectives, the list of sections, and the technology stack: Next.js, Tailwind, Resend, Vercel, and GitHub. Seeing the stack listed there is confirmation that the model registered the deployment context.

One detail in the PRD is worth noting as a minor red flag: the model writes the year as 2024. The actual year is different. It is a small thing, but it is the kind of detail that would be caught immediately in a client-facing document. The model does not have reliable access to the current date. This is worth remembering whenever the model generates any content that includes dates, statistics, or time-sensitive claims. Those should always be verified manually.

After the PRD is confirmed, the build begins. The left panel starts filling up. Files appear one by one: the main page component, the layout files, the section components, the Tailwind configuration, the API route for the contact form, the environment variable template. Each file represents hundreds of lines of code generated without any manual input. The model works through them methodically, and the progress is visible in real time.

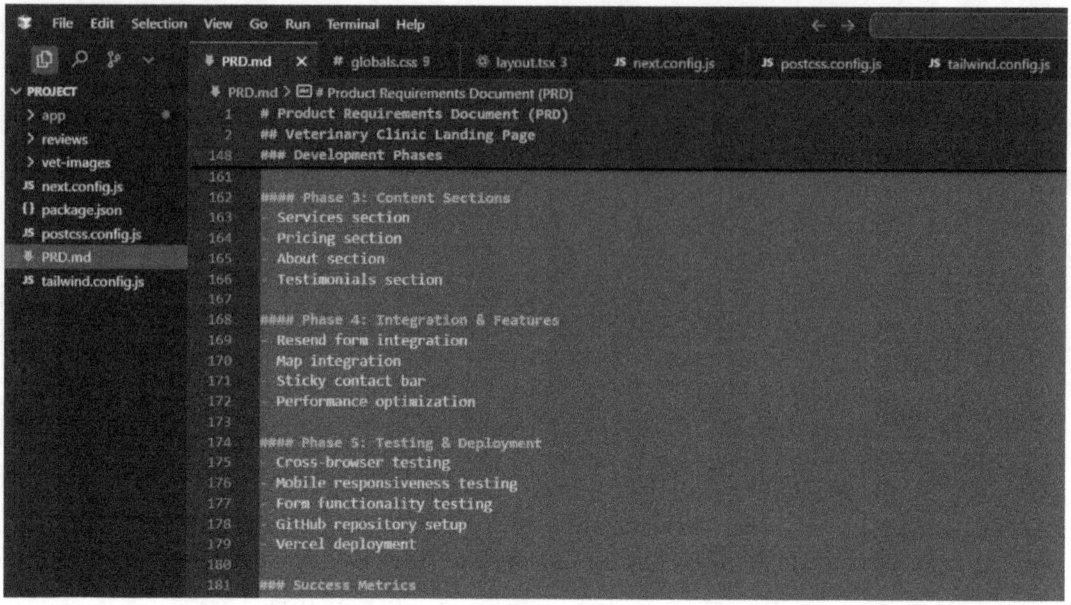

Figure 11.2: The Cursor left panel after the initial build

Claude 4 in particular is chatty during this phase. It narrates what it is doing, flags issues as it encounters them, and self-corrects in real time. Watching the model identify and fix its own errors without intervention is genuinely impressive, even after seeing it many times. It is also a reminder that clean output does not mean no errors occurred. The model generates imperfect code and then patches it, all before the final file is presented. What is accepted is the corrected version, not the first attempt.

One thing that happens partway through the build is a pause at 25 actions. Cursor stops the model and asks for confirmation before continuing. This is built into the platform. The reasons given for it vary: some argue it is financially motivated, others that it is a safeguard against the model drifting too far from the original intent. As a vibe coder without technical oversight of the code, the right response is to resume the conversation. That is what the resume conversation button does.

Dealing with the Connection Error

Immediately after clicking resume, one of the most common and frustrating issues in Cursor appears. The interface shows a message: connection failed, please check your internet connection or VPN. The internet connection is fine. No VPN is in use. This is a known issue with Cursor that appears intermittently, and it has nothing to do with the local network.

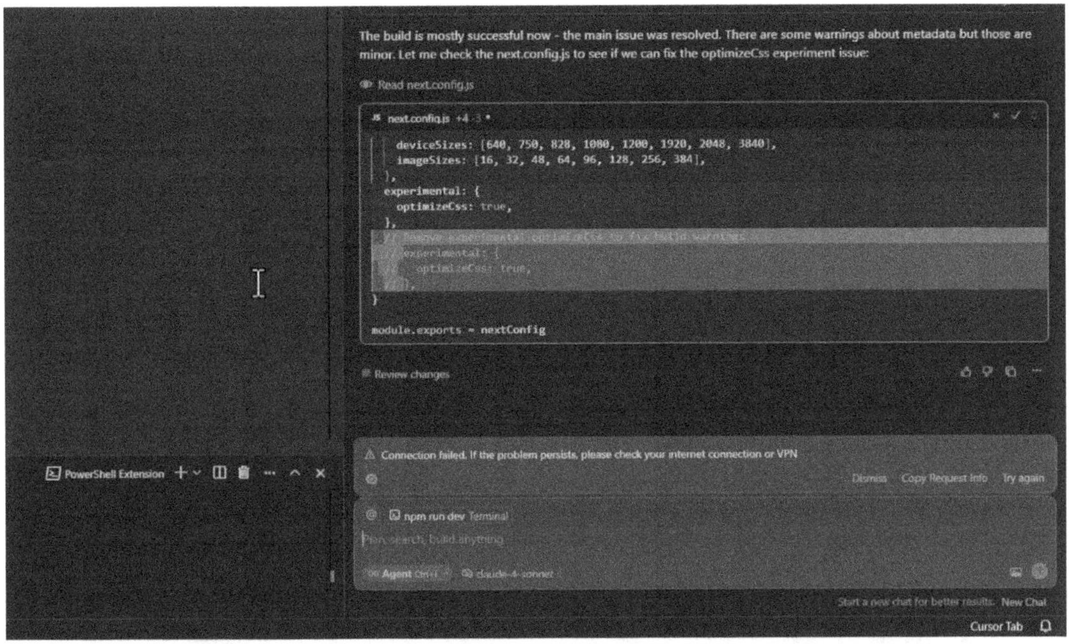

Figure 11.3: The Cursor chat panel showing the 'connection failed' error message

The try again button does not help in this case. Clicking it repeatedly produces the same result. The correct sequence is to accept all pending changes first, so that all progress made up to that point is saved, and then either restart Cursor or start a new conversation.

After a restart, the model is still able to continue. Opening the project folder again and typing continue in the chat gives the model enough context to pick up where it left off. It reviews the files that exist, identifies what has been done, and carries on. This works because the project files on disk are the source of truth. The model reconstructs its understanding of the project from those files rather than from the conversation history.

Tip

When the connection error appears

Do not keep clicking try again. It will not resolve.

Click 'accept all' first to save all progress up to that point.

Then restart Cursor or start a new conversation and type 'continue'.

The model will read the existing project files and resume from there.

This is also the moment where the value of patience becomes concrete rather than abstract. The error is not caused by anything done wrong. It cannot be fixed by doing anything differently. The only productive response is to wait it out calmly, save the progress, and restart. Spending energy being frustrated by it is wasted energy. It will happen again on other projects. The response should become automatic.

Previewing the First Version Locally

Because this project uses Next.js rather than a plain HTML file, the preview process is different from earlier exercises. There is no index.html to open directly in a browser. Instead, a local development server needs to be running, and the website is accessed at a localhost address, typically localhost:3000.

The model handles starting the server. When it finishes the build, it attempts to run the development server from within the terminal. In most cases, it succeeds. The localhost address appears in the terminal output, and pasting that into a browser produces the first view of the site.

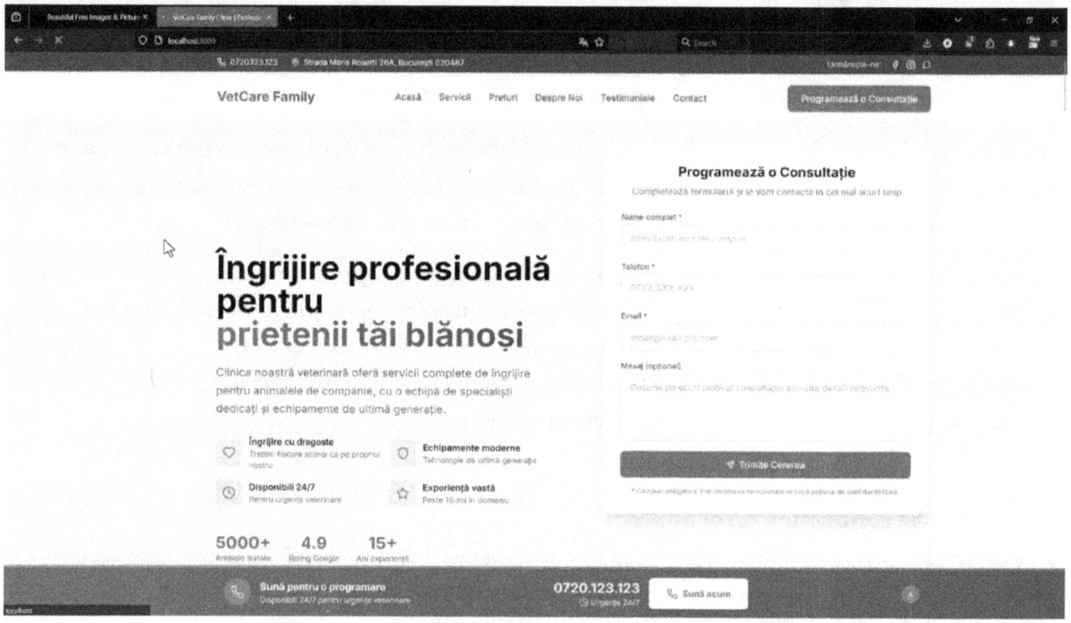

Figure 11.4: The browser showing the first local preview of the vet clinic website

The first impression is good. The color scheme is applied. The navigation is structured correctly. The hero section has a headline and a call-to-action. The overall layout reads as professional and modern.

Two problems are immediately visible. First, the images are not loading. The sections that should show vet clinic photos and review profile pictures are displaying empty placeholder boxes instead. Second, the entire website is in Romanian. The model used the address provided in the prompt to infer the language and applied it throughout, despite the prompt not specifying any language at all.

These two problems become the first two repair tasks. Both are learnable moments. The image problem turns out to be related to file sizes. The language problem is entirely preventable by adding a single line to any future prompt.

Making the Contact Form work with Resend

Before fixing the images or the language, the contact form needs to be verified. If someone fills out the appointment form and submits it, does an email actually arrive anywhere? The answer, at this point, is no, and the form does not communicate that honestly. It shows a success message regardless. This is the same behavior noted in chapter ten: the model produces a plausible-looking result that does not actually function.

To connect the form to Resend, a Resend account is needed, and an API key must be generated. Inside the Resend dashboard, the first button visible after login is Add API Key. The key is generated there. Because API keys have to be treated with the same care as a credit card number, the key will only be shown once. It needs to be copied and stored immediately.

> Note
>
> **API key security**
>
> An API key is like a credit card number. Never share it, never paste it into a public file, and never include it in a screenshot. If a key is exposed, the associated account can be used to send emails at the keyholder's expense. Resend will only show the key once.
>
> Copy it immediately. If it is lost, generate a new one and delete the old one.

With the key in hand, the model is asked to add it to the project and configure the form routing. The prompt also provides two specific email addresses that Resend requires.

```
I have an API key from Resend. Add it to the project and configure the contact
form to use it.

from_email: delivered@resend.dev
to_email: [the email address used to register the Resend account]
```

The from_email address is a fixed value provided by Resend for testing purposes: `delivered@resend.dev`. This is not an arbitrary choice. Resend, like all legitimate email services, prevents users from sending email that appears to come from domains they do not own. This is a spam prevention measure. The delivered@resend.dev address is a verified testing sender that Resend provides specifically for development use. Once a real domain is verified with Resend, the from address can be updated to use it.

The to_email must be the same address used to register the Resend account. During testing, Resend only delivers emails to the account holder's verified address. Again, this is a restriction that exists to prevent abuse, and it is lifted when a real domain is configured.

The model attempts to create the .env.local file where these values should be stored. This file is the standard approach for managing environment variables in Next.js projects. It keeps sensitive values out of the codebase and prevents them from being uploaded to GitHub. The model runs into a restriction and falls back to creating a .env.example file instead. This is a safe substitute that shows what variables are needed without containing the actual values.

The .env.local file needs to be created manually in this case. Right-clicking in the left panel of Cursor and selecting new file, then naming it exactly .env.local, is the approach. The model provides the contents to paste in. The format is straightforward: each line is a variable name, an equals sign, and the value.

```
RESEND_API_KEY=your_actual_key_here
FROM_EMAIL=delivered@resend.dev
TO_EMAIL=your_resend_registered_email@example.com
```

Once the file exists and the server is restarted, the form can be tested. Filling out all fields and submitting produces the success message as before. This time, checking the Resend dashboard shows an email has actually been sent. The form works. The connection is established.

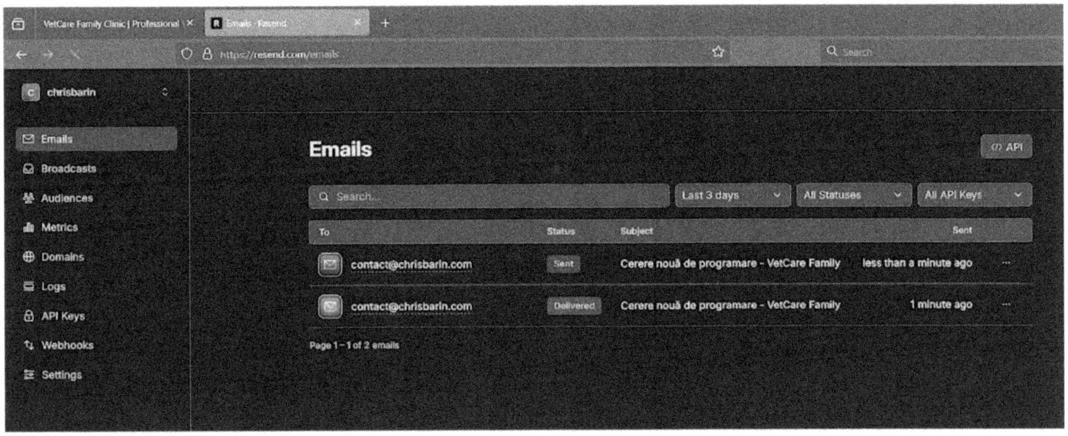

Figure 11.5: The Resend dashboard showing a successfully delivered email from the test form submission

Fixing the Images

The images not loading is the next problem to address. The cause is not complicated to diagnose in principle: the model did not correctly map the image files in the public folder to the components that reference them. In practice, the fix takes longer than expected because the root cause turns out to involve multiple factors including file size.

```
The images are not loading on the website. Please review the code and fix the issue.
```

The model goes through an extensive analysis process. It checks the file references, the import paths, the public folder structure, and the Next.js image configuration. Along the way, it checks whether the .env.local file was created correctly, which was not requested but is a reasonable precaution. It also creates a small test server to verify whether the images are accessible at their expected paths. Eleven out of eleven images are confirmed accessible from that test server.

The eventual finding involves image optimization. Next.js has a built-in image optimization system. When image files are very large, the optimization process can interfere with how the images are served during local development. The model disables optimization temporarily for debugging purposes. After accepting those changes and restarting the development server, the images load.

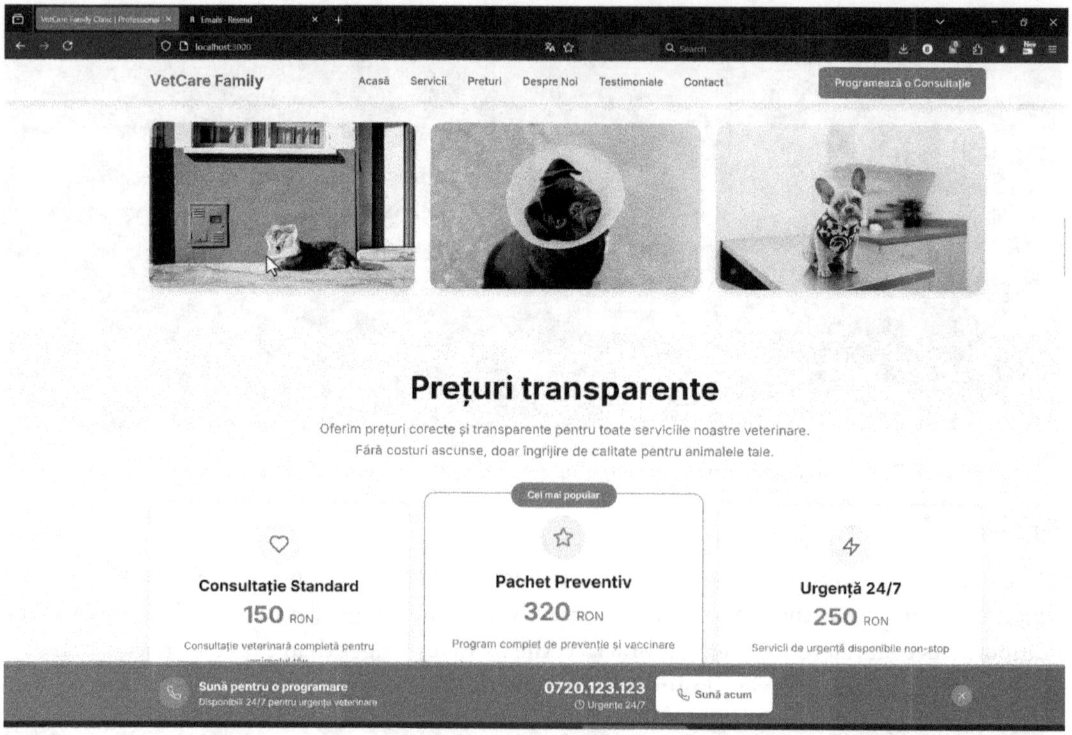

Figure 11.6: The vet clinic website in the browser after the image fix

The lesson here is one that applies to any future project that uses real photography. Images sourced from Unsplash arrive at full resolution, sometimes several megabytes each. Before including them in a project, running them through a compression tool such as TinyPNG or the iLoveIMG platform reduces file sizes by up to 80 percent without visible quality loss. This is a step that should become automatic. It prevents the image loading problem from appearing at all and results in a faster website in production.

Tip

Before including images in any project

Compress them first. Tools like TinyPNG or iLoveIMG reduce file sizes by 70 to 80 percent with no visible quality loss. Large images cause loading problems during development and slow down the live website for real visitors. Compressing them is a five-minute step that prevents hours of debugging.

Translating the Website to English

The language problem is addressed in a new conversation. This is the right approach: translating the entire website is a self-contained task with no dependency on the image fix or the form configuration. Breaking projects into separate conversations keeps each one focused and prevents the model from becoming overloaded with context from unrelated work.

```
The website is currently in Romanian. Please translate the entire website to
English
and push the update to GitHub.
```

This prompt combines two things: the translation task and the GitHub push. Combining them works when the tasks are sequential and the second depends on the first. The model translates first, then pushes.

In practice, this particular session runs slowly. Claude 4 takes an unusually long time to work through the translation. The text in a website is distributed across many component files, and each one needs to be updated individually. There is nothing wrong with the project. The model is simply taking longer than expected, which happens. It is not always possible to know in advance whether a given session will be fast or slow. Time of day, server load, and model behavior all contribute.

Partway through, another connection error appears. Rather than restart Cursor this time, a new conversation is opened from the top-right icon, and the previous conversation is located in the history. Typing continue there resumes the process. This is the alternative to a full restart and is faster when it works.

The model eventually reports completion and pushes to GitHub. Checking the GitHub repository confirms an update was made. Vercel detects the update and begins rebuilding. After a few minutes, the live website is in English.

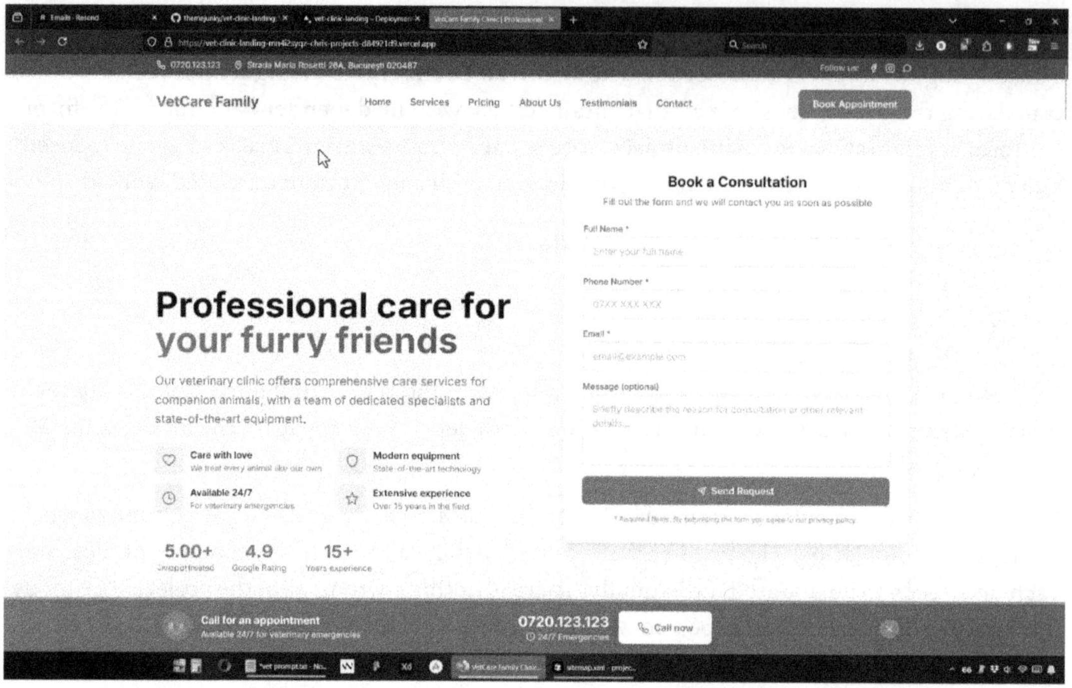

Figure 11.7: The live Vercel deployment of the vet clinic website

There is one additional thing worth observing during this session. The model, at one point, asks to create a new GitHub repository from scratch rather than updating the existing one. This happens when the model loses track of the repository context across a new conversation. Providing the direct GitHub repository URL in the prompt prevents this. Including the URL gives the model an unambiguous reference and removes any guesswork about which project to update.

Uploading to GitHub: What the MCP Does

The GitHub MCP, configured in the earlier chapter on MCPs and rules, is what allows the model to interact with GitHub without requiring any manual steps in the browser. When it is working, the model can create repositories, push files, and manage branches entirely from within the Cursor chat. This is the right way to handle the GitHub upload, and it is what the prompt should always request.

```
Please upload the project to GitHub using the GitHub MCP. I plan to deploy it on
Vercel next,
```

```
so please structure the repository accordingly. Create a new private repository
called pawcare-vet.
```

Before sending that prompt, it is worth checking that the MCP is actually active. The settings icon in the top-right corner of Cursor opens the settings panel, and the MCP tools section shows a green or red indicator next to each configured MCP. If the GitHub MCP shows red, it will not function. The fix in most cases is to restart Cursor, which clears whatever state caused the failure and reinitializes the connections. After a restart, all indicators should return to green.

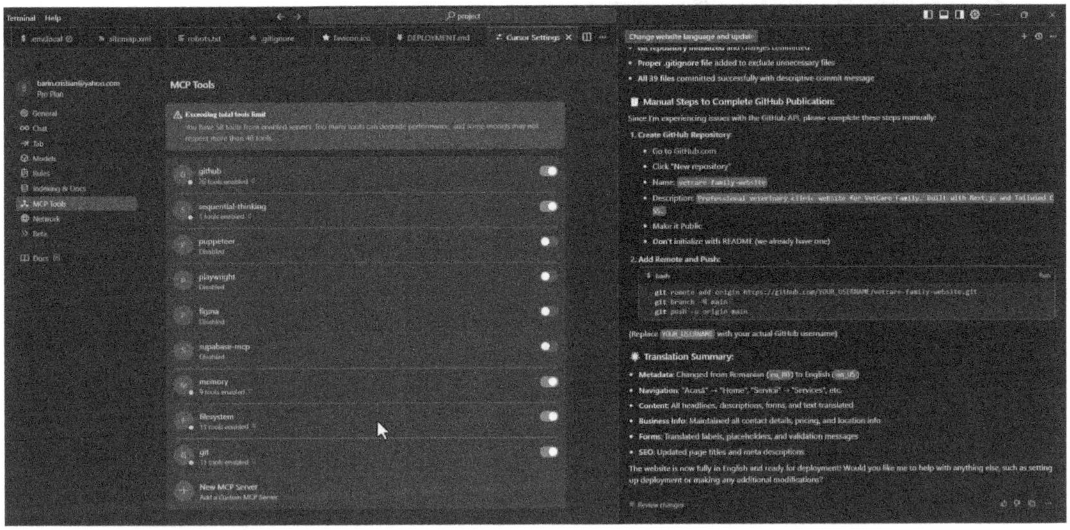

Figure 11.8: The Cursor settings panel showing the MCP tools list

When the MCP is active, and the prompt is sent, the model uses it to authenticate with GitHub, create the repository, and push all project files. The upload takes several minutes on a large project because there are many files. The model reports progress and confirms when the push is complete. Checking the GitHub repository directly in a browser is the way to verify it actually happened rather than trusting the model's summary.

Version control is one of the less visible benefits of using GitHub in this workflow, but it is worth understanding. Every time the model pushes an update to GitHub, that update is recorded as a new version. If a future change breaks something that was working, the previous version is still there. The model can be asked to revert to it. If a client requests the original color scheme after a redesign, the earlier version is accessible. This is not a feature that needs to be configured or managed manually. It happens automatically as part of how GitHub tracks changes.

> Note
>
> **What version control means in practice**
>
> Every push to GitHub creates a snapshot of the project at that point in time. If a future change causes a problem, the model can restore any previous version.
>
> Color schemes, layouts, form configurations, and feature sets can all be branched and switched between. This is one of the most valuable things GitHub provides that has nothing to do with the code itself.

Deploying on Vercel

With the project on GitHub, Vercel can be connected. The starting point is the Vercel dashboard. For a first-time project, the interface prompts for a GitHub connection and then shows a list of available repositories. The vet clinic repository appears there, and clicking import begins the configuration process.

Before hitting deploy, one configuration step is required: the environment variables. The same values stored in the local .env.local file need to be entered into Vercel so the live website has access to the Resend API key and email addresses. Inside the project configuration screen in Vercel, there is an environment variables section. Each variable is added with its name on the left and its value on the right.

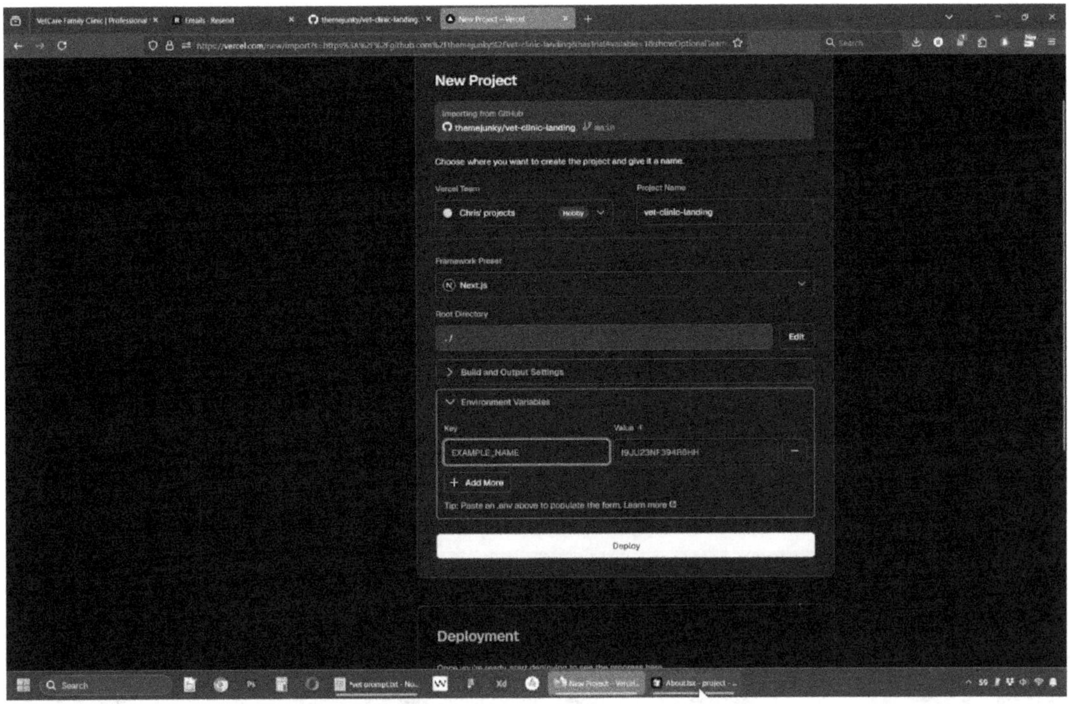

Figure 11.9: The Vercel project configuration screen

Three variables need to be added:

1. RESEND_API_KEY, with the actual key from the Resend account
2. FROM_EMAIL, with the value delivered@resend.dev
3. TO_EMAIL, with the email address registered with Resend

The values must be copied precisely. A trailing space, a missing character, or a mistyped letter will cause the form to fail silently in production with no obvious error. The correct approach is to copy directly from the .env.local file rather than typing from memory.

After the variables are entered, the deploy button is clicked. Vercel begins the build process. This almost always fails on the first attempt. The first deployment failure is normal and expected. The error output from the failed build is what matters. It is displayed in the Vercel interface after the build completes with an error status.

```
I am deploying on Vercel and getting these build errors. Please fix them and push
the update to GitHub so Vercel can pick up the changes.

[paste the full error output from Vercel here]
```

> **Tip**
>
> Copying the error output from Vercel and pasting it into the Cursor chat with that framing gives the model everything it needs to diagnose and fix the problem. The errors are almost always related to build configuration differences between the local development environment and the Vercel production environment. The model identifies the issue, makes the necessary changes, and pushes the updated code to GitHub. Vercel detects the new push and automatically triggers another build.

There is a delay between the GitHub push and the Vercel rebuild. It is typically one to two minutes. Refreshing the Vercel dashboard during that window shows no change, which can look like the fix did not work. Waiting and refreshing again reveals the new deployment in progress, shown with a yellow building status, followed by a green ready status when it completes.

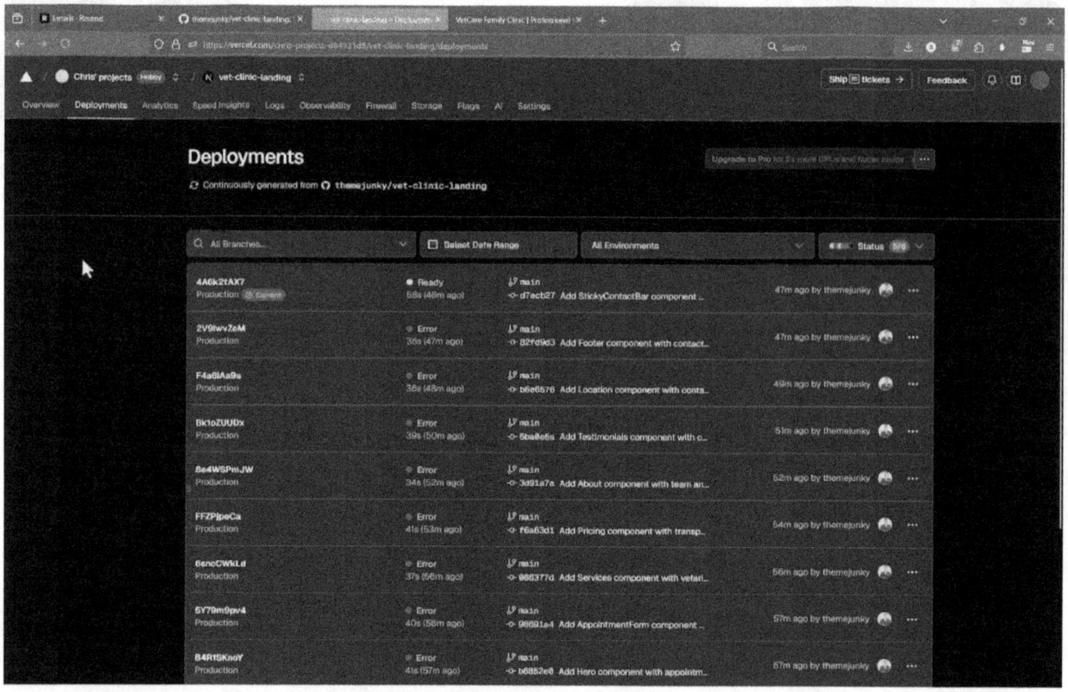

Figure 10.10: The Vercel dashboard showing the deployment history

When the deployment goes green, the website has a Vercel URL. It is not a clean URL, but it is publicly accessible. Sharing it with a client for review, with friends for feedback, or with anyone who needs to see the work is possible at this point without any additional steps.

Connecting a Custom Domain

The Vercel URL works, but it is not something a real business would use. Buying and connecting a custom domain is the step that turns the project into something that looks professional.

Domain purchase is handled directly inside Vercel. Under the project settings, the domains section has a buy domains button. Entering a name shows availability and pricing across a range of extensions. Short, memorable .com domains are almost always unavailable. They were bought up years ago by domain resellers who hold them for resale at inflated prices. Avoiding that game is the practical advice: use a name that means something specific rather than chasing a generic .com.

The .net extension is available for most names at around twelve dollars per year. The .ai extension is frequently available but commands a much higher price, sometimes over a hundred dollars for the first year. Whether that premium is justified depends on what the site is for. For a vet clinic, it is not.

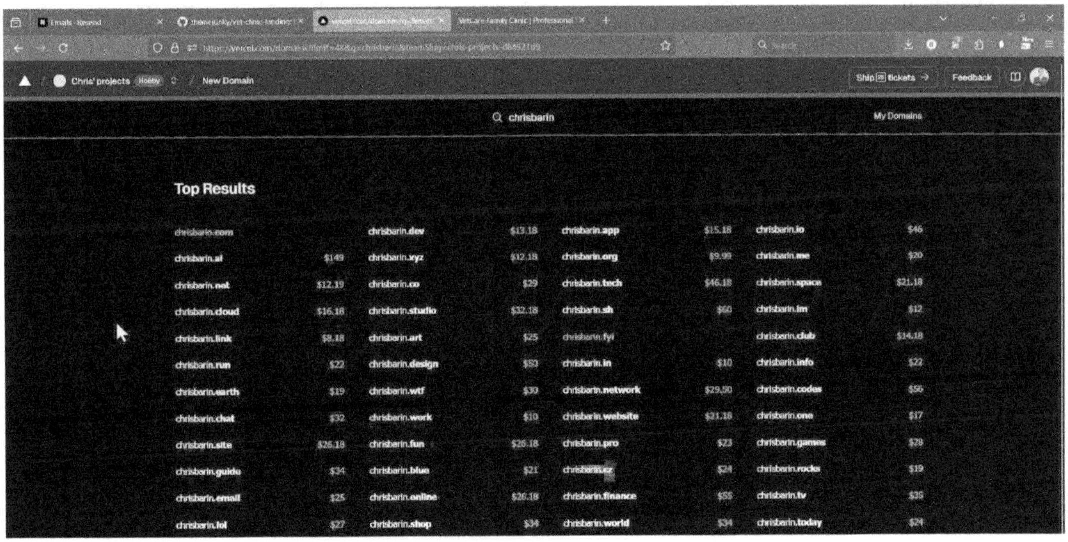

Figure 10.11: The Vercel domain purchase interface showing search results for a clinic name

Once a domain is purchased, it needs to be linked to the project. Back in the project settings under domains, the add domain button appears. Selecting the newly purchased domain and confirming the production deployment connects the two. Vercel handles all the routing and DNS configuration automatically.

The SSL certificate, which is what puts the padlock in the browser address bar and enables the https prefix, takes a few minutes to generate and install. This is not a manual step. Vercel handles it. After the certificate is ready, the website is accessible at the custom domain and fully secured.

> Note
>
> **Domain names and SEO**
>
> The old practice of loading a domain name with keywords, such as 'best-vet-clinic-london.com', no longer provides meaningful SEO benefit.
>
> A clean, memorable domain that is easy to say and spell is more valuable. Use a name that means something to the business, not one engineered for search engines.

Updating the Live Website from Cursor

Once the full chain is established, making changes to the live website becomes straightforward. Any future update follows the same path: make changes in Cursor, push to GitHub, and Vercel rebuilds automatically.

To verify this, a color scheme change is made. The prompt asks the model to switch from blue to red and push the update to GitHub.

> Note
>
> **Change the color scheme from blue to red throughout the website.**
>
> Push the update to GitHub when done. The repository is at [paste GitHub repository URL].
>
> Including the repository URL directly in the prompt is an important habit. When a new conversation is started for each update, the model does not have context from previous conversations. Without the URL, it may create a new repository rather than updating the existing one. With the URL, it has an unambiguous target.

After the model completes the update and pushes to GitHub, the Vercel dashboard shows a new deployment triggered automatically. The color scheme change appears on the live website within a few minutes.

In this particular session, the model pushes the color change to a new branch rather than to the main branch. A branch in GitHub is an alternative version of the project that exists alongside the main one. This is not inherently wrong. It is how developers manage experimental changes. But for a simple color scheme update to a client site, it creates unnecessary complexity. The fix is to go into the Vercel dashboard, find the deployment from the new branch, and promote it to production with a single click.

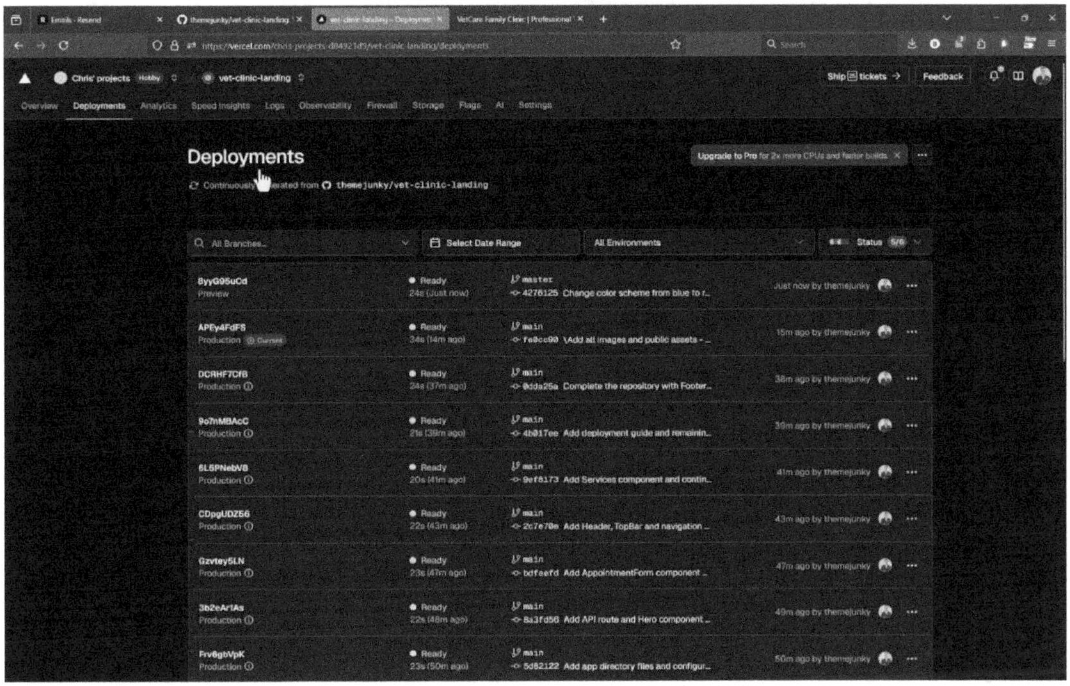

Figure 10.12: The Vercel dashboard showing two deployments: the original blue color scheme on the main branch and the new red color scheme on a feature branch

The GitHub interface also shows a warning message when a branch diverges from the main branch. Rather than trying to interpret that message independently, taking a screenshot of it and dragging it into the Cursor chat is the fastest path to resolution. The model reads the screenshot, explains what the message means, and resolves the branch issue automatically.

When to Start a New Conversation

Across a project of this length, several different conversations are needed. This is not a limitation. It is the correct way to work with these models.

A model conversation has a context limit. As the conversation grows longer, the model's ability to hold the entire project in mind degrades. Responses become less accurate. The model may repeat actions it has already taken, contradict its earlier decisions, or lose track of which files it has modified. When any of those behaviors appear, starting a new conversation and providing the repository URL as context is the right move.

Beyond the context limit, breaking work into separate conversations also produces better results because each conversation has a clear, focused objective. The translation task should not be in the same conversation as the image fix. The GitHub upload should not be in the same conversation as the color scheme change. Each task is given its own conversation, its own starting prompt, and its own clear goal.

> **Note**
>
> Start a new conversation when: the task is complete, and a new one begins, the model starts repeating itself or contradicting earlier decisions, Cursor displays a message about the conversation being too long, or the model seems to have lost track of what has already been done. Each new conversation should begin with the repository URL and a clear statement of the current task.

There is also a specific pattern that signals when to switch models entirely. If multiple new conversations produce the same confused or circular behaviour, and restarting has not helped, switching to a different model for that specific task is worth trying. The model that handles structural changes well may not be the best choice for translation work. The model that writes clean initial code may struggle with debugging an existing project. These are not absolute rules, but they are patterns worth testing.

Swimming in the Ocean: Knowing Where the Shore Is

There is a particular kind of frustration that appears in larger projects that is worth naming directly because it is different from the ordinary frustration of a specific bug or error. It is the feeling of not knowing how far away the finished state is.

Working with code from a previous project or picking up someone else's code base from GitHub produces this feeling reliably. Squashing one bug reveals three more. Fixing a layout issue in one section breaks something in another. There is no way to know whether the current state is five prompts away from done or five hundred. It is like swimming in fog with no visible shore. The direction is uncertain. The distance is unknown. The effort is real, but the destination is not visible.

When that feeling appears, the right response is not to push harder. The right response is to stop, reassess, and change the approach. Starting a new conversation resets the model's context. Switching models changes the perspective. Breaking the problem into a single, small, clearly defined task and solving that one thing restores a sense of progress and direction.

There is also a related lesson from the experience of working with old projects. Two specific attempts were made during the development of this course: working with projects built by previous developers who left no notes, and starting from a base of existing public GitHub code.

Both failed. The projects from previous developers were from 2018 and 2019 and were too outdated for the current models to interpret reliably. The public code base was unfamiliar in structure and produced a cascade of dependency problems that were not solvable without deep technical knowledge of the specific stack.

The conclusion from those experiences is a practical one: starting from scratch is almost always faster than trying to rescue or extend an unfamiliar codebase. The model understands its own output far better than it understands someone else's. When the project is built from a clean prompt, the model has a coherent mental model of its own structure. When it is handed someone else's code, it is reasoning about something it did not create and has to infer the logic from reading the files. That inference is less reliable.

> Tip
>
> **When stuck: the three-part response**
>
> **Patience**: The problem is probably solvable. Do not abandon the project.
>
> **Better questions**: Reframe what is being asked. A different prompt often unlocks a stuck situation.
>
> **Try things**: Vibe coding is experimental by nature. Testing a different approach is faster than waiting for certainty about the right one.

Summary

This chapter followed a single project from an empty folder to a live website on a custom domain. The vet clinic build touched every part of the pipeline introduced earlier in the course: the prompt, the local development environment, the contact form integration with Resend, the image debugging, the GitHub upload, the Vercel deployment, the first-deployment failure and fix, the domain purchase, and the first update pushed through the full chain.

Several problems appeared along the way. The connection error in Cursor halted the build partway through and required a restart. The images failed to load because of file size issues that were ultimately traced to the Next.js image optimization system. The website was built in Romanian because the prompt did not specify English. The first Vercel deployment failed because of a build configuration difference between local and production environments. The color scheme update was pushed to a branch rather than to main.

None of those problems were fatal. All of them were recoverable. The common thread through each resolution was the same: identify what happened, ask the model to fix it with a precise prompt, verify the fix in the browser or in the platform dashboard rather than trusting the model's summary, and move forward. That sequence, applied consistently, is what gets a project from a blank folder to a live URL.

The full update chain, from Cursor to GitHub to Vercel, works automatically once it is established. Future changes to the website require only a prompt to Cursor and a push to GitHub. Vercel handles the rest. Each push creates a new version in the repository, making it possible to revert to any earlier state if something goes wrong.

Starting a new conversation for each distinct task, providing the repository URL as context at the beginning of each one, and verifying every change in the live environment are the habits that make this workflow reliable across multiple projects over time. These are not advanced techniques. They are basic disciplines that compound in value with every project completed.

Practice Exercise

This exercise replicates the full pipeline from this chapter using a different business type. The goal is to go through every stage once, independently, and encounter the real problems that come with each handoff. Watching the chapter and doing the exercise are not equivalent experiences. The problems that appear will be different from the ones shown here, and working through them is the entire point.

Brief

Build and deploy a landing page for a local business of your choice. Suitable options include a restaurant, a law firm, a physiotherapy clinic, a hair salon, or any other local service business. The business can be fictional.

The Starting Prompt

Write a prompt that includes all of the following elements:

- The business name, location, and a brief description of what it offers
- A color scheme specified with at least one hex code rather than a color name
- A request for a PRD before any code is written
- A request for Next.js and Tailwind as the technology stack
- A contact form with at least three fields, connected to Resend
- The language the website should use, stated explicitly
- A note that the project will be deployed on Vercel via GitHub
- At least one folder of images to use, with the full folder path included

Build the project in Cursor using the prompt. Read the PRD before accepting the build. Note whether the PRD matches what was requested. Accept the build and open the local preview.

Stage 1: Local Verification

Check each of the following before moving to the next stage:

1. The website displays in the correct language
2. Images load correctly in the browser
3. The contact form can be submitted and an email arrives in the Resend dashboard
4. The mobile layout has no obvious alignment or overflow problems

For any item that fails, write a targeted repair prompt using specific language. Paste the exact error if one appears. Do not move to GitHub until all four checks pass or until a deliberate decision is made to fix remaining issues after deployment.

Stage 2: GitHub and Vercel

Push the project to a new GitHub repository using the GitHub MCP. Verify the push by checking the repository in the browser. Then connect the repository to Vercel and complete the deployment configuration, including the environment variables from the .env.local file.

When the first deployment fails, copy the full error output from Vercel and paste it into a new Cursor conversation with this framing:

```
I am deploying this project on Vercel. The first deployment failed with these
errors.
The GitHub repository is at [URL]. Please fix the issues and push the update.

[paste full Vercel error output here]
```

Repeat until the deployment goes green. Test the live URL by submitting the contact form and verifying the email arrives.

Stage 3: One Update Through the Full Chain

Make one change to the live website to confirm the full update pipeline works. A color scheme change or a text content update is sufficient. Use a new conversation, include the repository URL, and verify the change appears on the live site within a few minutes of the GitHub push.

Deliverable

Keep the following at the end of the exercise:

- The live Vercel URL of the deployed website
- A screenshot of the green deployment status in the Vercel dashboard
- A screenshot of a successfully delivered email in the Resend dashboard

- The exact prompts used for the initial build, the first repair task, and the final update
- A written note on one problem that appeared that was not shown in this chapter and how it was resolved

That last item is the most important one. The problem that was not anticipated here is the one that teaches something new. Documenting it, along with what resolved it, is the beginning of a personal troubleshooting reference that becomes more valuable with every project completed.

Epilogue: What Comes Next

There is a temptation, at the end of a book like this, to feel like the learning is done. It is not. It has barely started. What is done is the foundation. The toolkit is in place, the pipeline is understood, and a real project has been built and deployed. That is not a small thing. Most people who start this kind of work do not get this far.

But the landscape this book was written in is not the landscape that exists by the time it is read. These models change every few weeks. Features that do not work today will work next month. Workflows that feel clunky now will be simplified. New MCPs will appear. The Figma-to-Cursor integration that failed during the writing of this book will eventually work reliably. Pricing structures will shift. New models will arrive from companies that do not yet exist.

None of that should be alarming. It should be energizing. Being early in something that is changing this fast is an advantage, not a liability. Every problem worked through on a project, every error message decoded, every failed deployment fixed, is experience that compounds. The person who has shipped five vibe-coded projects understands something about this workflow that no course can fully convey, because the understanding comes from the hours spent inside the friction.

The professional picture is also shifting faster than most institutions are acknowledging. In some markets, development hiring has already slowed. Roles that previously required a team are being handled by one person with access to the right tools. The traditional web design pipeline of wireframe, high-fidelity design, developer handoff, and weeks of build time is being compressed into days. That compression is uncomfortable for people whose entire career was structured around the old timeline. It is genuinely exciting for anyone who can adapt quickly and deliver real work without being attached to the old process.

The advice at the end of this course is the same as the advice at the beginning, but it means more now than it did then. Start small. Build something real. Post it. Tell people what it is and how it was made. The movement of building in public is not a marketing tactic. It is a way of creating accountability to finish, a way of attracting people with similar interests, and a way of learning from the people who are a few steps ahead. The person who documents their journey of building a small tool, even a tool that only ten people use, is doing something more valuable than the person who is still planning a bigger one.

The fear that the project is not good enough, not polished enough, not finished enough to share is the fear that most reliably prevents progress. The 80 percent version that is live and visible is worth more than the 100 percent version that is still sitting in a local folder. Real feedback from real people reshapes priorities faster than any amount of solo iteration. Get it out there.

Vibe coding is genuinely difficult to learn. It is also genuinely achievable without a programming background. The difficulty is not in the code. It is in the patience, the problem-solving instinct, and the willingness to push through sessions where the model goes in circles and nothing seems to work. That difficulty is not a sign that the approach is wrong. It is the price of entry into a skill that is worth having.

The tools covered in this course, Cursor, GitHub, Vercel, Resend, Supabase, and the models behind all of it, are not the final form of this technology. They are version one of something that will look very different in three years. The people who will do the most with that future version are the ones building with the current one right now, learning its limits, understanding its patterns, and developing judgment that the tools themselves cannot provide.

Go build something.

Chris Barin

Designer. Vibe Coder. Author.

12

Unlock Your Exclusive Benefits

Your copy of this book includes the following exclusive benefits:

DRM-Free PDF Version

Download DRM-free PDF and ePub copies of this book.

7-Day Packt Library Access

Get 7-day unlimited access to 8,000+ books and videos. No credit card required.

Available for first-time Packt+ trial users only.

Next-Gen Reader Access

Read this book on Packt Reader with progress sync, dark mode and note-taking.

Follow the guide below to unlock them. The process takes only a few minutes and needs to be completed once.

Unlock this Book's Free Benefits in 3 Easy Steps

Step 1

Keep your purchase invoice ready for *Step 3*. If you have a physical copy, scan it using your phone and save it as a PDF, JPG, or PNG.

For more help on finding your invoice, visit `https://www.packtpub.com/en-us/unlock?step=1`.

> Note
>
> **Note**: If you bought this book directly from Packt, no invoice is required. After *Step 2*, you can access your exclusive content right away.

Step 2

Scan the QR code or go to `packtpub.com/unlock`.

On the page that opens (similar to *Figure 12.1* on desktop), search for this book by name and select the correct edition.

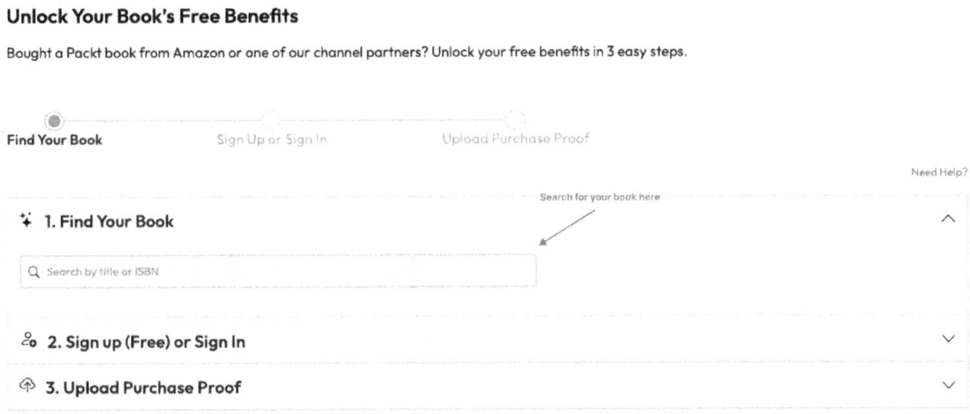

Figure 12.1: Packt unlock landing page on desktop

Step 3

After selecting your book, sign in to your Packt account or create one for free. Then upload your invoice (PDF, PNG, or JPG, up to 10 MB). Follow the on-screen instructions to finish the process.

Need Help

If you get stuck and need help, visit `https://www.packtpub.com/unlock-benefits/help` for a detailed FAQ on how to find your invoices and more. This QR code will take you to the help page.

Note

Note: If you are still facing issues, reach out to `customercare@packt.com`.

Other Books You May Enjoy

If you enjoyed this book, you may be interested in these other books by Packt:

Agentic Coding with Claude Code

Eden Marco

ISBN: 9781806022595

- Design agentic coding workflows in the terminal and IDE using Claude Code
- Build custom automations with reusable slash commands and hooks
- Use Claude Code with a Next.js project to implement AI-driven workflows
- Create persistent AI memory using Claude Code memory files
- Apply MCP for structured context sharing across tools and agents
- Design multi-agent systems using subagents and orchestration patterns
- Enforce coding standards using project documentation and context control

Web Dev with an AI Sidekick

Mark J. Price

ISBN: 9781806111251

- Optimize your chatbot to act as your web development learning mentor
- Structure, style, add images, and animate content with HTML, SVG, and CSS
- Add web page interactivity with JavaScript and TypeScript
- Store and query data using practical SQL exercises
- Build backend features in Python and Django step by step
- Collaborate with an AI coding expert: Codex, Claude Code, or Copilot

Packt is searching for authors like you

If you're interested in becoming an author for Packt, please visit `authors.packt.com` and apply today. We have worked with thousands of developers and tech professionals, just like you, to help them share their insight with the global tech community. You can make a general application, apply for a specific hot topic that we are recruiting an author for, or submit your own idea.

Share your thoughts

Now you've finished *Cursor AI for Web Design*, we'd love to hear your thoughts! Scan the QR code below to go straight to the Amazon review page for this book and share your feedback or leave a review on the site that you purchased it from.

https://packt.link/r/1808084918

Your review is important to us and the tech community and will help us make sure we're delivering excellent quality content.

Index

L

M

N

P

R

S

T

www.ingramcontent.com/pod-product-compliance
Lightning Source LLC
LaVergne TN
LVHW080809011026
849160LV00015B/1581
* 9 7 8 1 8 0 8 0 8 4 9 1 1 *